Praise for *Concealed*

"**A moving, honest, and compelling memoir** that unveils the little-known world of Persian-Jewish immigrants in America in the 1950s and 1960s. Amini's storytelling is masterful, her prose poignant, and her characters leap off the page right into your heart."

—**Ronda Spinak**, Co-founder and Artistic Director, Jewish Women's Theatre

"***Concealed* is an extraordinarily eloquent narrative** that provides a humanizing glimpse of the underground Jews of Iran, their story of oppression and assimilation, and how a gifted, intelligent girl growing up in the States struggles to reclaim the past while propelling herself into the future. Amini's dignified, honest, and probing voice resonates throughout her journey of self-discovery."

—**Angella M. Nazarian**, author of *Pioneers of the Possible*, *Visionary Women*, and *Life as a Visitor*

"**Esther Amini renders the joys, travails, and history** of her immigrant Mashhadi-Jewish family with deep insight, humor, and disarming honesty. This brilliant memoir raises timely questions that will continue to haunt long after the last riveting page is turned."

—**Dora Levy Mossanen**, author of *Scent of Butterflies*

"**Esther Amini's memoir is masterfully written** from the heart of her personal history. Courage and conviction overcome fear and restriction as Esther emerges revealed."

—**Eve Brandstein**, Writer/Director/Producer, Eve Brandstein Productions

"**How does one speak up under the rule of a dictatorial father** and in the shadows of a louder-than-life mother while battling hundreds of years of cultural misogyny, anti-Semitism, illiteracy, and oppression? Rich with reflection, character portraitures, vibrant anecdotes, and often surprising history, *Concealed* tracks one Jewish-Iranian-American female's transformation from silent child to confident woman as she sheds layers of cultural chador and not only finds but asserts her own voice."

—**Heather Siegel**, author of *Out from the Underworld* and *The King & The Quirky*

"**Esther Amini has written a beautiful memoir.** *Concealed* tells an immigrant story of generations past, yet rings as current as tomorrow. With imaginative prose, Amini tracks her parents from their harrowing beginnings living as closeted Jews in Mashhad, Iran, to their new home in America. When they pass on the fear and secrecy that remain embedded in their psyche to Amini, she discovers that she, too, is growing up concealed and longs to break free. This is a moving story to be appreciated by anyone who has struggled toward self-knowledge and love, yes, love for the ones who have unwittingly done harm."

—**Marcia Butler**, author of *Pickle's Progress* and *The Skin Above My Knee*

"*Concealed* is Esther Amini's remarkable account of growing up in a house where books and education are for boys and a prearranged and stultifying marriage is supposed to be her destiny. It chronicles the journey of a sensitive and curious girl who from childhood has to create her own story. Against her parents' wishes and cultural mores, Amini not only survives but thrives and reinvents herself in extraordinary ways. Lucky for us she grew up to be a writer with a keen eye and ear who has produced a wonderful memoir."

—**Patty Dann**, author of *Mermaids*, *Starfish*, and *The Butterfly Hours*

"*Concealed* is a poignant, amusing, compelling story of immigration and dislocation as experienced by a family trying to bridge dramatically clashing cultures—Iranian versus American. Amini chronicles the dangers of being a Jew in Mashhad, Iran; her escape from ancestral illiteracy, underground concealment, and a historical legacy of voicelessness; and her decision to pursue a career devoted to breaking silence and helping others use their own words and find their own voice. This insightful, artfully written, and totally absorbing memoir will have universal appeal."

—**Carol S. Thea, LCSW**, President, New York School for Psychoanalytic Psychotherapy and Psychoanalysis

"*Concealed* is a heart-wrenching coming-of-age memoir** by the daughter of hidden Iranian Jews who immigrate to America but never escape the emotional prison of their previous existence. Esther Amini grapples with the shadow of the chador even while tasting Western freedom. You will cheer for her as you ponder the eternal question: how do we survive our families?"

—**Sally Koslow**, author of *Another Side of Paradise* and *The Widow Waltz*

"*Concealed* is a fascinating account of growing up** in an immigrant Jewish family from Iran, deftly told with affection intermixed with ambivalence. Amini portrays the inevitable conflicts between tradition and modernity confronted by American daughters from Middle Eastern families with all the skills of a traditional storyteller. Her finely etched cameos provide insights into the process of Americanization and the bonds of family within this ancient Jewish community. Amini's memoir contributes a rich personal note to our understanding of the process of uprooting and adaptation that characterizes this era of nationalism and forced migrations."

—**Jane S. Gerber, PhD**, Professor Emerita of History, Director of the Institute for Sephardic Studies, The Graduate Center, City University of New York

"**In this beautifully crafted memoir**, Esther Amini weaves a riveting portrait of her family life as the daughter of Iranian-Jewish immigrants in New York City struggling to emerge from the shadows of medieval Mashhad. It is a life fraught with contradictions, a constant push-pull between tradition, trauma, and the need to be free. It is a deeply personal tale, painfully honest and brilliantly told."

—**Susan Mailer**, psychoanalyst and author of *In Another Place: With and Without My Father, Norman Mailer*

"**Are we what we reveal? Is our hidden self ours?** Are nature and nurture adversaries? Esther Amini has written a unique, courageous, heart-wrenching, and humbling memoir in which gender, religion, country, and individual character battle it all out. I couldn't stop reading."

—**Ilan Stavans**, author of *On Borrowed Words*

CONCEALED

Memoir of a Jewish-Iranian Daughter
Caught Between the Chador and America

ESTHER AMINI

CONCEALED

Memoir of a Jewish-Iranian Daughter
Caught Between the Chador and America

ESTHER AMINI

GREENPOINT PRESS
NEW YORK, NY

ISBN 978-0-9906194-2-0

Library of Congress Cataloging-in-Publication Data

Book Designer: Robert L. Lascaro
LascaroDesign.com

Illustrations by Edmund J. Sullivan (1869-1933)
From *The Rubaiyat of Omar Khayyam*, translated by Edward FitzGerald and illustrated by Edmund J. Sullivan (Methuen, 1913)

Greenpoint Press
A division of New York Writers Resources
greenpointpress.org
200 Riverside Boulevard, Suite 32E
New York, NY 10069

New York Writers Resources:
· newyorkwritersresources.com
· newyorkwritersworkshop.com
· greenpointpress.org
· prisonwrites.org

Printed in the United States on acid-free paper

To my children, grandchildren, and future generations,
who may want to know where they come from.

CONTENTS

Prologue: Invisible – 1

PART ONE: A FORCE OF NATURE

1. Closet Full of Oscars – 5
2. The Box – 17
3. Scalped – 21
4. Public Secret – 29
5. Runaway Bride – 43
6. Shepherd in Queens – 47
7. Kosher at Christmas – 53
8. Tuti – 57
9. Rearview Mirror – 63
10. On Ice – 69

PART TWO: FROM MASHHAD TO MANHATTAN

11. David's Earlobe – 75
12. Queen Esther's Tomb – 83
13. Exodus – 89
14. Crossing – 97
15. Welcome – 101
16. Thinking Goats – 107

PART THREE: OLD WORLD MEETS NEW

17. Showering with Mom – 119
18. Neet – 127
19. Cornell –133
20. Friday Night Cleavage – 141
21. Protégé – 147
22. Kitchen Confidential – 153
23. Lady Liberty – 157
24. About Face – 159
25. Origins – 167

PART FOUR: BREAKING AWAY

26. Behind Bars – 175
27. Booklegger – 181
28. Risky Move – 189
29. Change Subject! – 195
30. Barnard – 203
31. Confession – 209

PART FIVE: LOST AND FOUND

32. Homecoming – 219
33. Matrimony – 227
34. Jerusalem – 229
35. Scandal – 235
36. Second Chance – 239
37. Ira – 245

PART SIX: BIBI

38. Persian Paranoia – 253
39. Gin Rummy – 259
40. Outnumbered – 265
41. Yateem – 269
42. Broken Door – 275

Epilogue: Visible – 281

FAMILY PHOTOS: IRAN – 113
FAMILY PHOTOS: USA – 213

GLOSSARY – 283
ACKNOWLEDGMENTS – 289
ABOUT THE AUTHOR – 291

Author's Note

In writing this memoir, I've done my best to verify factual aspects of the memories and stories shared and have relied on my recollection and that of many others for details I couldn't confirm. I've tried to be truthful and apologize for any errors this memoir may contain.

The names of my ancestors and family members are real, as are the names of my parents' beloved rabbi, the late Morris Goldberg; my dear friend Lin; and my esteemed art history teacher at Barnard, Barbara Novak. All other names have been changed to protect the privacy of people with whom I've lost touch and often out of respect for the émigré Mashhadi-Jewish community, which holds secrecy and privacy as core values. Readers may wish I wrote more about certain events, but I have to weigh that wish against the wishes of those dear to me who would rather I wrote nothing at all.

I include a number of Persian/Farsi/Mashhadi words, phrases, and foods in this memoir, along with a few Hebrew, Hindi, and Yiddish terms. In every case, I've tried to use the most common standardized spelling of the English transliteration. In some cases, however, I've used my own spelling of uniquely Mashhadi terms.

IRAN
Three Key Cities in Family History and Lore

❶ **MASHHAD** — Holiest Muslim city in Iran; the Aminoff and Levi families' ancestral home

❷ **TEHRAN** — Capital of Iran, where Esther's parents lived during World War II

❸ **HAMADAN** — Site of Queen Esther's Tomb, where Esther's mother prayed for a daughter

The past is never dead. It's not even past.

—William Faulkner

INVISIBLE

"Estaire is not here!"

Gwendolyn, my third-grade classmate, had come over to play. As soon as she walked through our front door, dressed in pink-and-blue argyle socks and a matching cardigan, my father gave her a stabbing stare.

"Estaire is not here!" he said icily.

I was standing right there, right next to him, in plain view. Gwen's eyes met mine. I quickly looked away and tried to hide in the spaces between his words. With a ferocious wave, Pop sent her away and swept back into the living room without a glance in my direction. I was invisible to him. I looked at my feet, touched my elbows, then began shaking like a rag doll. My mind gunked up. *Could he be right? Am I imagining me?*

The shame was immense. A heart punch. Would Gwen tell our entire class what had just happened? Would she say, "Esther's father is Iranian and that's what they do"?

It wasn't the first time Pop had insisted I wasn't visible when I was, but I was no less mortified. How could I be unseen when seen? How could I disappear upon demand?

I didn't call out, "I am here!" I was afraid of words. Pop often cautioned, "Speech makes lips unclean." So at age eight, fearing his angry outbursts and wanting clean lips, I chose silence.

I wished my mother were home. She, born with sword in hand, would never have let this happen. She would have shoved Pop aside, invited Gwen in, and offered her trays of piping hot homemade Persian pastries. Gwen would have loved my mother and been fooled into thinking my home was much like hers. She'd never know what I knew.

By third-grade, I was practicing shrinking, abiding by Pop's rules to avoid his wrath. I ate little, spoke minimally, breathed soundlessly while my mother worked at becoming ever more visible, expanding to the point of bursting, no matter the consequence.

I was a consequence. ▧

PART ONE

A FORCE OF NATURE

CHAPTER 1

Closet Full of Oscars

Born in 1925 Iran, Mom had been forced to live as an underground Jew in the fanatically religious city of Mashhad, a Shi'ite stronghold and pilgrimage site with a long history of maiming and massacring infidels. Head bent, breathing through a black *chador*,[1] peering through an eyeslit, she slunk through alleyways, faceless and shapeless, passing as Muslim.

The chador was more to her than just a cloth covering. It was the symbol of her suppression and target of her rage. Years later, Mom told me about one sun-scalding summer afternoon when she and her stepmother, Yocheved, were hauling sacks of fava beans home from the market. Both were heavily shrouded, properly groomed, Islamicized for outside eyes. My mother, 14 and recently married to my 34-year-old father, was already three months pregnant. As her cloaked face dripped with sweat, she spat out in Farsi:

"I hate chadors. I'm ripping mine off. Why are we hidden? Why can't men look at us? We're allowed to look at their hideous faces, their bare arms and legs."

"Shh!" Yocheved gestured for her to lower her voice. "The Imams are keeping us safe. A woman's lips, hair, elbow, even her ankle can drive a man crazy. If we conceal ourselves, men can control themselves."

"*Kooft-e balah!*[2]" Mom cursed through blasts of sticky air and suffocating drapes. "I'm not responsible for their unruly penises. Men should learn to lock their crotches."

1. *chador* (Persian/Farsi)—long, loose garment that covers a woman's head and body
2. *Kooft-e balah* (Persian/Farsi)—a curse, wishing someone pain, disaster, misery, and disease

While chadors were designed to hide women, hers incubated visions of a headlong and noisy break for freedom. Eight years later, urged on by an older brother who had already emigrated to the United States, she uprooted her husband and two young sons and spearheaded the family's fretful, lengthy, circuitous migration from Mashhad to Manhattan. On the eve of their departure, Mom lit a match and torched her black chadors, turning heavy cloths and the weight of their meaning to ash.

In New York City, unveiled and thoroughly seen, she speed-sorted through Saks Fifth Avenue's dress racks, searching the very finest. She ran her fingers along crushed velvet, squeezed densely sequined organza, and fondled sumptuous chiffon, scanning for plunging necklines that screamed: *Look at me.* At home she donned bright colors, convoluted patterns, 3-D textures that made me cringe as an adolescent. To this day I can't wear fire engine red, her color of choice.

At home, she'd hand-grind steaks; pickle every conceivable vegetable; tend a garden packed with plum tomatoes, Persian cucumbers, mint; and insist on ironing all bedsheets, undershirts, even cotton underpants. Between waxing floors and polishing walls, she baked, broiled, and basted. Mom scoffed at women who were slow and celebrated those who were hyperactive.

My father shuddered with disapproval and deepened their divide by labeling everything she did "unnecessary and excessive." Too much huff-puff, too much noise, too much upheaval.

In Mashhad, Pop had also relied on duplicity to survive, kneeling and bowing in public squares, reciting the Koran,[3] and chanting *namaz*,[4] while inwardly praying to *HaShem*,[5] the God of Abraham, Isaac, and Jacob. However, he had experienced Iran quite differently than Mom. While my mother's face was always concealed, his was always visible, easier to identify as an underground Jew. Even in the secrecy of their home, behind shuttered windows, they both lived in constant fear of being outed.

Treasuring silence, happy with dry toast and tea, he implored Mom to stop the constant activity. "Your noisy hands and feet give me a migraine!" Mom deafened her ears and soldiered on. As *Ghormeh Sabzi*[6] bubbled for hours on the kitchen stove, its thick

---

3. Koran (Arabic)—*Quran*, central Islamic religious text
4. *namaz* (Persian/Farsi)—Islamic prayers sung five times a day
5. *HaShem* (Hebrew)—a name for God
6. *Ghormeh Sabzi* (Persian/Farsi)—Persian stew made with veal, dill, parsley, scallions, lima beans, turmeric, cinnamon, dried lemons, and mint

aroma of dill, parsley, scallions, veal, lima beans, turmeric, cinnamon, dried lemons, and mint blanketing our home, Mom was crocheting shawls, embroidering four-yard-long tablecloths while rhythmically pedaling our Singer sewing machine with her right foot, churning out floor-to-ceiling red velvet curtains.

By adolescence, I knew Mom wasn't the woman I wanted to be. Her hustle and bustle wasn't repugnant to me; however, her driving need to be the best backbreaking housewife who ever lived was. By out-cleaning, out-cooking, she felt she was outshining all other wives. Striving for perfection as she tackled domestic chores seemed foolish, trite—a waste of life. While she stood on top of a ladder, triple-checking ceiling moldings in search of a missed speck of dust, I vanished into *Moby Dick*, *Popular Mechanics*, whatever printed matter I could lay my hands on. The more she scraped and scoured our spick-and-span home, the more I dove into schoolwork, disappeared into textbooks, acing every exam. She was loud, latchless, and emphatically visible. I, her polar opposite, navigated my path concealed, seeing much and saying little. While she publicly aired whatever crossed her mind, I conducted inner dialogues I knew no one could hear but me.

By my teens, I had renounced her, telling myself she was vapid and vain—just a random, reckless person I happened to be born from with no real relation to me. I distanced. As mother and daughter, we became intimate strangers.

One of Pop's weekday rituals was watching the 6:30 news in the den of our Forest Hills home. One evening, I sat down to watch it with him. Whenever on edge, unnerved, or incensed, he picked the hairs off his face. Pinching a whisker and twisting it out seemed to keep combustible rage in check. As Walter Cronkite reported on the escalating war in Vietnam, showing clips of American soldiers on the battlefield, reading counts of those captured, wounded, and killed, Pop picked his left cheek bare. I wasn't sure why. Were these reports resurrecting memories of his Iranian past? Or was he angry I was sitting beside him, alert, curious, thinking, undeniably present? Did that make him rip out his hair?

Privately, I questioned the ethics of U.S. involvement in Vietnam. I asked myself: If born male, would I enlist in the Army and risk my life for this war? When high school classmates debated heatedly in locker rooms, cafeterias, classrooms, hallways—"hawks" versus "doves"—I listened intently, gathering data, jumping from side to side, eager to hear each group's truth, keen to develop my own.

Pop wasn't a talker. He watched the evening news in dark silence, and if I sat beside him, I was expected to do the same.

Vietnam did not interest Mom. That evening, as Pop and I sat in front of the TV, she stepped into the kitchen, sank into a chair after a day of heavy housework, released an *I am depleted* sigh, and reached for a magazine. When I came in later, she was sitting at the table, slowly flipping through *Vogue*. She couldn't read—she'd never been taught to read or write—but she loved looking at swanky, high-end clothing and fantasizing about which dress she'd wear to the next gala Persian party. Turning pages, she came across photos of Oscar de la Renta's shimmering evening wear. From boleros to ball gowns, my mother loved this couturier's designs. The Chantilly lace, gold metallic brocade, mink trimmings, and beaded rhinestones exuded a regal elegance she craved. She cupped her mouth and muttered in Farsi, "Oscar understands me." His jewel-encrusted costumes smacking of Louis XIV opulence made her heart pound. Down deep, Mom was certain these gowns, worn by Hollywood starlets, fashion icons, and former First Lady Jacqueline Kennedy, were also designed for her.

On the center of our kitchen table sat an enormous metal tray holding rolling hills of uncooked Persian rice. Automatically, Mom began to separate the individual grains with her long fingers, plucking out tiny black impurities. Hours of mindless finger-flicking gave her plenty of time to think. After prolonged silence, she turned to me and said, "Estaire, look Yellow Pages. Geeve me Oscair add-dress."

Not sure what she was thinking and doubtful I'd find an address, I complied. Sure enough, there was the listing for Oscar de la Renta's showroom, tucked away in the Garment District. I scrawled the information on a scrap of paper, handed it over, and watched her slide it into her bra.

The next day she sprayed underarms and earlobes with Chanel No. 5, put on her finest two-piece, camel-hair suit, and slipped on caramel stilettos. Crafting a face, she stood in front of a full-length bathroom mirror dabbing a thin layer of concealer, outlining her eyes with panther-black, dusting her lids with eggshell-blue. She rouged her cheeks, loosely powdered her forehead, nose, chin, and carefully filled in her full lips with red. Meticulously masked with an ornamented Marie Antoinette hairdo, Mom grabbed her alligator bag, clutched the scrap of paper, and reached for me.

All I wanted was to dissolve, slip away on a wisp of air back to the safety of my bedroom. Mom was up to no good. I was certain of it. I'd been down this road with her before. She wanted me along simply to serve as a dictionary, translating English into Farsi in case linguistically she faltered.

I also knew I was about to feel shame—the same kind I had felt when Pop had told Gwendolyn I wasn't there. My presence wouldn't matter. My humiliation—discounted. Mom was about to be false, and I would have to stand there beside her, witnessing her lies. All alone, with no one interjecting the truth. I wouldn't know what to do with me, and that was most frightening. Nowhere to hide...no camp to call my own other than my taut center. Again, I would wish I were invisible.

Why did I obediently trail her broad back? Why couldn't I say, "No, Mom, this time you're on your own"? Was I tagging along as her protectress, knowing there was no telling what kind of rash, impulsive mess she could get herself into? Or did I shadow her out of some voyeuristic impulse, just so I could see? Fully aware she was lawless, did I get a thrill watching her get away with things I'd never dare do? Or was it that I just couldn't say "no," that I didn't feel I had that freedom? Struggling with shifts of horror, awe, and dread, I followed her out the door, feeling bond and bondage.

Thirty minutes later, ascending from the subway, we emerged into direct sun on Seventh Avenue.

Manhattan's Garment District.

We found our way to Oscar de la Renta's showroom. My mother knocked on the steel door. Her face blossomed into entitlement. The door opened an inch. A tall, blond gatekeeper, wearing patrician airs and reeking of aftershave, jutted out a hip. "...Yes?"

Mom swung the door open, plunged forward, tossed her chin upward like an operatic diva. Even more haughtily than he, she replied, "I, FROM PAIR-JEE-AH. BOUTIQUE IN TE-HER-AN. I BUY FOR BOUTIQUE." It was the 1960s, and many Americans didn't know much about Iran. It wasn't on their mental map. Mom had quickly learned to say, "Pair-Jee-Ah. I, from Pair-Jee-Ah, like Pair-jee-an cat...Pair-jee-an car-pet."

"Madame," the gatekeeper asked, "do you have an account with us?"

My heart clenched. My mother shot me a look. I stared at her stage face, trying to summon mine.

"I HAVE CHIC BOUTIQUE. BOUTIQUE NAME TE-HER-AN, TWO TAU-SANT. ADD-DRESS VON HUNDERED PAHLAVI STREET, TE-HER-AN."

Not one word was remotely true. I swallowed extra hard.

The room was painted antiseptic white. A welcoming bowl of pastel-colored mints had been placed on a white marble table in front of a white leather couch. Seated under a gooseneck lamp, a sleekly dressed Peter O'Toole look-alike salesman wearing a silk bowtie and chest-hugging shirt, quickly rose to shoo us out the door with his manicured hand. Finely attuned to Mom's slightest nuances, sensing she wasn't finished, I stood bolted in place. She opened her alligator bag, rapidly began pulling out wads of $100 bills and stacking them on the table.

O'Toole's mouth dropped open. His brow twitched as he stared greedily at the growing pile.

"I PAY CASH!" Mom announced haughtily. "My cust-o-mair buy my drezz becauz unique. I buy von drezz size four, dif-fair-ent drezz size seex, dif-fair-ent drezz size eight, dif-fair-ent drezz size fourteen. UNIQUE! My boutique UNIQUE! Pair-sian vee-men don't like vair same drezz." She lifted her chin and tightly pursed her bright red lips.

Unique was a word she had learned a few nights before watching her favorite TV program, *The Lucy Show*. She loved the sound of this impenetrable word. Her capacity for deception was epic; her ability to bluff her way into places that forbade entry, riveting. Standing beside charlatan Mom, I shuddered, expecting police to pounce and imprison us behind razor wire.

Oscar's staff huddled in one corner, the pupils of their eyes shrunk to tiny pinpricks as they whispered into one another's ears. Our salesman disappeared, then reappeared, bearing a plate of madeleines and cups of freshly brewed coffee. He smiled graciously as he seated us on the plush white couch.

"Ladies, please. Have a bite to eat while I pull together our upcoming fall line for your viewing."

As he exited, Mom picked up the porcelain cup. Sipping coffee, she snickered in Farsi, "Did you see how at first he didn't want to let us in?" She continued in a whisper. "Hundred-dollar bills legitimized me, *tokhmeh sag.*[7] Give them cash and they feed you cakes. Estaire, they're crooked, two-faced, just like the Mullahs of Mashhad. They can all be bought." With guarded eyes she bit into a second madeleine. I stared at stacks of $100 bills, wondering where

---

7. *tokhmeh sag* (Persian/Farsi)—from the egg of a dog

this cash had come from. Mom was good at stretching the money Pop gave her for household expenses, but it was hard to believe she had saved this much. There was no use asking, since I knew she wouldn't tell.

Out rolled two tall racks of Oscar's evening gowns. Lowering the corners of her mouth, Mom walked over and began flipping through apparel as if rummaging through some basement thrift shop.

"Fresh off the runway," O'Toole injected.

"No good," Mom balked. "I vhant see bettair drezz." She arched a disapproving brow.

I couldn't find any part of myself in her. *Blood ties, that's all*, I told myself. *We share nothing but blood.* She acted with her lips, fore-head, eyebrows—each feature playing a role of its own, cunningly timed. The more theatrical she became, the more anxious I grew, pushing down a chemical urge to flee. When she snubbed Oscar's world-renowned designs, I trembled, certain she had gone too far. O'Toole would now unmask her. Instead, he rushed into the back-room and rolled out three more racks of opulent gowns that drew from 17th-century fashion at the Court of Versailles. How quickly roles had reversed. Now she was nobility and he, her lackey.

My mother made her selections. *"Khoda hafiz,*[8]*"* she cooed in a sweet and sticky voice, cracking a bulletproof smile as we swag-gered out.

In addition to her handbag, she now carried two Oscar de la Renta evening gowns while I carried the other two. The size 4—a midnight blue, cowl-necked, satin cocktail dress—became mine. The size 6—a strapless brown velvet with ruched skirt—was given to my brother Albert's wife. The size 8—gunmetal gray, beaded and ruffled tulle—was given to my brother David's wife. Mom took tri-umphant possession of the size 14—a red and black silk Flamenco dress with mermaid hem.

Accompanying Mom home, toting two hefty garment bags on my teenage shoulders, I felt a seismic shift—a bodily earthquake, as if somehow I was forever changed. This de la Renta escapade wasn't just another one of her brazen stunts. For me it was a pivotal caper. My firecracker mother had duped, deceived, and majestically triumphed. I had watched her will herself into being someone she wasn't—and carry it off. Her message, distilled to its essence: *Just perfect the act.*

8. *Khoda hafiz.*(Persian/Farsi)—God protect you.

Even though I had fully rejected her, I now felt there was something to learn. I had dreams, pounding wishes, secret needs of my own. *If she can do it, so can I. I, too, can come out on top. I, too, can win.*

Later that evening, with pistons firing, she staged a biting parody of the tight-ass gatekeeper and greedy salesman, winning a round of applause from her sons and daughters-in-law: Mom had outwitted the West. My father's short neck wrinkled as he shook his head, arms thrashing in the air. *"Khejalat bekesh!*[9]*"* he shrilled in Farsi. Cinching his robe at the waist, he threw back his head and scolded. "This is criminal behavior! You've gotten yourself and us into deep trouble! You're ruining our reputation, our family name. For thousands of years our ancestors have lived obediently, abiding by the laws of the land. *Khanum,*[10] I forbid you ever to return to Oscar de la Renta. You must never go back!"

Standing a foot taller than Pop, Mom towered over him. She breathed calmly, evenly, as if he hadn't said a word. Her brown eyes gleamed with satisfaction. Mom was beyond right and wrong.

In Farsi, she washed his words away: "The Garment District is fraudulent. Only now, they've met their match."

She shot me a conspiratorial wink. Returning her wink, I half-smiled. I was only a half-conspirator, more spectator than cohort. Watching her perform, I was of two minds—proud of and appalled at her gall. I was convinced her ease at negotiating multiple identities came straight from her early years in Iran, where she had first honed them. As for me, I had difficulty lying even when it was in my own best interest; but, on this day, I envied Mom's dissociative strength. Cherry-picking, I teased out what I admired—her willfulness, fearlessness—and wanted to make mine. A Herculean task. *If only I had a fraction of her courage coursing through my veins.*

As she stood before her bathroom mirror wiping off makeup with gobs of Pond's Cold Cream, I asked, "Why did you have to go to Oscar de la Renta's and do what you did?"

With a 747 wingspan, Mom swept her arms open and bellowed, "Vee all die soon! Een-joy!"

She returned to the showroom whenever in need of *bar mitzvah,*[11] *bat mitzvah,*[12] wedding, or *bris*[13] attire. Salesmen now warmly

9. *Khejalat bekesh.*(Persian/Farsi)—Shame on you; be ashamed of yourself.
10. *Khanum* (Persian/Farsi)—Madame
11. *bar mitzvah* (Hebrew)—Jewish coming-of-age ceremony for boys
12. *bat mitzvah* (Hebrew)—Jewish coming-of-age ceremony for girls
13. *bris* (Hebrew)—Jewish circumcision ceremony

welcomed her, this exotic Persian woman with her alligator purse. She opened an account under the name of her nonexistent shop, Tehran 2000. Illiterate, mathematically limited, Mom computed on her ten fingers. The thrill of defying all odds, settling all scores, and disproving naysayers stroked a deep, soft, pleasure spot. Taking her far away from the chador.

That same evening, after Mom had waved aside all of Pop's rebukes, I walked into my upstairs bedroom and found my father neck-deep in my backpack. Prickly chills raced down my spine. It was as if I'd walked in on a ransacking burglar.

He pulled out his head and bellowed, "Enough books!" For years, ever since I turned eight, he had been warning, "Books are evil, they poison girls' minds," and ordering me not to read. My love of books angered and frightened him. My parents came from a city and culture that kept girls out of school and far from the written word—a world that firmly believed female illiteracy was a blessing that helped shape young girls into good wives. No female member of my mother's or father's family had ever learned to read or write. I was the first from both lines to enter a classroom. My mother, at certain times, found my math and reading skills useful to her, which was all she really cared about. However, according to Pop, literacy was a liability: Each year of schooling made me less desirable and harder to marry off.

Whipping a paperback copy of Shakespeare's *Romeo and Juliet* out of my backpack, he ranted in Farsi, "Love! Love is for degenerates." Pop's eyes hardened as he peered over the tops of his thick black-framed glasses. "American love is cheap, full of lifelong trouble, always ending in divorce. I've lived longer than you. You're only a child. I judge character. You can't. When you're matched with a man I know and approve of, someone with our values, there's permanence."

In our home, dating was prohibited. "Your mother and I didn't do this thing," Pop often boasted. "We didn't speak to one another until we were wed. What was there to talk about?" A lot, actually. If they had had a chance to get to know each other before marrying, they might not have married at all. Even so, Pop wanted his children to adhere to the old ways. I was to live under his Persian tent, wear blinders, and avoid all men until told to look. This American notion of finding one's own mate, he warned, "is the road to self-ruin."

That night, frustrated by Mom, unable to control her, Pop came down doubly hard on me. Marshaling support from the Torah,[14] he preached, "The Lord commands you to honor your mother and father. That means obey." He scowled at me. "Enough school!" He gave his forehead a powerful smack, leaving behind a red splotch. "I will choose your husband. He will be an Iranian Jew from the city of Mashhad. I will know his mother, father, the reputation of his grandparents and great grandparents. I will know if they kept *kosher*,[15] if their ancestors were hardworking, their wives good cooks. These things you can't know. How can you choose a lifetime husband? I will find someone *najib*,[16] a man who is kind, trustworthy, honest in business, and you will become his wife."

Close to tears, my eyes cranked shut—a survival skill. None of it made sense. He didn't have a clue who I was. How could he know what was best for me? I'd live confined, behind bars, under some husband's vigilant guard. He'd be a watchdog, just like Pop. I'd be restricted, shushed, and deadened. Images of straitjackets, manacles, a harness of leather and iron flashed through my mind. I wouldn't be allowed to think, much less differ. I felt myself sinking into quicksand, engulfed. I had to escape. How could I smuggle me out of my life? I wasn't quite sure, but I promised myself I'd find a way.

It was the 1960s, which compounded confusion. Marijuana, Flower Power, communes, Women's Lib, and a sexual revolution sweeping the country. My classmates wore miniskirts, marched down Fifth Avenue braless carrying "Make Love, Not War" signs, and dated John Lennon and Mick Jagger look-alikes. Strolling with friends through hashish-scented Central Park, I saw guitar-strumming hippies leaning against trees sharing moist kisses and wondered what that felt like.

But Pop had outlawed love. "It's for heathens," he swore. Now, after Mom's Oscar de la Renta coup, he outlawed spending time with friends. He insisted I come straight home after school and stay home, embroidering tablecloths, hemming skirts, and mastering the art of Persian cooking. The not-so-hidden subtext was: *Your life belongs to me.*

I didn't protest. I rarely spoke my mind and hardly ever stood up for myself. But on this day, after watching Mom leap over de la Renta hurdles, I felt the stirrings of resistance. I didn't want design-

14. Torah (Hebrew)—Old Testament containing the Five Books of Moses
15. keep *kosher* (Hebrew)—follow Jewish dietary laws
16. *najib* (Persian/Farsi)—kind, caring, trustworthy

er dresses, Mom's closet full of Oscars. I wanted school. I wanted to read, hear other people's ideas, and explore mine. I wanted a say in who I was, who I wanted to become; I wanted to draft a different version of me.

Years earlier, I had bought a diary and begun making daily entries. It had become a trusted confidante, holding my most precious thoughts. Feeling unseen and unknown, I wrote to hear *my* voice even if my parents couldn't.

As soon as Pop left my room, I sobbed, bit my nails, then opened my diary and penned: *We're in this world differently. Can I escape their grip and still keep them? I want two things at once, them and me. Can I be their daughter and live in twentieth-century America? Having a life I call my own requires deceit and high risk—the risk of being disowned.*

Later that night, the kitchen phone rang. I surged down the stairs, needing to beat Pop to it.

Knocking me down like tenpins, he snatched the receiver.

"She's not home!" He slammed the phone into its cradle.

I got up off the floor. The phone rang a second time.

I reached out. Pop shoved my hand aside. He lifted the receiver just to jam it down again.

Expecting to be whacked, I covered my face. "Who just called me?" I stuttered through bars of bitten fingers.

Stroking his chin in search of errant whiskers, he found and tore out three.

"No one called. Go to bed!"

"Pop, these are classmates. They want to discuss homework assignments." I summoned some courage. "They have every right to call and I have every right to talk."

Pop, like a lion tamer, gripped me by both shoulders and pressed me against the wall. His breath was hard, sour. "No one is to call you. Not now or ever. If they do I'll rip the phone out. Go to bed!"

Pinned, I went dark. Pitch-black dark. His slimy, pulsing sweat belonged to a flesh-chomping cannibal. Finally, he let me go. Staggering upstairs, twisted out of shape, I retreated into my bedroom, my foxhole, imagining myself strangling him. Tying the thick black phone cord around his Adam's apple and tugging real hard.

Cut out friends, cut out books, cut out my tongue; scrape out thought and wonder—whatever grows inside. Leave me hollow, an empty shell to be filled by some random Iranian husband. If he could, my father would slice off the ears bookending my brain.

The next morning, burdened by Pop's dictates and my weighty backpack, I trudged into Forest Hills High's massive auditorium. My friend Bernadette pulled me aside.

"Who the fuck slammed the phone on me last night? Not once but twice?"

"My father."

"What's wrong with him? I felt I was trying to reach a P.O.W."

"You're close. I'm not allowed to talk when he's home. From now on, call before five p.m. while he's still at work."

"Es, I don't get it. Why can't I talk to you?"

"It has nothing to do with you. He's convinced every American is out to corrupt or abduct me. One day I'm going to crack."

Bernadette gave me a pained, sympathetic stare. *Roll of the dice, we each got a raw deal*, she messaged through heather-gray eyes. She had her own long skein of secrets and knew how it felt to be different. A year earlier, after swearing me to secrecy, she had told me her mom was not only a sleep-all-day-on-the-couch alcoholic, but also a practicing lesbian. I had never heard the phrase "practicing lesbian" and thought it was some Far Eastern religion. Bernie set me straight. She also described in detail the secret life she was living: cooking, cleaning, running the home, discreetly disposing of empty liquor bottles while concealing her mother's sexual escapades.

"Truth in my home doesn't exist," Bernie had told me, her lower lip quivering. "Mom and I share lies. She has a long line of lovers, so when neighbors, the cleaning lady, or our superintendent ask, I say they're my mother's sisters."

In the 1960s, if lesbians lived in our Queens neighborhood, no one knew. "If the super of our building ever found out," Bernie explained, "we'd be thrown out on our asses. We'd be homeless, Es, 'cause the word would spread that my mother is a dyke. No one would take us in."

Bernie lived her own brand of fear and shame, so she easily understood mine.

I invited her over many times, always making sure to slip her out early, before Pop got home. Mom, opposing Pop's rule that no friends come to the house, greeted Bernie with a broad smile and trays of freshly baked cakes. She didn't know Bernie's backstory but would have welcomed her even if she did.

CHAPTER 2

The Box

The image of my 1950s mother in the kitchen handing out homemade sweets to my school friends may evoke nostalgic feelings. Descriptions of her Persian cakes and cookies may suggest an attentive, nurturing, even protective mama.

Mine was not quite that.

I learned this early and received constant reminders.

One winter day, when I was four years old, Mom zipped me into my snowsuit, buckled me into my stroller, and took me with her to S. Klein on 14th Street and Union Square to shop for bedsheets. I remember this toddler-afternoon as if it were yesterday. Pushing me along ahead of her, she sped down aisles, rifled through bins of bedding, inspected stacks of fitted and flat sheets, until she found exactly what she wanted.

I, too, found what I wanted.

"Mommy," I pointed upwards. "Can I have her?"

Mom looked up. Sitting on a high shelf was a doll almost as tall as I was. She had copper-colored ringlets and black lashes fringing bright green eyes; a brass-buttoned pea coat was draped over her white velvet shift.

In a loud, magnanimous voice, Mom answered in Farsi, "If you want her very much, I'll buy her for you."

With a rosy glow Mom placed the life-size doll on my lap. In a rush of gratitude, I grabbed her hand and kissed the back of it. Pulling her hand out of mine she recoiled, as if bitten by a snake. "Stop it, you know I don't like it when you touch me," she chastised in

Farsi. I didn't mind since she had just given me a playmate I knew I could kiss as much as I wanted. I named her Vicky. Gently I traced the curve of her nose, lips, earlobes, and carefully stroked her silky curls. Vicky winked. She didn't pull away.

Mom took the doll, swung my stroller around, and told me to stay still while she paid the cashier. A smile stretched across my face. Vicky, the sister I longed for, was coming home with me. I'd seat her on a chair and invite her to a tea party with all my stuffed animals. I'd tuck her in bed with me and whisper into her ear all my nighttime secrets. I'd tell her I'm afraid of words. Of talking. Afraid of what Mom and Pop might do if they heard me. She'd understand and tell me she was afraid, too. She'd be my best friend.

As soon as we got home, I popped out of my stroller, unzipped my snowsuit, and asked, "Can I play with Vicky? Please?"

Mom waved her permission as she headed for the kitchen.

Lightning fast, I ripped off the brown wrapping paper and opened the box. I shut and reopened my eyes, thinking something was wrong with me. With both hands I groped inside the box—turned it upside down. It was empty. There was nothing inside, not even tissue paper.

I ran into the kitchen. "Mom, there's no doll!"

"Okay," she said, and continued chopping onions.

"Let's go back and get her. We have to tell the store. You paid and she isn't in the box."

Calmly, Mom peeled another onion.

Crying furiously, I begged her to do something.

Mom handed me three Barton's chocolate lollipops and walked away.

Candy in one hand, empty cardboard box in the other, I ran sobbing up to my bedroom and began banging my head against a wall.

"Where is Vicky?" I wailed.

Bang!

Frenzied thoughts tumbled in my mind.

Empty box. Bang!

Mom doesn't care? Bang!

Didn't she carry my doll home? Bang!

Maybe there was no doll. Maybe I imagined it. Mom has magic powers. Maybe she made Vicky disappear. Bang!

Each bang shook loose the dark thought I was locking inside.

Maybe Mom lied.

My whole body buzzed.

No! No! I scolded myself. *I'm bad for thinking she's bad.* Bang! Bang!

Lost, haunted, I beat the front, back, sides of my head against my bedroom wall until the room began to spin—faster and faster.

Barton's chocolate dripped from my lips as I sank to the floor. Dizzy. Muddled. Learning.

CHAPTER 3

Scalped

I n S. Klein, I had a burning need not only for Vicky but also for her ringlets. I stroked her curls, buried my nose in her nylon locks, and breathed their scent with envy. At age four, my head had already been shaved six times.

I remember sitting on a lidded toilet with a dish towel tied around my neck as Pop, first with scissors and then with a handheld safety razor, mowed my scalp. I must have been two at the time. The room was chillingly white. Shivering in a cotton undershirt, I watched my chestnut hair fall onto the tiled bathroom floor. I couldn't see myself. I didn't have to. I knew my naked, stubbly head looked ugly. I was ugly. As tears trickled down my cheeks, my father said: "Estaire, when you grow up and become a young lady you will thank me. Because of me, you will have a beautiful thick head of hair." Throwaway lines. Tomahawked, is what I felt.

With each stroke of the blade, my heart pounded. My body wasn't mine; it belonged to him. Head, hair, limbs were Pop's to do with as he pleased. What else would he decide needed cutting?

I squeezed my eyes shut, wondering if my tongue was next. Butchered for having a tongue. I paired hair with speech: both unwanted.

I have photos of myself at age two wearing a one-piece, leopard-print bathing suit topped by a shiny, bald head, looking neither male nor female. I didn't understand the long, sad stares I received, but I remember families on neighboring beach blankets gasping, perhaps thinking I was dying from a terminal illness. Neither of my brothers had their head shaved; nor was my mother ever fleeced during her Persian childhood. Pop justified his scalpings by assuring me a more beautiful me. I was never convinced. He certainly wasn't invested in making me more physically alluring. On the contrary, raising a daughter, especially in America, was terrifying for him. He needed to make sure desires were repressed—those coming *from* me and those coming *at* me. Perhaps he thought that, with scissors and razors, my womanhood rested in his hands. He could postpone it. It didn't have to begin until he was ready, until he said so—until he allowed my chestnut locks to grow.

Mom went along with Pop's bathroom ritual. My father had attended school for two years in cosmopolitan London, where Mom assumed he had learned many things unknown to the Mashhadis of Iran. She believed that through frequent shavings I *was* being ensured a thick, enviable head of hair.

The head-shavings stopped by age four. Pop never explained why. And due to shavings or not, my hair did grow back thick and bountiful.

Only years later did I learn that my childish lumping of unwanted hair with unwanted speech wasn't so far off. When I was 14, I grilled my mother about my father's childhood, desperate to know why Pop demanded I tiptoe around the house, living as quietly and as invisibly as possible. I was told that my father's father, Moshe Aminoff, had slid his blade over Pop's young scalp just as Pop had slid his over mine. And, as I had suspected, my grandfather hadn't limited himself to cutting off hair. Moshe's child-rearing credo was that children should be neither seen nor heard. Preferring his own sullen company to that of others, he terrorized his wife and seven children into mutism, choosing to reside in unproblematic, unintruded silence. He believed that speech fouled his home, as if releasing deadly toxins, just as Pop believed it fouled ours.

Everything I knew about Pop's early life came from Mom, who willingly answered all my questions. Questioning my father was taboo. Whenever I asked Pop about his father, his face would darken and he'd numbly reply, "My father was a great man"—a rote response accompanied by bodily twitches, cold sweats, and stomping out of the room.

Tuti, my paternal grandmother, married to Moshe at the tender age of nine, had accommodated his every demand, soundlessly cooking, cleaning, darning socks. I met her for the first time when she came to New York for Albert's bar mitzvah. In no way did she resemble a *tuti*[1]—a parrot, the loquacious bird she was named after. Instead, she spoke only when spoken to, and then in bareboned monosyllabic responses. Mom told me that during Friday night dinners, Moshe made sure his wife, three sons, and four daughters welcomed the Sabbath eating in deathly silence. If a chair squeaked, if the tine of a fork scraped against a plate, if a youngster burped, Moshe would bang his fists on the table, enraged that the evening had been defiled. Tuti would limply look down at her folded hands while Pop and his six siblings ran trembling to their bedrooms, fleeing their father's sight.

Deprived of height, my Iranian father, who stood five feet tall, always wore lifts and British tweeds, which he fondly traced back to those two years he spent in England. My grandfather Moshe Aminoff came from a long line of landowners, merchants, and traders and wanted my father, his oldest son, to carry the glory and dazzling success of the Aminoff Dynasty into the 20th century. Moshe believed a British education would teach my father how to think and negotiate like other barons of business, eventually turning him into another Rothschild or Rockefeller. So at age 16, as part of his intellectual grooming, Pop was sent from Mashhad, Iran, to Townley Castle, a boarding school for well-to-do Jewish boys in Putney, London. Raised in nerve-rattling fear and deafening silence, he was nonetheless expected to instantly engage with the world and become a financial genius. Only then would he become worthy of his father's love and respect.

The problem was that, while Pop adored London, he hated school. He would slip out of his German classes, snag bread from kitchen pantries, and hide in the dorm bathroom, munching on stolen rolls. He never learned a word of German, French, or Italian. He did, however, master English. As for all of his other classes, he found them worthless. Pop felt his time was better spent strolling through the fashionable city streets, purchasing custom-made fitted shirts, tailored tweed suits, ankle-length camel-hair coats, Cordovan shoes, and delicately patterned silk pocket squares for his suit jackets. After two years in London, he returned to Mashhad wearing a feathered fedora hat—stunningly dashing and dapper, but uneducated.

1. *tuti* (Persian/Farsi)—parrot

Upon his return, his father disowned him. Why? What did he do to cause such a rupture? I never learned the full story. Pop was a man of secrets, and this was a well-kept one. Mom suspected that while studying in London, he mishandled his father's money, perhaps mounted up debt. He was able to work when he returned home and had accumulated some wealth by the time he married my mother, so it's possible Pop and Moshe eventually healed their breach. If so, it didn't last. Not only were Pop and his father not speaking by the time my brothers and I came along, but many of Pop's siblings had stopped talking to one another, too. In fact, this Aminoff family, with its long history of feuds and exhausting vendettas, had more members who weren't speaking to one another than who were.

Was silence their way of gagging rage? Making sure it remained contained, one step removed from homicide? But by not talking to one another for 50, 60, even 70 years, weren't they, in fact, killing off one another? All sailing through their separate lives as if the others didn't exist.

Once my father married and had a family of his own, he fell back on his father's teachings. Nursed on fear, whenever a conversation became animated, he would frantically holler, "Enough talk! Talk is evil!" Pop found language potentially lethal. In his worldview, discussion led to raised voices, disputes, anger—and, yes, bloodshed. Opposing voices reaching peaceful resolution was inconceivable to him. Pickled in the brine of Moshe's jar, Pop loathed sound of any kind, especially if it came from his wife and children. Whether it was intentional or unintentional didn't matter. It was all viewed as defiant and subversive and met with his father's screaming, room-clearing temper.

Hearing me joyfully run through the house as a child enraged him. The thump of my feet hitting the carpeted stairs registered as nothing but detested noise. As I raced back up the stairs one evening, Pop tore after me. His short physique coupled with cheetah strides sent me into a white-hot panic. His flaming-red face and flailing arms told me I had committed an unforgivable crime. As he was about to grab me, my mother torpedoed in behind him, banging a sling-back, silver stiletto heel on his head. Mom's sexy stiletto was always within reach when she needed an assault weapon. Occasionally, missing his balding crown, her spiked heel left haphazard marks on his wide forehead.

Taking the steps two at a time, I rushed to the safety of our second-floor bathroom. Quickly locking the inside latch, gasping for air, I pressed my spine against the bathroom door and sank to the floor.

The buzz of the doorbell, the ring of the telephone, the screech and slam of the screened door opening and closing, the squeak of my rubber-soled shoes on the floor, laughter—even mild-mannered conversation and audible breathing roiled my father. While the rest of us were asleep, he patrolled the house with deep, dark eyes, searching and listening for sound.

I learned to walk on the balls of my feet with one hand covering my mouth. It was as if Pop's hand was covering my mouth, or was his father's hand covering his mouth and mine? I became soundless. When reading a book or lost in thought, I'd look up and find my father glaring at me, grimacing, which made me wonder if he could also hear me think. I imagined that even the inner workings of my mind were too shrill for his liking.

While Pop was at work, Mom encouraged full release. *You make the rules!* she'd proclaim. Unrestrained, my brother David and I broke loose, explosively jumping onto the backs of our living room couches, pretending to ride our horses, Silver and Scout.

"High Ho Silver!" David whooped. "A fiery horse with the speed of light! A cloud of dust and a hearty 'High Ho Silver!'"

David was the Lone Ranger. I, seven years younger, was his sidekick, Tonto. While he, the masked man in a cowboy hat, was armed with metal guns and caps that smoked, I, his faithful Comanche companion with a gray feather stuck in my hair, stabbed our enemies with a rubber knife. David's hat flew in the air as we straddled our couches, wildly kicking the cushions and snapping our jump-rope reins.

Hiding behind dusty Montana mountains—our bulky armchairs—I mumbled, "Kee-mo-sah-bee...me help you fight outlaw."

"Tonto, don't you have a family?" the Lone Ranger asked.

"No, Kee-mo-sah-bee. Me lone like you."

David was a fine Lone Ranger. He looked me dead in the eye and said, "We'll ride together, Tonto."

"Me glad. Me fight good for you. Tonto risk life for Kee-mo-sah-bee," I faithfully whispered, galloping behind him into the wide-open wilderness.

At the sound of Pop's key turning in the rusty lock, the canon of quiet clamped down again. David and I vanished, taking with us all evidence of the Lone Ranger, Tonto, and the Montana mountains, leaving no trace of guns, knives, smoking caps, or our strong voices.

Weekday evenings were usually mellow when I was little. After dinner, Pop sat in his winged armchair and read the *New York World-Telegram and Sun*, the only newspaper he brought home. His intense facial expressions led me to believe he was understanding world affairs on a level far beyond that of any other father. I was afraid of the clean, sharp lines of his face, signaling displeasure.

Sitting next to him on my short wooden chair, I flipped through the pages of *Humpty Dumpty*, *Little Red Riding Hood*, and *The World of Dogs*. When he turned his page, I turned mine. Noticing that he read with a slight tilt of the head, I did, too. As I watched Pop reach for his scalding, freshly brewed tea, I pretended to sip mine. Staring absently out the window, I provided soundless neutral company. Every so often I'd look up to receive his nod of approval. When we sat side by side, not speaking, breathing softly, and holding our chosen texts, I felt loved. My father and I were orbiting the same sun, sharing his silence.

Silence took root in me, and my need for solitude grew. On my eighth birthday, my eldest brother, Albert, bought me an easel, palette knife, canvas boards, and tubes of Grumbacher oil paint. From then on, I spent Sundays in my room with alizarin crimson, burnt umber, Indian yellow, and thalo blue. After mixing fleshy heaps of pigment, I'd scoop, fling, and scrape. Leaving behind Mom, Pop, P.S. 99, and any need for friends, I sailed into zones of shrieking colors that couldn't be heard by anyone other than me. Each hue had a breath, pulse, and tongue of its own. In this soundless space my paints spoke loudly, and I listened intently, dabbling in portraits and landscapes, but preferring to lose myself in blissful, freedom-finding abstracts.

I discovered I didn't want to put the world into words—that not every sensation had a matching name, not every image or impulse could be explained. I began to believe that spoken language was artificial, formulaic, forcing me to shoehorn feelings into sentences while losing so much in translation. I preferred the primal feel of paint. Paint that sang, cried, and killed. Paint that said, *I'm not rational, not civilized, not neatened up. I'm straight from the gut—muddy and messy. You can't tell me who I am. I'll tell you.*

I studied hard, did well in school, but struggled with an undisclosed secret: Words did not come easily. They came out backwards, in the wrong order, haltingly. I had to fight hard to retrieve a word, to verbalize thought, to translate flutters of feeling into language. My innards had potholes that swallowed up nouns, verbs, and adjectives before I could reach them. Words felt like little rebels, fugitives on the run, each with a warring will of its own. They made their own decisions, whether to stay or scram, help me self-express or leave me tongue-tied. And so I thought and spoke in shades of color.

Were my brain cells diseased? Pop thought of me as his *inconvenient daughter.* By disowning words was I becoming more convenient?

CHAPTER 4

Public Secret

I wrote Pop off as deranged, in need of psychotropic drugs. His ban on books, thought, speech was not normal. None of the other girls in our Mashhadi émigré community had a father like mine. They weren't sneaking phone calls, concealing friendships, or hiding high school textbooks under their beds. Their fathers smiled, softly conversed, and comfortably inhabited two worlds: inner Iran and outer America. Having escaped persecution and oppression in Mashhad, these dads were grateful to be in the States and kept gratitude in mind as they adapted to New York City. Pop, on the other hand, brought the terror with him.

One afternoon, when I was 14, Pop marched past David's book-laden bedroom, peered into mine, and caught me writing in my diary.

"Stop!" he commanded. "Close your mind!" My father believed that thinking robbed women of beauty. It creased their foreheads, caused hair loss and bald spots, yellowed nails, and made them barren—incapable of producing heirs. Looming over me, he scratched furiously at his white tufts of hair. "Men marry beautiful women with smiling eyes, not shriveled eyes wedded to thoughts! Estaire, stop thinking. No man will marry you." His breath scalded my face.

Cracking all ten knuckles, Pop left the room.

As the sun drew a sharp line on my bedroom wall, my thoughts tumbled. *Words express ideas. Do ideas belong only to men? Is wrestling with thoughts a masculine sport, leaving gashes that never heal? Was he saying if I step into that ring I'll end up alone, with pea-sized eyes that don't smile? That I'll become disagreeable and combative and no one wants a combative woman?*

Such a heap of rubbish. What if I had two people inside me—one who had smiling eyes and another who wrestled? Then again, maybe Pop knew something I didn't. *Am I headed for disaster? Should I go into deep freeze and become who he wants?* A steep price to pay for safety. Yet, here I was, once again *thinking*, doing exactly what he forbade. Could he be right? Was I breaking a law of nature? Had I been born only to breed? Was my every thought making a beeline for my ovaries, zapping and destroying my eggs? Was I trading in future children for forbidden thoughts?

Wearing out at 14 years old—a harbinger of doom. The very age my mother was when she married.

By then I had heard bits and pieces of my parents' underground life in Mashhad but had not questioned them about it. I only knew they felt their story continued with me, and they were determined to turn their past into my present and future.

Caught between Mom's flamboyant personality and Pop's strict edicts, I felt my insides rapidly evolving from silent Iranian daughter with no real say in her future to silent daughter with a plan. I decided I'd listen closely to their tangled tales and find out as much as I could about the details of their history. I'd learn why they fled Iran, what risks they took, and how they managed to make a new life in America, so I could, too. I'd find out why Pop was so terrifying and why Mom had thought nothing of giving me that *empty box*. I'd need all the information I could gather before plotting my own escape. I'd take notes, log dates, stockpile justifications, and, when the time was right, sound the bell and flee.

It was a long and lazy *Shabbat*[1] afternoon in Forest Hills Gardens. My mother and I lounged on French Provençal couches; the samovar gurgled as we sipped freshly brewed tea. A Sarouk carpet warmed our living room, and silk Persian rugs with scenes of birds peeking through branches, eavesdropping, hung on the walls. I was burning to know more about this child bride, illiterate homemaker, explosive rebel, this force of nature I called Mom. So I dug.

"There's so much I've never asked. Ma, tell me about your childhood, your life growing up in Iran."

She didn't need coaxing. Mom loved to gab. Cracking pumpkin seeds with gapped front teeth, she crossed her thick thighs, spit

1. *Shabbat* (Hebrew)—Sabbath, day of rest, Judaism's seventh day of the week

shells, and reminisced, returning to her beginnings.

"I vas stra-ong girl! I luv sing, dance, laugh, joke."

She said she had no real memory of her father, who had died when she was two. She had been raised in Mashhad by Yocheved, her stepmother, whom she'd been led to believe was her birthmother, her beloved *mammon joon*.[2]

"I not know she not my mud-dair. I tink she eez mud-dair."

"What happened to your mother?"

"She die ven I vas born."

"But you didn't know that?"

My mother shook her head. "No."

"When did you find out Yocheved wasn't your mother?"

Mom frowned as she cracked more pumpkin seeds. "Later. Ven I vas ten."

"You never talk about her. You've never shown me a picture of her. Was she kind? Did you love her?"

"*Zan pedaer*[3] vas quiet voo-men. No talk much. Good cook. She nevair, nevair say *no* to me."

Mom said that when she and Yocheved would stroll through Mashhad's outdoor markets, Mom was forceful and demanded all she craved: pomegranate juice, pistachios, plums, bolts of colorful fabric to be hand-stitched into dresses for her.... Yocheved would snap open her purse and quickly buy whatever my mother desired.

"Alvays, she say *yes*. Vhat I vhant, I get."

My mother said this without any affection; she didn't say she loved Yocheved. I wondered why.

Mom's words, *What I want I always get*, aroused my envy and resentment. How self-centered, how selfish—always having to get what she wanted. Was this the source of her might? Was this why she was so powerful, so confident, never caring what others thought—able to stand alone, not needing anyone's approval? Did Yocheved strengthen Mom's will by never saying no? Did she do it on purpose? If so, why? Aren't there times when every mother must say no? Was Yocheved afraid of Mom—meek, cowardly, sidestepping temper tantrums? Or was she fearful of what her tightly knit underground community might think as they watched her mother a daughter who wasn't hers?

My parents grew up in Iran's holiest Islamic city—one of the

2. *mammon joon* (Persian/Farsi)—dear mother
3. *zan pedaer* (Persian/Farsi)—father's wife

holiest cities in the Muslim world. Its name, Mashhad, means place of martyrdom. Millions of Muslims make pilgrimages to Mashhad every year to worship at the shrine of the ninth-century martyr Imam Reza, who's buried there. Located in northeast Iran, close to the borders of Turkmenistan and Afghanistan, the city was a major oasis along the ancient Silk Road and grew into an important center of industry and trade. Nader Shah brought the first Jewish families to this city from other parts of Iran in the 18th century. After his assassination in 1747, anti-Semitism in Mashhad ran rampant, preparing the ground for a mob attack on the Jewish community in 1839 that left hundreds wounded and dozens dead. Survivors were given a choice: Convert to Islam or die. This day is known to Mashhadi Jews as *Allah Daad*.[4]

Jews who didn't flee, lived double lives, outwardly appearing to be Muslim while secretly observing Judaism. Generation after generation they hid their faith, leading underground lives through wave after crashing wave of anti-Semitism that peaked again with the spread of Nazism in World War II and Muslim fury over the creation of the State of Israel.

Mom didn't tell me all of this during one sitting. Some came out in future conversations, and the rest I later learned on my own. But once she began talking, her memories streamed.

Mom said she and Yocheved would scurry down streets and alleyways to *Eidgah*,[5] the Jewish ghetto, hidden behind their chadors, never knowing if or when they'd be unmasked, stoned, beaten, or lynched.

"Ma, how could you live that way? Weren't you scared?"

"Vee all scaired and steel vee stay." Her voice deepened. "Stoopeed. Vee all stoo-peed!"

In Farsi, she said, "We were a public secret." The Muslims of Mashhad knew who the Jews were, and from time to time, when hatred and prejudice boiled over, stonings and beheadings returned. Jews relied heavily on *reshveh*[6]—monetary bribes, paying Imams to look the other way, hoping to buy a few days or weeks of peace while praying for benign neglect. Muslim leaders went along with the charade. Sufficiently compensated by reshveh, they colluded, pretending these Jews were true converts, some of their own. However, on any random day of the year an Imam could decree that

4. *Allah Daad* (Persian/Farsi)—God's justice
5. *Eidgah* (Persian/Farsi)—Jewish ghetto in Mashhad
6. *reshveh* (Persian/Farsi)—monetary bribes

day another Allah Daad, granting Muslims license to pilfer, raid, and ransack homes of the *Jadid al-Islam*[7]—Jews who had outwardly converted to Islam.

On those days, from behind bolted doors, my parents heard mobs rushing through their ghetto, shrieking: "You're filthy! Despicable! Deserving of death!" Rioters pelted windows with rocks, crashed through gates, and broke into homes, terrorizing young mothers nursing their infants, ailing grandparents cowering in bed, and husbands on their knees, begging that their families be spared. Gun-toting pillagers took whatever struck their fancy—household furnishings, gold, silver, rugs. Eyeing the pubescent girls, calling them "whores," the invaders seized and raped, leaving behind grotesquely swollen heads and severed limbs.

One of my father's communal duties, I learned, was to periodically grease the local Imam's open palm, lavish him with bribes and fawning attention with hopes of averting a preselected day of Allah Daad.

Mom grimaced, remembering the Imams. "A swinish lot," she sneered in Farsi.

For generations my ancestors hid in plain sight, living a lie, blending, pretending, adapting to a culture that wanted to annihilate them. They befriended Muslim neighbors and shopkeepers, spoke in their vernacular, danced to their Islamic melodies, cooked their foods, used their spices, and shouted their curses. Mirroring Muslims, they painted the palms of their hands with henna, rubbed it on their hair, slapped *dayerehs*,[8] wore chadors, only to go home and braid *challah*,[9] light Shabbat candles, strictly keep kosher, perform circumcisions, and marry solely amongst themselves.

Stunned, I drank in each word. So much I didn't know. Did others know? Or did their story remain concealed, known only to those who had lived it. I mopped a stray tear and thought about what I had just been told. Would I have had the will and strength to survive? Could I have braved a community, a nation, a world turned against me? And, if so, at what price?

For sure, history's tentacles had attached themselves to Mom and Pop. Two hundred years of ancestral hiding must have left its imprint on their neural pathways. *Could centuries of enforced duplic-*

---

7. *Jadid al-Islam* (Persian/Farsi)—literally "new to Islam"; a term for Jews who had outwardly converted to Islam
8. *dayereh* (Persian/Farsi)—framed drum with jingles resembling a large tambourine
9. *challah* (Hebrew)—braided bread made with eggs and eaten on the Sabbath

ity and deceit alter genetic coding? Could it have altered Mom's DNA? I
answered *Yes.* A resounding *Yes. Yes* helped me endure and understand her. It explained her natural proclivity for twisting the truth,
distorting the facts, altering who she was, so she could always come
out on top. Perhaps she wasn't lying just for the fun of it, I told
myself. Perhaps even in Oscar de la Renta's showroom she was surviving Mashhad.

And as for Pop, the threat and dread of an Allah Daad day must
have hung over his head like a guillotine blade. Mashhad, New York
City—it made no difference. Allah Daad continued to hover, as if it
could happen anywhere and at any moment.

During my parents' years in Mashhad, the city was considered
the boondocks by the highly cultured and cultivated Iranians living
in Tehran. It was a city stuck in the Dark Ages, lacking electricity,
plumbing, toilets, hospitals, physicians, antibiotics, and any form
of anesthetics. Even though it was the second most populous city
in Iran, refrigerators, washing machines, and central heating were
unknown. Water running through gullies was brought into the
village by hand pumps and carried home in buckets. Toilets were
nonexistent, my mother said. Instead, families shared outhouses,
which amounted to huge, deep holes dug in the ground. Adults
took turns standing with one foot on either side of an open pit, and
children were held high because their legs weren't wide enough to
spread and stand. When I asked Mom if they used toilet paper, she
laughed.

"Neh.[10] Vee yuze vatair from *aftabeh.*[11]"

"Mom, didn't you leave the outhouse wet?"

"Vee pour vatair and dreep dry."

I gasped.

Mom refilled our glasses with steaming hot tea and leaned back
on silk turquoise pillows which she, at age nine, had embroidered.
In our living room, prominently displayed on an end table, were
a number of framed, jewel-toned Persian miniatures—intricate
scenes painted on ivory in a broad, rich palette of lapis lazuli blue,
yellow ochre, and bright orange flecked with gold leaf. The one
my parents treasured most, oddly enough, propped on a doily, por-
trayed love: a turbaned male and his chadored sweetheart curled
up on a Persian rug under a peach tree, sharing a loaf of bread and

10. *neh* (Persian/Farsi)—no
11. *aftabeh* (Persian/Farsi)—metal pitcher

a jug of wine—a scene illustrating a verse by the 12th-century Persian poet Omar Khayyam. It was odd because Mom and Pop's was a loveless marriage. I studied the painting, wondering if it was a painful reminder of what they secretly pined for and would never have.

Under this corner table sat an enormous pewter pot. I had never questioned its purpose and had just assumed it was some Persian planter in need of a tree. I decided to ask.

"Mom, why did you bring this with you, all the way from Iran?"

She told me it wasn't a planter but a cauldron she had used in Iran to boil chickens for chicken soup. Women cooked communally, and extended families always ate together in Eidgah.

"How many chickens did you fit in this tub?"

"Ten...may-bee twelf," she answered with pride.

Married couples never lived alone, all by themselves, Mom said. Grandparents, parents, uncles, aunts, cousins, married children, and grandchildren all lived under one roof. While women shopped, cleaned, and cooked together, men supported their extended families and protected their combined financial interests by working in the same trade. Some families were metal smiths, jewelers, tailors, rug dealers, while others were merchants who traveled between Mashhad and Boukhara, selling sugar, cinnamon, cardamom, and returning with bales of fur to market in Mashhad. Pop was a merchant, living off the Aminoff family's stellar reputation, traveling back and forth between Mashhad and Boukhara before Mom learned to walk.

Houses in Eidgah were purposefully interconnected, my mother said, sharing central courtyards that allowed men secret access into one another's homes for daily *minyans*.[12] In Farsi-inflected English, Mom told me that they learned to live like mice: running, hiding, everything done secretly. A terrible life.

Suddenly a thought punched me full in the face: *Isn't that my life?* Aren't I a muted mouse, scurrying about, hoping not to be seen? Hiding from Pop? Concealing friends? Bringing them in and out of the house in secret? I felt another eerie parallel.

Apart from fury, Mom also held fond memories of life in Eidgah. Flat pigeon-gray rooftops brought families together. On hot summer nights, men, women, and children stepped from roof to roof, spread out mattresses, picnicked on chicken kabobs, roasted pista-

---

12. *minyan* (Hebrew)—quorum of ten Jewish men age 13 or older required for communal worship in Orthodox Judaism

chios, and homemade *torshi*.[13] After trading tales, eating, drinking, and smoking their hookahs, they drifted into sleep.

Remembering cool, cozy twilights, nestled against Yocheved, gazing up at a navy blue sky brilliant with stars, Mom heaved a sigh. In Farsi she said, "Estaire, we loved sleeping on our roofs. There was no such thing as air-conditioning in Mashhad. The evening breeze was our refreshment. Climbing honeysuckle, clinging to our ghetto walls, perfumed the air. A honey scent I'll never forget. No matter where I am, once I smell honeysuckle, I return right away to Eidgah."

However, at the age of ten, Mom's life was ripped asunder. A meddlesome Mashhadi pulled her aside and scolded in Farsi: "Hana, stop calling Yocheved *mammon joon*. She isn't your beloved mother. Esther Levi was your real mother, and she died right after your birth. Your father married Yocheved to raise you. Your real mother is dead!"

Words that cut hard and deep. "Liar! Liar!" my mother screamed, as she ran off to find mammon joon. Beating Yocheved's chest with clenched fists, she pleaded, "Tell me! Tell me she's a liar!" My mother pressed her head against Yocheved's hammered breasts and wept. "Mammon joon, tell me the truth. Tell me you're my *real* mother." Yocheved held her as they sank to their knees, sobbing. Their long, tousled hair intertwined, sticking to each other's wet cheeks.

"This woman is cruel," Yocheved cried. "She had no right speaking to you this way. It's the wrong time. I was waiting for you to grow up." Yocheved blotted her face and reached for Hana's hands. "I was going to tell you everything once you had a husband, a family of your own, once I knew your husband's love would heal you."

Yocheved told my mother that her father, David, had first married his cousin Hana, who had given birth and died. David then married Hana's 12-year-old sister, Esther—my mother's mother. Esther provided him with four children: two sons and two daughters. The last, my mother, was born when the others were already grown. Esther died shortly after my mother's birth. Following his wife's death, David married Yocheved to care for his newborn daughter. Soon, Yocheved became pregnant with her own child, Solomon, my mother's younger half-brother. Then Death, like a sniper, struck again. When Mom was two, tuberculosis killed her father.

My mother didn't want to hear Yocheved's words. She tried to cover her ears, but Yocheved tightly held her hands. When she let them go, Hana gave Yocheved a sharp shove and hollered, "I HATE

13. *torshi* (Persian/Farsi)—pickled eggplant and cauliflower

YOU! You've lied to me! You're not my mother! You're a filthy liar!"

From that day on, my mother no longer addressed Yocheved as mammon joon. Instead she demoted Yocheved to the impersonal rank of zan pedaer.

From the age of ten until her death at 75, Mom never trusted again. Fixated on lies, on betrayal, she experienced the world as traitorous.

Swallowing a raw lump in my throat, I felt an unfamiliar tenderness. "Your mother died after childbirth and your father died when you turned two," I softly repeated. "You don't remember them. But Yocheved, your stepmother, raised you. You had *her*. She was kind, patient, generous, always looking out for you, never a harsh word." I took her hands, stroked her long, slender fingers. "Ma, you had a mother right from birth, and it was Yocheved. Why couldn't you love her?"

She pulled both hands away. Her face turned gray. "Vie you cheat me and say dees?"

Cheat meant betray, and betray meant not siding with her. My words lodged in her chest like darts. Why was I turning against her, not buying her story? Why was I robbing her of all justifications and entitlements to her version? As I spooned her Yocheved, Mom spat her out. Glaring at me from beneath a furrowed brow, stuck in childhood, she saw me as her enemy.

Feeling slapped across the face, I wanted to charge out of the room, convinced she was hopeless—always feeling sorry for herself when, all along, she had actually had a doting devoted mother.

Undeterred, she continued recalling her past.

Mom said that in the early 1920s, when she was born, Mashhad was hundreds of years behind Tehran, not having even some semblance of a medical facility. As women in labor writhed on bedroom floors, pushing, midwives instructed them to scream. This was called assistance. Many women died during childbirth, while others delivered stillborns. Lacking sufficient breast milk, new mothers left their twins and triplets out in the cold to perish. Mom shook her fists as she spoke of her parents' deaths, reliving anger at her double loss. Not only had she lost her mother and father but she didn't even remember them; she couldn't even call them to mind.

Mom said over and over that she was large-boned. Too big, too much, too strong, and so her explosive birth had killed off Esther, her frail mother. I listened, stupified. Had someone actually told her this? Or had she decided it for herself? Did she really believe she had caused her mother's death? For some, carrying this burden of guilt would be reason to speak softly, cower, hide, welcome a chador, and incarcerate that inner, mother-murdering force. Mom, on the contrary, exuded power. Some have a passion for restraint; she had a passion for full release.

She was not yet 14 when my 34-year-old father, Fatulla Nissan Aminoff, laid eyes on her. Fatulla was his Muslim name, and Nissan his underground Hebrew name. My mother's aboveground Muslim name was Agh Bibi, and Hana, her Hebrew name. They were both attending a Jewish wedding in a neighbor's basement when Fatulla peeled back the cloth *mekhitzah*[14] separating men from women and spotted her. Mom was tall, fair-skinned, full-lipped and dark-haired. Surrounded by gaggles of giggling girls, she—a natural comic—held court telling jokes. The other young women howled, begging for more. Blinded by her chiseled cheekbones, alabaster skin, fetching figure, Pop decided then and there Hana Levi would be his wife. He didn't speak to her, didn't know her thoughts or feelings, never even heard the sound of her voice, but he was certain she was perfect.

In Mashhad, it was common for pubescent girls to marry men 20 to 50 years older than themselves. Minorities, such as Jews, were at a higher risk of being raped, and once a girl's virginity was lost no man would wed her. So fathers protected their young daughters by marrying them off as soon as possible. Early marriage also helped maintain the Jewish community, safeguarding daughters from being taken in matrimony outside the faith. If a Muslim knocked on a door to claim a girl, parents could honestly reply: "She is spoken for."

Back then, Mashhadi Jews didn't just wed within their own community but, more specifically, within their own bloodline—often, as Mom's father had done, to first cousins. Aminoffs were promised to Aminoffs, Levis were matched with Levis, Hakimis with Hakimis.... Parents paired infants as future mates and placed them side by side in cradles. Generation after generation of in-breeding not only safeguarded against intermarriage but also helped keep possessions and property within each extended family.

Pop, a hardcore traditionalist, broke from tradition. Convinced he was the best judge of character, he refused to marry the Aminoff cousin his parents had chosen for him and instead selected my

14. *mekhitzah* (Hebrew)—partition or divider separating men from women during a religious service

mother—a Levi. Pop chose beauty and desire over blood and duty, a decision his father, Moshe, held against him his entire life. A difficult man under the best of circumstances, Moshe did not attend my parents' wedding and forbade Tuti from attending. He didn't send a gift and refused to have any contact with my parents after their marriage. My brothers and I never even met him.

In any case, Pop chose Mom. Thoroughly smitten, he must have forgotten he hated parties, despised hysterical laughter, and was a die-hard social recluse.

The very next day Pop sent a *khastegar*[15] to Yocheved's home, requesting Hana's hand in marriage. Overjoyed, Yocheved was certain Hana's deceased father had intervened and made it all happen— that he had reached down through the heavens, placed his hands on the crown of Hana's head, and blessed his orphaned daughter. Coming from a financially successful, highly respected Jewish Mashhadi family, Pop was viewed as a great catch. His tweed jackets and thick, wavy black hair cut British-style recalled two years spent at a London boarding school. And with or without his father's help, he had done well for himself, owning acres of farmland and fruit orchards, raising sheep, goats, and chickens, all attended to by hired hands. "He's aristocracy—a gentleman with princely means," Yocheved informed Hana. "Marrying into the Aminoff dynasty will heal all wounds and give you a lush life of love and luxury."

"Fatulla is an old man!" my mother fired back. "He could be my grandfather! And to make it worse, he's a full head shorter than me. I don't want him!"

"At your age, you can't possibly know what's best for you," Yocheved replied. "Fatulla is najib. He will become your father, mother, husband, and best friend. Once you grow up, you'll see I am right. He comes from very respectable stock, the finest Jewish family."

Never before had Yocheved defied my mother, but on this day she did.

Despite Mom's howling protests, Yocheved agreed to the marriage, and, even though Moshe disapproved, a regal wedding took place. The streets of Mashhad were lined with festive lanterns and red roses. My father wore a top hat and tuxedo; my mother, a French wedding dress. Pop had purchased Parisian lace embroidered with baroque pearls and had it stitched into a gown for his bride in Mashhad. Radically mismatched, they rode through the streets in a

15. *khastegar* (Persian/Farsi)—matrimonial representative who speaks on behalf of the suitor

chariot drawn by eight rose-festooned horses. It was 1938, and the pomp and pageantry outshone all other weddings.

None of this meant anything to my mother. Her heart was all used up. Repeatedly betrayed, she turned tough. She held both the city of Mashhad and Yocheved responsible for her misery: Mashhad for allowing her mother and father to die; Yocheved for taking her mother's place, deceiving her, and handing her over like crated cargo to some old man.

Mom began crying as she told me her story. Face flushed, she looked at me and said, "I suff-air, Estaire. Vonce I suff-air, I all-vays suff-air." According to her, people never healed from past hurts. It just wasn't possible. One of her lines was: "No one gets over anything, and I can't either." Looking like wreckage, like a human ruin, she reached for a box of tissues and wailed, "Estaire, I broken!" Her tears, a monsoon.

I found her story shocking and infuriating. A child forced to marry a stranger more than twice her age. Abduction, I called it. Sexual slavery. Rape.

"Mee-stake," Mom hissed through gapped teeth. "My life mee-stake. Iran burn me!"

For the first time, I felt I understood. She *had* been cheated: not allowed to live her own life, the one she deserved. Her life had been predetermined, locked into place. Mom had protested. She had never agreed to marry, had never given her consent, but in Mashhad female dissent was meaningless. Mournfully, she said, "Mashhad lit a match, charred my youth, and robbed me of choices."

There were questions that struck me later: Why, then, did she mock my studiousness and ridicule my wish to go to college? Brain scrambling. How could she curse her lot and want that same lot for me? How could she cry, feeling trapped, caged, and not fight for my freedom? Didn't I matter? Was she the only one who mattered? She stood up to Pop, wasn't afraid of him. That, I knew. So why didn't she support my will, defend my choices? I didn't know where she stood: Was she for me or against me? Didn't she want me educated, able to fend for myself? I, too, felt cheated. Maybe Mom wasn't my true birth mother, after all. Maybe, in years to come, I'll learn that mine had also died and Mom, just like Yocheved, was a stand-in.

Later, in a calmer state of mind, I told myself, *This is who she is. Accept her. She won't change.* But soon after, I found myself again wholeheartedly wishing and believing she would. I lived in a shifting space of longing and loathing, hope and despair, while Mom remained herself, rabidly fixed.

CHAPTER 5

Runaway Bride

By age 14, Mom was expected to coast through sex, pregnancy, natural childbirth, and parenthood without hitch or complaint. Unlike some other young girls, she couldn't. Instead, she came apart, cursing, smashing, storming out, leaving husband and child behind. In a rush to abandon her married life, she fled to neighboring houses with satchel in hand, vowing never to return to Pop. Decades later, a number of women from our Mashhadi émigré community confirmed Mom's stories, telling me how my hot-headed teenage mother charged into their homes seeking refuge, all the while cursing Pop and her wretched life. The very next day, after shooting off steam, she would trot back home feeling wisps of triumph.

But, by then, I already knew the stories were true, because as far back as I could remember, she repeatedly fled our home, too.

My parents frequently fought. They fought over what she said, what she shouldn't have said, what he didn't say, what he should have said, where she wanted to go, and where he forbade her to go. In the privacy of their red velvet bedroom, they fired Persian curses at each other that penetrated thin walls: *Tokhmeh sag. Pedaer sag.*[1] *Jendeh.*[2] *Bemir.*[3] As a child, I plugged my ears and cringed, imagining one killing the other, leaving behind bloodstained Persian rugs.

If divorce was not an option for Mom, running away was. Fleeing became a way of life; her quick response to matrimonial misery.

1. *pedaer sag* (Persian/Farsi)—fathered by a dog
2. *jendeh* (Persian/Farsi)—whore
3. *Bemir.* (Persian/Farsi)—May you die.

"I'll never return to this hellhole!" she'd shriek in Farsi. As a child, I was certain I was her hellhole. My gut told me I was bad...worse than bad...evil. If I was good, she'd want to stay. But she didn't. She wanted to leave. Slumped in a corner, sucking my thumb, I'd watch her drag a suitcase from deep inside a closet, throw it onto her bed, and frantically stuff it with belts, boots, and bras. Spewing curses, crying, she'd grab her traveling bag and fly out the door, leaving me behind.

As she ran, I'd run after her, wailing, begging her to come back. Sobbing, heaving from the pit of my stomach, I'd chase her down the sidewalk with short strides until her broad back vanished from sight. Pop would scoop me up and carry me back home.

Back in my bedroom, I'd hide under my bed, shut my eyes, clutch my chest, and try to wish it all away. I wanted Pop to stop her, take charge: barricade the doors, rope this bull, toss her over his knee and slap her butt.

But instead of meting out discipline, he condoned.

When I was older, Pop would say, "Estaire, every time she misbehaves, you must forgive her. She never had a mother or father." His eyes would well with tears. "Your mother is heartbroken." Then, in a charged whisper: "She's a *yateem*.[4]"

Yateem. A lame excuse. I didn't buy it. There had to be millions of grown-up orphans who didn't wail endlessly, tugging at their hair, who didn't pitch plates and routinely run away from their husbands and children—disappearing for days and hiding their whereabouts, wanting to create as much distress as possible, then sashaying home victorious, refusing to answer any questions.

While she was quick and loud, I remained soundless—not uttering a word for the first two years of my life. With enormous trepidation, fearing she had birthed a mute, she took me to a string of pediatricians, always asking if I had missing parts. Checkup after checkup, doctor after doctor assured her: "Esther has a working tongue and healthy vocal chords. All parts are in place." It was Dr. Horowitz who moved his chair to the side of his desk, smiled at my mother, and offered a solution.

"Hana, you've been talking to your daughter in both Persian and English. She's confused. If you drop Persian and speak only in English, she'll start using her voice." Influenced, no doubt, by the McCarthyist mood of the late 1940s and early 1950s, he believed

4. *yateem* (Persian/Farsi)—orphan

immigrants should rid themselves of all old-country ways—language, accents, clothing, rituals—and become 100 percent American. Backed by medical degrees and decades of experience, he staunchly pronounced that exposing children to multiple tongues led to neurological confusion. At the time, Mom could barely speak English, so she ignored his advice.

Dr. Horowitz was well-meaning but off the mark. At age two, I *was* confused and frightened. Not by a bilingual home, but by home. Curled up on the floor behind my brown crib, eyes stinging with tears as my parents fought, I chewed my nails until they bled. I'd pull my pink satin blankie through my crib's narrow slats, hide under it, and nervously sniff and suck a blissful blend of nighttime breath, sweat, and spit. Fluids. All mine, but they felt like someone else's. Another, wrapped around me, calmly swaying, lulling, never leaving.

Staying voiceless felt right. I sealed my lips, crawled inside myself, and spun a protective cocoon.

CHAPTER 6

Shepherd in Queens

Walking through the open streets of Queens with my mother, my face fully exposed, all I wanted to do was hide. Six years old, three feet tall, I was dressed in a pair of silky gold, ballooning pantaloons. My short arms barely protruded from a heavily brocaded sheepskin vest tailored to fit a mountainous, nomadic male. In blackest of black, Mom had penciled my brows and raccooned my eyes. On my head she had mounted a turban to match the vest—stitched with gold and silver coils, thickly banded in sequins, beads, and jingling bells. Satisfied, she had handed me a seven-foot-tall, hooked shepherd's staff. We were headed to the Adath Jeshurun Synagogue in Kew Gardens, Queens for the Hebrew School's Purim Costume Competition. Mom had entered me as a Boukharian shepherd.

Purim[1] is a holiday that commemorates the saving of the Jewish people from Haman, a heinous Persian minister who reported to King Ahasuerus (Xerses I). The story is told in *Megillat Esther—The Book of Esther*. Esther was an orphan who lived with her cousin Mordechai as a concealed Jew in the city of Shushan in the fourth century BCE. When King Xerxes I of Persia saw Esther, he was smitten by her beauty and immediately proclaimed her his Queen. Haman, the King's evil Prime Minister, hated Jews, and tricked the King into signing a decree stating they all be killed. When Esther learned of this from Mordechai, she courageously approached the King, revealed her true Jewish identity, and pleaded for her people. Swayed by love, Xerxes

---

1. Purim (Hebrew)—festival commemorating the defeat of Haman's plot to kill the Jews

reversed his decree, and the Jews of Shushan were saved. Esther had heroically risked her life in order to save the lives of her people.

Mom, certain she was a direct descendent of this Queen, claimed the holiday as hers. Not only did she believe her ancestors dated back to the Persian Empire, and not only had she lived as a hidden Jew in Mashhad just as Esther had concealed her Jewishness from King Ahasuerus, but her mother, also named Esther, had died after giving birth, orphaning Mom, just as the Queen had been orphaned. Outspoken and ravishingly beautiful, Mom identified with her heroine, convinced that she, too, would have used her wiles to sway the King, just as Queen Esther had done.

It was the 1950s, a decade committed to conformity and assimilation. Everyone watched *The Adventures of Ozzie & Harriet, Father Knows Best,* and *Lassie.* An impenetrable barrier separated those who ate Wonder Bread, Twinkies, and Campbell's Tomato Soup from those who didn't; girls who wore poodle skirts, cardigan sweaters, saddle shoes, single-strand pearl necklaces from those who didn't. If you had darker skin, spoke with a thick accent, drank rose water tea, and ate saffron rice, wore *saris*[2] and chadors, you were a pariah.

Kids in our neighborhood threw stink bombs at buck teeth, freckled faces, wiry hair—anyone who was different. On my first day of first grade, I wore three Persian gold bangles to school, only to be teased, taunted, reduced to tears by classmates proudly wearing Mickey and Minnie Mouse watches. One white boy with a flattened nose and swollen eyes rubbed my head with both hands and asked if I ate watermelon. I didn't understand why he was asking but figured it must have something to do with my jingling bracelets. If any of my classmates had heard Mom's discombobulated English, felt Pop's stinging stare, heard my parents speak to me in Farsi, I knew I'd be dead meat. And so I didn't invite other six-year-olds to our home. Sure, Pop forbade it, but I also knew our home was odd, and odd meant being an outcast. In the school cafeteria, I concealed my green lunchbox packed with Persian spinach patties wrapped in pita bread instead of peanut butter and jelly sandwiches. A total giveaway. Quickly, I learned a *never:* Never reveal the sounds and smells of Mashhad. If girls in my class knew how different I really was, they'd never again play hopscotch or jump rope with me. This was a fact.

That evening, I quaked as I entered the synagogue in my Boukh-

2. *sari* (Hindi)—length of cloth worn draped around the body as a skirt and shoulder or head covering

arian shepherd costume. The musty vest, brought to the States by my mother, reeking of sunbaked manure, smelled like a desert camel. Blanketed beneath layers of fabric, releasing a stench, I withdrew inside myself.

At age six, I had fantasies of my own and imagined myself dressing up as a woman of valor. Annie Oakley, the sharpshooting cowgirl, was my first pick. The vest, the pantaloons, the spangly turban and shepherd's staff had nothing to do with me.

Still, I didn't protest. I didn't say a word. Talking brought on heavy palpitations and made me sweat. I was nonconfrontational, one might say spineless, but I knew words led to trouble, especially if they angered Mom. She was quick to scream, quick to feel attacked, and quick to counterattack. This holiday of costumes, masks, swinging *graggers*[3] carried my mother back to her homeland. When I imagined myself saying, "I don't want to wear your Boukharian shepherd costume," all my what-ifs crept in: *What if she decides that means I don't love her? What if she decides that means no one loves her? What if she bawls hysterically? What if she runs away?* I couldn't see her as someone who would stay, so I held my tongue.

In the synagogue, my Hebrew school classmates came skipping into the auditorium dressed as doctors, nurses, firemen, policemen, school teachers, ballerinas. As they passed me and my seven-foot-tall shepherd's staff, their faces contorted.

"Yuk! What are you supposed to be?" They squealed with laughter.

No one but Mom and I knew the answer. Mortified, my cheeks burning, I zipped my lips and gazed enviously at my friends Nancy, Susie, and Amy. Each wore the garments of their future dreams: Nancy was dressed as a school teacher; Susie, as a nurse; and Amy, in a powder-pink tutu, as a ballerina—all New York possibilities, unlike a Boukharian shepherd.

After eating *hamantashen*[4] and harmonizing in song, my classmates and I were instructed to stand on stage so judges could take a good look at our costumes and decide who would take First Prize and be the lucky winner of a Brownie camera. It sat atop a tall chrome pedestal at one end of the stage. Brownies were a luxury item that my fellow classmates and I never dreamed of owning. We stared at its shiny black and silver face, almost drooling.

3. *graggers* (Yiddish)—noisemakers
4. *hamantashen* (Hebrew)—triangular Purim pastries

Fearful of tripping, I clutched my trailing pantaloons and shut my mouth tight as we filed onto the stage. The jingling band over my brow vigorously announced my presence. No one could miss those bleating bells even if they had somehow missed my towering staff. I stood on stage in costume, feeling unclothed. Our outfits, lit by yellow floodlights, were now blindingly luminous. Standing with my classmates in a single row, I tried to hide behind Susie, proudly dressed as a Red Cross nurse. She looked divinely American: bright white nurse's uniform, white nurse's shoes, and a triangular boat-shaped hat stamped with a Red Cross. Her doctor-father's stethoscope was draped around her neck. In one hand she held a medical prescription pad and in the other a thermometer. Thoroughly authentic, thoroughly in tune with the times. Becoming a doctor was a dream belonging only to boys. Nursing was our female equivalent. Susie came across as a classy, self-assured, six-year-old career woman. I could see in her upturned face that she knew the coveted Brownie would soon be hers. And so did I.

After clearing his throat, the assistant rabbi reached for the mike. Finding the tension unbearable, I left my body on stage and traveled to a sunny, deserted, tropical island where I felt grains of sand between my toes and a balmy breeze blowing through my loose hair. My jagged breathing settled into a calm rhythm. Leaving my body felt awfully good. Through the sound of crashing waves and the scent of salt air, I still could hear the assistant rabbi speaking. He had collected and tallied the judges' ballots, and the first-grade Grand Prize winner had been chosen.

The room grew still. Parents huddled, anticipating the moment they could clap and scream with joy.

"Tonight, every first-grader deserves to win," the rabbi announced in an attempt at reassurance. "You are all wearing such delightful costumes..."

Dozens of children nervously shifted their weight from foot to foot.

"...and each lovely costume adds to the joyful *ruach*[5] of Purim...."

Battling stomach cramps, I tuned out the rest.

Through squinting eyes, I vaguely registered parents in the audience half-heartedly applauding. Relieved it was over, my gaze flitted over the crowd and landed on Mom. Her hair glistened like wet coal. She was beaming, clucking, wildly waving her hands in the air.

5. *ruach* (Hebrew)—spirit

As my eyes latched onto hers, my knees knocked. This had to be a mistake. I had won.

My hyperventilating mother was jumping up and down, as if on a pogo stick, looking like a million-dollar lottery winner. Dressed as a Boukharian shepherd, I felt like the biggest loser of all, but, even so, I bent at the waist and bowed.

"Thank you," I said, trying with all my heart to mean it.

There were second- and third-place winners, but only the first-place winner took home a camera. Other children in costumes mirroring the American dream were going home empty-handed. Some stomped off stage looking cheated, while others meekly dried their tears with their sleeves. Susie gave me a backhanded wave as she passed by.

"Baa...baa...Go play with your sheep, prizewinner."

Drunk with success, Mom grabbed my wrist and paraded through the crowd with my camera held high.

Back then I didn't have the words, but I did feel this was Mom's triumph, not mine. In some awkward fuzzy way, I knew she was both the six-year-old child on stage and the 31-year-old mother clapping wildly. Winning, I now know, meant she and her Iranian roots had triumphed, beating all the pedigreed German Jews attending our synagogue. Here, in America, she was not only free to show her face but finally free to win, taking revenge on every educated American mother she felt had scorned her.

I studied Mom's exuberance as she waved the camera high. While she felt coronated, I felt shamed. At age six, Annie Oakley galloping over hills and through valleys was my wished-for self, with or without a camera strapped across my chest. But Mom was telling me, *No. You don't know who you should be. I know.*

Day after day, my own voice became more difficult to hear, as if through gauze and steady static. Trying to sort it out, I arrived at a seesaw equation: For Mom to spring up, I must sink down. For Mom to feel victorious, I must feel swindled. A sour deal that smelled like rotten eggs.

CHAPTER 7

Kosher at Christmas

Mom was a Radio City Music Hall Rockette junkie. The *Christmas Spectacular Starring the Radio City Rockettes* was our yearly December ritual. Months ahead, she'd stand in line to buy two tickets smack in the center of the Orchestra section.

On the day of the performance, pressed into a hooded snowsuit and galoshes, I'd hold her hand as we slogged through snow heading to the subway.

A sign in the theater's lobby warned in bold block letters: "No Food From Outside Permitted." When I translated the English into Farsi, Mom shot back, "So vhat!" *So vhat* was her trademark reply. No one was going to tell her what she could or couldn't do, not even Radio City Music Hall. Each year, we'd sit in the center of this heavily gilded, Art Deco, 6,000-seat theater, watching the Christmas Spectacular and strictly keeping kosher.

Mom's eyes devoured the show. In Mashhad she never saw rows of synchronized, seminude females bouncing uniformly and high-kicking their lean legs to "Winter Wonderland," "White Christmas," and "I Saw Mommy Kissing Santa Claus." Studying the straight line of broad-smiling dancers in their scanty red-and-white Santa Claus outfits topped with pom-pom hats, her lips would part as she slid another glazed almond into her mouth. Stealthily reaching into our smuggled-in brown bags, we'd munch on Mom's homemade walnut cake, her *Nan-e Berenji*[1] and her oven-roasted glazed almonds. We'd duck our heads, discreetly sipping from cans

1. *Nan-e Berenji* (Persian/Farsi)—Persian rice cookies

of Red Cheek apple juice. Watching the leg-swinging dancers, I secretly chewed, secretly swallowed, secretly drank, expecting to be caught and handcuffed. Each of our sneaked-in snacks reminded me I was Iranian, Jewish, kosher, and an outlaw. For Mom, consequences were inconsequential. She remained cool and calm; I sweated for the two of us.

After a quick change of stage scenery, the Christmas Spectacular's highlight would begin: "The Living Nativity." Trumpets, saxophones, flutes, violins, cellos, drums, and cymbals heralded the birth of Christ. The audience would gasp as the theater darkened and an ultramarine sky studded with twinkling stars enveloped the stage. Shepherds, kings, and the three Magi paraded across the stage with sheep, camels, and a donkey to stand shoulder to shoulder before the Virgin Mary, Joseph, and the Baby Jesus, welcoming the haloed son of God. Women to my left and right rapidly crossed themselves while fingering their rosary beads. Nuns in black-and-white habits shut their eyes and entered a meditative trance. My mother thought nothing of letting me watch scantily clad dancers high-kick on stage. But a celebration of the birth of Christ was something different. "Estaire, don't look," she'd whisper in Farsi. "This is *asoor*.[2] Just eat your cake."

I did as told. I shut my eyes to orchestra, Magi, Mary, Joseph, Baby Jesus, Christmas carols. It made no sense. Mom was telling me to enjoy the show but ignore Jesus—pretend he wasn't there. But he was. He was the whole show. I had seen the pageantry, heard the music and singing. Even with closed eyes, "The Living Nativity" lived in my mind like a 3-D movie I couldn't turn off. I slouched down, curled into a ball of nerves, and bit my nails. *I'm sinning* scrolled across my brain. *If my Hebrew school teachers see me now, they'll kick me out of class and tell me never to return. What if one of them is here, spying on me?*

Sinking down deeper in my seat, I hid. During the birth of Christianity, I chomped on Mom's dense walnut cake and stared at my tightly laced Buster Brown saddle shoes, concentrating hard on remaining Jewish.

And yet, despite Mom's fear that this part of the Christmas Spectacular could trigger instant conversion, we returned every year. Each December, wrapped in woolens, we also made a special trip to see the Christmas windows on Fifth Avenue. Stoked by her mounting determination to reject her Mashhadi roots and conquer Man-

2. *asoor* (Hebrew)—not allowed, forbidden

hattan, Mom elbowed us to the front of each line snaking past Saks, Lord & Taylor, Bonwit Teller, and B. Altman. Coated with snow, shivering in the wind, my mother came to see the animated displays—the twirling princesses and dancing reindeer, the laughing Santas and hard-working elves.

Standing together in front of a Lord & Taylor window one December day when I was about ten, she told me that, growing up in Iran, she never had toys.

"Not even a doll?" I asked in disbelief.

"Not even a doll" she answered as she handed me a Barton's chocolate lollipop.

My chest cramped. I was whisked back to Vicky and the empty doll box. Mom often bought me toys. Why couldn't I have had that doll? Was she too pretty? Too American, with her green eyes and copper-colored hair? Why had Mom said *yes* when she really meant *no*? I still wasn't sure. But, I did know that when her yesses came too quickly, they were often empty and I shouldn't believe them.

I also distrusted my own recollections. Maybe I never saw Vicky. Maybe Mom never gave me an empty box. Maybe I was imagining it. Mom often tried to twist my memory, bend it out of shape, claiming that what I recalled had never happened, that the whole day had never happened. Was I supposed to trust her over myself? I needed her solidly on my side and didn't know how to get her there.

Mom said that in Mashhad there were no store-bought toys, no cartoons, no comic books, and certainly no walking-talking-dancing-flying animated puppets. Her childhood wasn't peopled with nationally known and loved characters such as Mickey Mouse, Donald Duck, and Porky Pig. Instead, Yocheved stuffed a sock, attached two buttons for eyes, and cross-stitched a long wobbly line to simulate a sealed mouth. Mom played for hours with this sock face, turning it into whoever she needed it to be. I imagined her very little, sitting on a cold wooden floor, talking endlessly to a sock, and wondered if this had anything to do with Vicky's disappearance.

Our annual trek to Macy's on 34th Street marked the culmination of Mom's Christmas pilgrimage. She enjoyed the window display, but that wasn't the purpose of our visit. She wasn't interested in the holiday sales. Instead, she had a pounding need to visit Macy's in-house Santa Claus. A holiday highlight.

I was five years old the first time she took me to stand on the Santa Claus line. With clenched jaw, she let me know this was not negotiable. I said nothing. Heavy-hearted, I stood behind American children eagerly waiting their turn to sit on Santa's lap.

We didn't believe in Christmas or Santa Claus, and we never had a Christmas tree in our living room. Instead, our kosher kitchen was decorated with brightly lit *Hanukkah*[3] *menorahs*,[4] multicolored *dreidels*,[5] and chocolate coins. I didn't know why I was on this line. Did she want me to lie...grow up to be a liar?

My turn came. Barely three feet tall, hair tied up in twin ponytails, I inched my way toward a big, white-bearded, red-and-white-clad Santa. With a fleshy stomach leaking out from under his brown belt, he thundered: "Come, little girl! Sit on my lap."

I timidly obeyed.

"What do you want Santa to bring you on Christmas Eve?"

I didn't answer.

"What do you want me to fill your Christmas stockings with, my little friend?"

He wasn't my friend. My mind went blank. I was scared. Pleadingly I looked up at Mom for help.

"*Begu*,[6]" she commanded in Farsi.

All I wanted was to slip off of his lap and run home, but I knew that wasn't an option.

"A toy," I said softly.

"What kind of toy, little girl?" He was now annoyed.

This was asking too much of me. I didn't want to be sitting on this strange man's fat thighs in the first place. I remained silent.

Losing patience, he smiled, slid me off his lap, nudged me toward Mom, and reached for the next child—a willowy black girl with tightly braided cornrows and red and green Christmas ribbons neatly woven through her hair. With a determined face, she climbed onto his lap and pressed up against his sagging belly.

"I want a doll with a red velvet dress and a white lace petticoat. I want my doll to have a baby carriage. I want a record player, a brand-new Slinky, black patent leather Mary Jane shoes for church, a navy blue wool coat with leopard cuffs and a matching leopard hood...."

My jaw hung. She spoke. She answered him. In a loud voice. She wasn't afraid. She had lots of words. She told Santa what she wanted. Why couldn't I?

3. *Hanukkah* (Hebrew)—Festival of Lights marking rededication of the second Temple in Jerusalem
4. *menorah* (Hebrew)—eight-branched candelabrum with a central socket used during Hanukkah
5. *dreidel* (Hebrew)—four-sided spinning top played during Hanukkah
6. *Begu*. (Persian/Farsi)—Tell him.

CHAPTER 8

Tuti

Mom always knew what she wanted. I was three-and-a-half when she announced to Pop in Farsi, "I'm sending a letter to your maniacal father telling him to release his wife. She's being suffocated by this brute, and just because you don't speak to him doesn't mean I can't."

My grandparents had left Iran shortly after my parents and had settled in Jerusalem. Tuti, married to Moshe from age nine and now in her eighties, had been held captive for more than 70 years by her vitriolic husband. Albert's bar mitzvah was approaching, and Mom wanted to use this festive occasion as reason to bring Tuti into our fold, since she had not, as of yet, been allowed to meet any of us. According to Mom, Tuti would soon be crossing the Atlantic Ocean for Albert's bar mitzvah.

Everyone in the family laughed. No way would our grandfather allow his wife to leave his side—not to visit America, and certainly not to be with Pop. After doing poorly in boarding school, squandering Moshe's money in England, and making some careless business decisions after returning to Mashhad, my father had then committed the unpardonable sin of marrying my mother. He was more than a disappointment; he was a despised and disowned son. Mom's hot-headed demand that Moshe unlock his wife and send her skipping into our open arms would, we were sure, only further enrage him.

But with gut determination, Mom set out to overpower her father-in-law. First she dictated numerous letters to her brother, Aaron, who wrote on her behalf. It was Aaron who had come to the U.S. before Mom and urged her to follow. Aiding his younger sister, he now wrote letter after letter to Moshe, all of which Moshe ignored. Next, Mom had Aaron write more than 30 letters to Pop's siblings and their spouses living in other countries, and to the elders of the Mashhadi community in Jerusalem, insisting they pressure Moshe to set Tuti free. This was the father-in-law who hadn't attended my parents' wedding, had never acknowledged their union, and had never attempted to know us, his three grandchildren.

As expected, my grandfather adamantly said *No* and my mother relentlessly said *Yes*. Mom wouldn't give in. A pigheaded tug of war turned into a contest of wills. For her, this deadlock took on a meaning and magnitude of its own. Without it ever being said, it later became clear to me that she was campaigning with all her might not just for Tuti but for every oppressed, voiceless, third-world wife.

Three months later, in October, Tuti was seated on a TWA plane, bound for New York City.

Mom had performed a miracle. Every Mashhadi family living in Kew Gardens was in awe of her supernatural powers. To this day, no one fully knows how she triumphed over Moshe's obstinate will. Perhaps engaging the elders of the Jerusalem community shamed him into consent. He never broke his silence, so we'll never know.

Pop, Mom, my two brothers and I taxied to Idlewild Airport to anxiously await her arrival. We were extra early, afraid that Tuti, who had never before stepped foot in the States and was unable to speak a word of English, would arrive before us. Mom, towering over Pop in the backseat of the taxi, broadcasted her worst fears, rapidly making them ours: What if this huge international airport, with all its convoluted, multileveled glass corridors and soaring crisscrossing escalators, made Tuti feel weak, dizzy, and terrifyingly disoriented? What if her head started to spin and she suddenly fainted and, when revived, couldn't even utter her own name? What if she felt lost and abandoned?

Strutting through the airport with the rest of us trailing in her wake, Mom headed directly for the Baggage Claim area. Ignoring a sign stating "Passengers Only," she pushed through the swinging doors and began weaving her way around the luggage conveyor belts, shouting at the security guards, "Tuti no can find suitcase! I find suitcase!" Meanwhile scanning with darting eyes for a frightened-looking mother-in-law she had never met and instinctively loved.

Standing with Pop outside the closing doors, I saw perspiration drip down his face and watched him wipe his wet forehead with a soggy hanky. He pulled out a cigarette, smoked one after another. I didn't know if he was chain-smoking because Mom was on the prohibited side of the swinging doors or because he was about to meet a mother he hadn't seen in more than 15 years. Then again, perhaps he was feeling his father's rage all the way from Jerusalem. Pacing and sweating, veins bulging at his temples, Pop inhaled an entire pack of Camels, sending streams of smoke towards the ceiling. Since he was shaking, I shook too.

Suddenly, he dropped down on one knee, took both my hands in his and said, "My mother is a great woman, Estaire. Someday you will grow up, be just like her, and make me proud."

I listened, startled, not knowing what to think. Finally, the doors swung open and my mother appeared with my tiny grandmother, four feet tall, 80 pounds, her bony arm comfortably resting in the loop of my mother's arm. Small and delicate, half Mom's size, in slippered feet, Tuti shuffled toward us. Her white mousey bun was bound in a tight knot at the nape of her neck. Her baby-blue eyes looked blank and bewildered, as if they had never before seen the light of day. As she ever-so-slowly made her way to us, the corners of her thin lips gently lifted into a smile.

My father ran to his mother, bent over her, first kissing the back of her gnarled, calloused hands and then, with tearing eyes, kissing each of her sunken cheeks. Wide-eyed, we three children followed Pop's lead, mindful of her frailty when hugging.

With a look of childlike innocence, Tuti stood before us, clutching her passport, wearing a thin cotton housedress. Since she would be staying with us for two months, we expected to see suitcases. Mom asked Tuti for her baggage receipt, and Tuti said she didn't have any luggage. My mother looked at her, bewildered. Hadn't she brought any change of clothing—blouses, dresses, shoes, underwear, a winter coat?

Tootie smiled bashfully, "*Neh, Aroos joon.*[1]"

Her husband had tossed her into the plane empty-handed, without an overcoat or even a pocketbook. Mom shook her head in disgust as Persian curses rolled out of her mouth.

"*Tokhmeh sag, harum zadeh,*[2]" Mom hissed.

1. *aroos joon* (Persian/Farsi)—dear bride
2. *harum zadeh* (Persian/Farsi)—bastard

Tuti naively grinned.

At the mention of Moshe's name, Pop began twitching and sweating.

Eyeing tiny Tuti up and down, I felt warmly towards her but also a bit confused. This was who Pop wanted me to become? Still, I was glad she was here. I'd never had a grandmother before.

After we brought Tuti home, Mom sped off to Macy's. On a rampage, she raced around buying winter coats, matching hats, leather pocketbooks, long-sleeved wool dresses, cardigans, scarves, thick stockings, shoes, underwear, the works—all for her newfound mother-in-law.

Each morning Mom would carefully coordinate Tuti's wardrobe and slip her into well-matched outfits, as if she was a toy doll. Never before had she been so pampered. My grandmother let my mother dress her, softly giggling, enjoying being fussed over. And yet a lifetime of marriage to a man who demanded silence had taken its toll.

During Tuti's two-month stay, my mother made sure to take her to the major tourist attractions: the Statue of Liberty, the Empire State Building, Rockefeller Center, Times Square, and Central Park. My grandmother would return from these day trips looking dazzled and dumbfounded by all she had seen. But she said almost nothing, speaking only when spoken to and then very few words.

Whenever Mom needed to food shop or go downtown to Delancey Street for her kosher meat, she'd leave me at home with Tuti, who not only couldn't speak a word of English but seemed to have no interest in speech. Any fantasies I may have had about climbing into a grandmother's warm lap to squeeze, snuggle, and cuddle quickly vanished. Instead, when left alone with my *bibi*,[3] I sat on the carpet at her stockinged feet and silently played with my wooden blocks while she sat in an armchair, quietly stitching hems, darning socks, helping Mom with her basket of clothes that needed mending.

Albert's bar mitzvah celebration took place on a Saturday afternoon in our dining room. Some 30 members of the Kew Gardens Mashhadi community gathered in our home to mark my brother's coming of age. I don't remember much about the event. I do remember that for the entire week leading up to it, Mom spent whole days in the kitchen, cooking, basting, frying, and baking, with Tuti keeping her company. As my mother unleashed the full range of her remarkable culinary skills, my grandmother would sit

3. *bibi* (Persian/Farsi) — grandmother

silently in the kitchen on a wicker chair, hands folded in her lap, watching and looking delighted. When I think of her now, that is how I see her.

While my bibi had arrived in New York empty-handed, she returned to Israel with two huge suitcases stuffed with high-end American attire. We never found out what Moshe's reaction was. He maintained his silence until his death, which took place about seven years later. Pop sat *shiva*[4] for his father in our home, but did not attend the funeral.

My father saw his mother again only once, many years later, when my parents flew to Israel to pick out their own burial plots. After his father died, Pop decided he wanted to be buried in Jerusalem, too.

4. *shiva* (Hebrew)—seven-day period of mourning

CHAPTER 9

Rearview Mirror

Despite the pride and satisfaction she took in briefly prying Tuti free of Moshe's vice-like grip, despite her anger at having been married off as a young girl against her will, my mother seemed to possess the same fervent expectations for me that my father did.

I was in my bedroom, intensely studying for a high-school biology exam when Mom stormed in.

Wrapped in a Crisco-stained apron, shaking a stalk of rhubarb at me, she snarled in Farsi, "Estaire, forget books. You must learn to become a housewife. Come into the kitchen and help me make *sambooseh.*[1]"

"Ma, leave me alone."

"Leave you alone?" Her voice swelled and rolled over me like an avalanche. "If you don't learn to cook, you will be all alone! No man will ever want you. You'll be a *khaneh mandeh.*[2]"

Livid, I yelled back, "You cook all day long! That's all you know how to do!"

"When your husband comes home from work, tired, hungry, what will you give him? Maybe you'll put multiplication tables on his dinner plate?" She leaned back, chortling. "You think that will fill him?"

Hunched over my textbook, I ignored her and kept studying until she gave up and left the room.

Multiplication tables. What about words? Sentences? Thoughts and conversation? Not just for dinner but exchanged freely. What

1. *sambooseh* (Persian/Farsi)—triangular pastry filled with chopped meat
2. *khaneh mandeh* (Persian/Farsi)—colloquial for old maid, spinster

about a husband who didn't want me stupid and silent, but instead full of ideas and opinions.

Even though she was echoing Pop's anti-education tirades toward me, I knew she had always wanted better for herself. How many times had I seen her tears, witnessed her pain, how often had she told me in a tone tinged with misgivings that she wished she had been schooled?

Every day our front and back doors swung open as a posse of Persian women charged in, eager to be entertained by Mom. Her satirical tongue evoked howling laughter as she impersonated each housewife's Iranian husband. With the same natural talent for comedy that Pop had witnessed when he first set eyes on her through a mekhitzah at an underground wedding in Mashhad, Mom's words, timing, delivery and stage presence kept these women crying with laughter and guaranteed they'd come back for more. And yet, still, she lived with sharp pangs of loneliness, felt isolated, shut out by her illiteracy.

The first time she confessed this to me was when I was three years old. Unable to read books, newspapers, road signs, PTA announcements, worn thin by sadness, she grieved in Farsi. "Estaire, I am forever wounded. Because I cannot read I feel shot in the head. There's a bullet lodged in my brain. I'm a cripple—blind, lost, alone, sealed in a cave. Can you understand me?" She wept tears into Persian lace hankies that had traveled with her from her homeland.

Right then and there, I vowed: *I'm going to fix Mom. When I learn to read, I'll teach her.*

Three years later, carrying a satchel filled with notebooks, homework pads, a wooden ruler, a pencil box filled with No. 2 pencils, and a brand-new Pink Pearl eraser, I marched into my first-grade classroom holding my head high. I was in school for the two of us. Mrs. White had never, in all her years of teaching, come across such a fanatically diligent first-grade student. On Friday afternoons she decorated each page of my writing workbook with gold stars, not knowing I was soaking up her every word so I could run home each day and become Mrs. White for my 31-year-old mother.

Lessons were held at our dining table. Mom made sure freshly baked Nan-e Berenjis, *Nan-e Taftuns,*[3] and a tall glass of Bosco chocolate milk were awaiting me. Our home was cushioned with Persian carpets. Standing beside my mother as she sat at the table, I nervously dug my bare toes into our Kashan's beet-red, cinnamon, cor-

3. *Nan-e Taftuns* (Persian/Farsi)—Persian scones

al, and indigo pile as I tried to teach Mom what I had just learned.

Two-letter words like it, at, to, go, no were joyfully mastered; however, getting beyond two letters was a grueling challenge. Remembering the silent k's, the silent g's, the infuriating th's, the short and long vowels, was hopelessly difficult for her. Each day she forgot what I had taught her the day before. Tossing my short arms in the air, I yelled and threatened to quit. She slammed shut her black-and-white marbled composition book and cried in defeat. Days went by, then we tried again, and again, still making no progress.

I became a bully. I accused her of not concentrating. "Pay attention to me! You're not studying hard enough. You're not memorizing your lessons. Your homework is full of mistakes. You must work harder. Mom. If you don't improve, I'll quit!"

I didn't intend to quit. I was going to drag her with me from first to second to third grade, no matter what. I had to remove that bullet stuck in her brain. I also had a burning need of my own: the need for an educated mother—one I could look up to, learn from, and lean on.

Even though I had accused her of not working hard enough, I realized eventually that her study habits were not the problem. She didn't master even first-grade reading because she simply couldn't. Perhaps she could have learned to read during early childhood. Perhaps her young mind had missed the window of time when literacy readily sticks. In any case, hard as she tried, she could not learn. It was now too late.

This made her need me all the more. Among fruits and vegetables Mom was a wiz. She was the keenest shopper in all of Queens. Hawkishly smelling, squeezing, and shaking watermelons, honeydews, pineapples, pomegranates, coconuts, she did everything short of biting before making her pick. But once we entered aisles of packaged food, her face lost its steely confidence. She clung to me like a child, gripping my hand and making sure I stayed close. Handing me a pack of Vienna Finger cookies, she asked under her breath, "Estaire, dees ko-shair?" Standing on the tips of my toes, I whispered into her ear the listed ingredients, carefully making sure none of the other A&P housewives weaving through the aisles heard me. Mom didn't want them to find out we kept kosher, much less that she was illiterate. Assured by me that the cookies contained pure vegetable shortening, Mom studied the cellophane wrapping, tossed ten packs into her shopping cart, and sealed them in her memory—under the kosher column.

I grew ashamed of her. I was embarrassed by her booming voice, her thick Persian accent, her obsession with cooking, and her gypsy-esque slapping of her goat-skinned dayereh at family celebrations. I was humiliated when she cut into long, highly civilized American lines, busting in with jabbing elbows, claiming the front of the line as hers, forcefully gripping my hand, yanking me alongside. She always had to be the first to enter a movie house, a Broadway theater, a city bus, an airplane, and the first at a concession stand. Supermarket lines were hers to jump. Shaking their black, white, and brown fists at us, people in line would yell, "What the hell do you think you're doing, lady?" Rage escalated into hair-raising curses. In response, Mom lifted her chin, deafened her ears, and with a regal calm looked straight ahead, as if the angry protests had absolutely nothing to do with her. She wasn't budging. She felt divinely endowed with certain unalienable rights, one of which was the right to come before all others. I wanted to trade her in for an Anglo-Saxon mom who stood politely in line and read *Life Magazine*. I hated myself for thinking this way, but I did.

There were, of course, childhood roots to my mother's behavior. Orphaned soon after birth, she believed she had been cheated from the very start. Robbed of her biological parents, married off at age 14 against her will, she felt the world owed her big time. Mom demanded restitution, and being first was only one of her many collectable paybacks.

Unable to master the written word, she decided a few years later that she'd try her hand at driving. Pop didn't drive, but he purchased a red Valiant for Albert and David to use when they received their licenses. One evening Mom loudly announced: "I drive car." In Iran she and Yocheved traveled by *doroshkeh*.[4] Concealed from head to toe in their black chadors, they sat on a wooden bench behind the grizzly, toothless, threadbare driver. Driving a car was a far cry from riding in a horse-drawn buggy, but this didn't dissuade her.

Neither did my father's reaction. When she announced she was going to take driving lessons, he stomped through the living room, with clenched fists. "Why do you have to drive? Driving will only bring death and disgrace to our family."

"I must drive to buy my kohlrabi for *Chelow Nokhod Aab*,[5]" she replied in Farsi. "I have to drive to the vegetable stores in Corona to

4. *doroshkeh* (Persian/Farsi)—horse and buggy
5. *Chelow Nokhod Aab* (Persian/Farsi)—Persian stew made with beef, meat balls, green vegetables, kohlrabi, lima beans, and mild spices

find firm, fresh ones. They can't be found in Kew Gardens."

All the other Hakimi, Azizollahoff, Djemshidoff, Ebrahimoff, Levian, and Aminoff wives bought their kohlrabies from the local A&P. They did not drive. No woman in our Mashhadi community drove a car, except for my Auntie Millie, my Uncle Aaron's wife, who was raised in London.

"You behave like a man!" my father yelled, grinding his teeth. "This is not dignified behavior. This is not womanly. A woman should not drive a car. This cheapens you and brings dishonor to our family name."

With her hands tightly squeezing her wide hips and her nose snapping in the air, my mother retorted: "I drive!"

She began taking lessons. Each morning Mr. Goldschmidt, her driving instructor, pulled up in front of our gabled house. He was a 10:00 a.m. punctual man. Short, stout, doubled over, and in his eighties, he'd help her into the passenger side of the front seat of his car and whisk off.

Pop clutched his head as Mom got ready to leave. "You will murder a stranger crossing the street or end up killing yourself in a car accident. We will be dragged through courts and you will be thrown into prison. Your children need you. Think of them."

Undaunted, she, with a Mae West strut, headed out the door to meet Mr. Goldschmidt.

Unable to stop her, Pop was reassured by the fact that Mom could not read or write. He was certain she'd never be granted a license. He endured her lessons with Mr. Goldschmidt by counting on the brilliance of the American system: She'd fail all her written exams and be found out. But on her very first try my mother passed her written and driving tests. To this day, I don't know how.

And drive she did—to Corona, Queens, to purchase her produce, but that wasn't all. On oppressively humid summer nights, after feeding her family, she would turn to me and say wistfully, "Estaire...you vhant go to airport?" That was my cue. We would climb into the Valiant and take off for Idlewild Airport, later renamed John F. Kennedy International Airport.

Riding up front next to her, I knew my life was at risk. For Mom, rearview mirrors were used only to reapply lipstick. Side mirrors were for decoration. Entering and exiting frenetic highways, weaving in and out of curving lanes on Queens Boulevard, and merging onto the Van Wyck Expressway, my mother drove with the unshakeable conviction that surrounding cars were all looking out for *her* and, as a result, she had nothing to worry about.

Other drivers honked like hell, their hands simultaneously slamming their steering wheels and foreheads. Male middle fingers shot out of rolled-down windows. In return, Mom with a carefree smile waved back and continued to blissfully cut in and out of speeding lanes. Riding shotgun in a time before seat belts, reading signs to her, watching for other cars, head swiveling, nails digging deeper and deeper into the upholstery, I was her navigator, co-pilot, and rearview mirror, shouting, "NOT NOW, MOM! WAIT.... NOW! GO!"

It was terrifying. And yet each time she asked, "Estaire...you vhant go to airport?" I went. I never said no.

Driving was my mother's fix. With windows wide open, she sped along and sung to the blast of rock 'n' roll radio like some daredevil teen. On steamy summer nights, as her hair blew every which way, she'd tell me to lift my arms, expose my armpits and cool off in the wild wind.

Mom's joyride peaked once she reached Idlewild. Gliding over ramps, racing from one airline terminal to another, recklessly flooring the gas pedal, we flew by Pan Am, TWA, Iceland Air, KLM, Swissair, and, of course, El Al. Sailing over intertwining lanes, her face softened; the unobstructed cobalt sky was hers now that my father was nowhere to be seen. Blithely, she was flying her own private jet. On these summer nights she rang of freedom. For an hour Mom cruised over every available ribboning ramp, over and over again, jetting away into the *can-do* night, before turning to me and saying, "Ready go home?"

If she was, then I was too.

These twilight trips began when I was ten and continued each summer into my teens. While Albert was studying architecture at Cornell and David was mastering English literature at Columbia, Mom and I were riding ramps.

By the time I turned 14, I understood that these evenings weren't just about cooling armpits or visiting an airport. Nor was I risking my life just to be compliant. I now accompanied Mom, summer after summer, with a very different agenda—hoping her intrepid spirit would seep into me. Each summer evening, I rode beside Mom, absorbing her *willfulness*, siphoning her strength. ▨

CHAPTER 10

On Ice

The minute I was born, Mom decided she was going to give herself an American childhood, both through me and with me.

I remember the winter day she came home with white leather skates, a red flared skirt appliquéd with winged blades, and a thick white cable-stitched turtleneck sweater with matching cable-stitched tights. I must have been six. Standing over me, she insisted I try everything on. I did. She quickly pulled a woolen pom-pom hat on my head, tightly tied it under my chin, and slipped my fingers into matching pom-pom gloves. I winced. I had *never* expressed interest in ice-skating

Should I want what I don't want? I wondered. *She must know what I should want. Maybe I'll want it once I learn how to do it. Learning to skate might be like learning to walk—something I need to know. Maybe I'll grow up and thank her for not asking me what I want. And if I don't complain and just skate, maybe I'll make her real happy. A happy that stays for lots of days. A happy that will make me happy.* Although Mom's wishes for me didn't match mine, I concluded: *I must be wrong and she must be right.*

There had been no ice-skating rinks in Mashhad. Muslim women and those who pretended to be Muslim didn't wear short, flared skirts, and they never twirled, balancing on the tip of a sharp blade in the middle of a frozen pond. Legs were never exposed. Thighs didn't cross and spin. Women kept them still beneath their chadors. And ice was scraped only to refrigerate food—never danced upon. Mom didn't tell me why she chose ice-skating for me, and

I doubt she even knew, since most of her decisions came straight from her gut. Looking back I think, through me, she was defying Mashhad.

Every Sunday, she reached into her grocery-money envelope and carefully counted out enough bills to pay for a private half-hour skating lesson at Rockefeller Center's ice-skating rink. And each Sunday, I was matched with the same tall, lean, handsome, white-gloved instructor. Tightly clutching his hands, I was pulled into the center of the rink. Piped orchestral music, floating over hard ice, sounded like a flat lie. Skating was brutal. My toes were squashed, both ankles ached, and my nose froze into a red nugget. As winter winds scoured my cheeks and teared my eyes, I let out puffs of pain and forced cheeriness. I didn't grumble or complain, just wore a fake smile.

Bundled up, Mom leaned over the tall railing watching my every move. I held my instructor's firm waist as he dragged me around the rink and waved with one hand as I passed by. She glowed. Then I agreed to hold his hands and glide first on my right foot, then my left foot, allowing the opposite foot to rest. She blew kisses. Weeks later, both feet were working together and neither one was allowed to just come along for the ride. She applauded wildly.

By the time I was ten, I was skating with two feet, no longer clutching my teacher. He and I skated backwards and forwards. I twirled on one foot and, with sudden starts and stops, even jumped. We reached a Sunday when we actually danced to the piped music. This sent Mom over the moon. I displayed strength, speed, endurance, perseverance—and masochism. Ignoring spastic aches running into my anklebones and through my arches, ignoring knotted muscles, ignoring my own likes and dislikes, I blinked back tears and skated. As she cheered with pride, I thought: *Mom likes me, admires me, maybe even loves me.*

Because I was a boney, shy, self-doubting child—the complete opposite of her—I believed I wasn't the daughter she had prayed for. Skating gave me the chance to prove myself wrong.

Money was tight, and keeping up with growing feet was costly, yet each year she insisted on buying me a brand-new pair of white leather skates.

"Ma, I don't need new skates. We can rent them at the rink. Everyone does. Anyway, it's not as if someday I'm going to compete in the Olympics."

Making sure Americans at the rink didn't overhear, she educated me in Farsi. "Estaire, never rent ice skates. They are all sweaty, smelly from the greasy feet of strangers. Feet spread rare diseases. Diseases that have no cure." Mom didn't want me to become a professional skater—that she made clear. But she wouldn't stoop to renting shoes. "It's low-class to wear someone else's shoes. You're not a homeless beggar. You are a *somebody*. Always remember you are a *somebody*. Never rent!"

I hated the cold and secretly loathed skating. But as my crushed, mangled toes and agonized ankles cried, I danced, spun, and jumped, always remembering that my lessons were coming from her grocery allowance. For a full half-hour, I cut across the ice with blazing speed, just to feel Mom's eyes resting on me. I hungered for her undistracted gaze. At Rockefeller Center she wasn't frying, baking, or grilling. She wasn't manically pedaling the Singer sewing machine, churning out floor-to-ceiling curtains. She wasn't railing over her orphaned childhood or cursing my father. She wasn't running away with packed suitcases. Instead, she stood still as I glided by. Mom actually stood still, silently staring at me. Her eyes, fastened on my limbs, traveled up my legs, and attached themselves to my waist. Although she didn't like to touch or be touched, when I twirled and jumped, her eyes held me tightly. As long as I was on ice, she was mine. When I skated, I didn't have to share her, not even with her own tumultuous self. How could I say *no*?

PART TWO

FROM MASHHAD
TO MANHATTAN

CHAPTER 11

David's Earlobe

B ack at home, Mom divided herself into uneven thirds: David, the middle child, received the widest wedge. Albert, the eldest, was given the next largest. I was handed a slim slice, though by far the most confounding. In some ways Mom's portion size didn't really matter, since I felt both brothers belonged to me. Growing up with Al and Dave, ten and seven years my senior, was an experience of its own. Together, ours was a story within a story—a sibling story. I felt bound and beholden to them, with a strong sense that my birth and fate were tied to theirs and that I owed them something huge—like my life. It was the way they looked into my eyes, the way they listened, the way they tried their best to shield me from homelife ruckus. How did they become so strong? So outspoken? How did they become their own people? Only after learning what happened to each of them in Iran did I begin to understand.

I t was 1939 when Mom, at the age of 15, became a mother. Pop took a long deep drag from his Lucky Strike cigarette and insisted their firstborn son be named Albert, after Britain's Prince Albert. Ever since his British boarding school days, Pop had felt a visceral tie to the Brits—as if in some former life he too had been an Anglo-Saxon who'd played an integral part in the creation of their empire. He wore their suits, fluently spoke their tongue, and with deep reverence, held onto his version of a British accent. He selected neither his father's name, Moshe, nor his grandfather's, Benyamin, which at that time was the cultural expectation. Instead, he named his son after British royalty and, sure enough, Albert, who also resembled Pop, became my father's prince.

Two years later, Pop tacked a floor-to-ceiling world map onto his living room wall and pierced Austria, Czechoslovakia, Poland, Yugoslavia, Denmark, Norway, France, Belgium, Luxembourg, the Netherlands, Libya, Egypt, Romania, Greece, and the USSR with straight pins: all countries invaded by the Nazis. Living in Jew-hating Mashhad, with the constant threat of stabbings, throat-slittings, and hangings in public squares, my father's fears exponentially grew as his fingers traced Hitler's push for world conquest and domination.

Germany and Iran were strong trading partners, and many Germans were living in Iran, helping Reza Shah Pahlavi, the crowned King, modernize the country. The Shah was a complicated man. He believed Germans and Persians were both part of the same Aryan (Indo-European) race, but he believed Iranian Jews were special, too—superior to the European Jews Hitler was trying to eradicate. He was the first Shah to show respect for Judaism by bowing to the Torah during a visit to a synagogue in the 1920s, and yet he allowed the Germans living in Iran to promulgate their Nazi beliefs and impose discriminatory policies on Iranian Jews. The birth of a Zionist movement in Iran disturbed him more. He didn't trust the imperialist motives of Britain or the USSR and tried to keep Iran neutral during the war. However, after Hitler invaded the USSR in June 1941, Britain and the Soviet Union thwarted these dreams. They invaded northern and southern Iran, targeting warships, naval and air bases, and lines of supply and communication, making sure the country's oil refineries didn't fall into German hands. The Iranian armed forces fought back but were quickly overwhelmed. Two months later, much of the country was in their control, and they forced Reza Shah to abdicate in favor of his pro-British son, 22-year-old Mohammad Reza Shah Pahlavi.

Strategically located, possessing essential oilfields, refineries, and a crucial north-south railroad corridor, Iran became an occupied country, run, exploited, and plundered by the Soviet Union in the north and Great Britain in the south. The old government collapsed. Foreign troops and refugees poured in. My parents dealt with air raids, water and food shortages, rampant inflation, unemployment, and swelling bread lines. Much of Iran suffered famine, resulting in massive deaths. Darkening Iran's blue skies with transport planes, monopolizing the railroad and other transportation routes, Allied forces moved five million tons of munition and other supplies across Iran into the Soviet Union.

During his reign, Reza Shah had also pushed the people of Iran to abandon traditional dress, going so far as to prohibit women from covering themselves and require men to wear western hats. These edicts sparked resistance that the Shah's regime violently crushed. More than 1,500 people were killed in Mashhad in July 1935 when troops attacked the shrine where devout Muslims had gathered to protest the Shah's push towards modernization. Religious leaders who spoke against these policies were arrested. The more Reza Shah tried to repress the backlash, the more the Muslim fundamentalists, led by the clerics, gained strength, paving the way for a different power grab. As the fundamentalists and the Germans spread their noxious beliefs in Iran, anti-Semitism became even more venomous.

Caught between the forces of religious oppression and backlash, combined with wartime occupation by foreign powers, Pop, with a family to support and no source of income, made the decision of many migrants before him: Head for the big city. He moved his wife and son from Mashhad to Tehran, hoping Iran's capital would offer some sort of financial opportunity. But famine, food shortages, and unemployment were just as severe in the capital, if not worse. After settling the family in a Mashhadi community in Tehran, weeks rolled by as Pop searched for a way to eke out a living. Hopeless and helpless, his heart heavily sank. With a wardrobe full of freshly pressed shirts, he lay idle in his bedroom, shades drawn, propped up against a bank of tear-stained pillows, mechanically thumbing a string of amber worry beads.

After three months of thumbing, Pop had each irregular-ly-shaped bead, with its own particular luster, crack, and curve, memorized. Mom, with no tolerance for inertia and lacking even a sprig of sympathy, finally stomped into the bedroom waving a broomstick, scornfully chastising in Farsi with her teeth digging into dry lips. "*Babai Albairt!*[1] Get up and out. English is your only asset. Use it! Use English to feed our family!"

On a raw rainy day in September of 1942, clad in cuffed her-ringbone gabardines, a custom-tailored shirt, silk paisley tie, match-ing ascot, his hair pomaded and slicked back, Pop stepped into Tehran's British Embassy. Quivering, he told the young man at the

1. *Babai Albairt* (Persian/Farsi)—Albert's father

front desk that he must see the British Ambassador. Reciting the three sentences he had rehearsed earlier that morning in front of Mom, he said: "My name is Fatulla Aminoff. I am here to offer aid. Perhaps I may be of service to the British."

To his surprise, an aide-de-camp welcomed him into his private chambers, offered him a leather seat, a shot of whiskey, and a hand-rolled, full-bodied Havana cigar. Pop's impeccable dress and strong command of the English language worked in his favor. Paring his fingernails, the assistant glanced up at my father. "Our soldiers are ill-prepared for Iran's cold, harsh winters. Would you be able to sup-ply our troops with parkas, gloves, sweaters, and wool-knit skull caps? This is what we desperately need."

Stubbing out his cigar, Pop instantly replied, "Of course I can! It would be my honor." The rest just tumbled into his trembling lap.

Having come from a long line of Silk Road merchants, trad-ers, and shepherds, my father drew from his mercantile past. He quickly located suppliers, set up deliveries, and became the point man for the British army in Iran. For the next several years, he not only dressed pilots and foot soldiers in parkas, sweaters, gloves, and woolen skull caps, but also sold the English tons of timber to build their much-needed shacks and tent supports.

Now flushed with success, Pop crossed wide boulevards in a dou-ble-breasted suit, charcoal-gray fedora, proud to be seen and known by fellow merchants and shop owners as an aide to the Brits. He strutted Lalezar Street—the Champs-Élysées of Tehran—like a true blue-blooded Aminoff and frequented Café Naderi, where Mr. Hakimzadeh, the proprietor and poet, would serve him a dish of vanilla ice-cream topped with a flourish of whip cream, always on the house.

It was here, in Tehran, that Mom gave birth to a second son. This time it was her turn to name their child, so she chose David in mem-ory of her father. Once again namesake expectations were fulfilled, and David, who resembled her side of the family, was instantly as-signed the role of surrogate father, a parent for whom she longed.

Rising above the masses, Pop left his shaded bedroom and, with newfound self-confidence, came out of hiding, feeling he could once again claim his rightful place in Mashhadi society. As a wage-earning resident of Tehran, Iran's enlightened capital, he now purchased coveted food items through its black market and elegantly clothed his wife and sons. He enrolled the boys in a posh private preschool and was even able to put money aside.

Having found his place, why would he ever want to leave?

Dusky-skinned, charcoal-eyed Layla was a fifth family member—a cherished and trusted Muslim nanny who had braved the move from Mashhad to Tehran. At age ten, Layla had been married off to a mean-spirited village drunk prone to alcoholic blackouts—an explosive brute who scarred her cheeks with cigarette burns and beat her unconscious. With his leather belt, he slashed her face, calling her "repulsive—as ugly as a cow's liver." She left him behind in Mashhad, accompanied my family to Tehran, and sent him her monthly pay. A satisfactory arrangement for both.

Layla meticulously cleaned the house, hand-washed laundry, shopped for fruits and vegetables, as my mother baked cakes and simmered stews. Albert, to this day, recalls Layla's rail-thin frame, her reassuring hugs, sweet words of praise, and Persian lullabies. She offered comfort, a steady even calm, all that Mom didn't have to give.

Albert was frail, soft-spoken, and shy, while David was round, robust, and quick to speak his mind. Even though their dispositions differed, they felt a twinship, always looking out for each other, whether it be in school or at home. Each morning, Layla prepared breakfast, cheerfully fed the boys, and neatly dressed them in their matching white shirts, khaki shorts, and sandals. With large, curious eyes framed by crisply cut bangs, they held hands as she walked them to and from school.

One afternoon, Layla rushed home with the boys, weeping. Three-year-old David was shrieking. Six-year-old Albert was crying and holding his brother close. David's earlobe, oozing bubbling bloodied puss, had been burnt to a crisp. Mom and Layla frantically attended to his ear while Albert, between sobs and gasps, told her that their Muslim teacher had accused David of misbehaving, then stuck a poker into an open fire. When it was red hot, she had grabbed David by the arm, pressed the poker against his earlobe and screamed, "Dirty Jew!"

Grief-stricken, Layla took David in her arms and rocked him in her lap, kissing and comforting him as if he were her own.

David's inflamed earlobe set Mom on fire. This teacher's abominable attack on her son did more than sear his ear; it seared Mom's soul and incinerated all ties to her ancestral home. She realized it made no difference whether they lived in insular Mashhad or cosmopolitan Tehran, whether Pop was earning a good income or not; life in Iran was vile. Mom wanted more for her sons, much more than she had ever known. She felt compelled to escape the flames of hatred, fanaticism, bigotry, prejudice before they devoured her boys.

"For generations, our ancestors have lived underground lives, disguised as Muslims," she lamented in Farsi to her husband in the presence of her children. "We've been beaten and killed simply for being Jews. What was done to us was done, but I won't let them *ever again*, I say *ever again*, touch my sons!" Opening her collar, Mom spat three times onto her chest—*teh, teh, teh*—warding off the evil eye.

With or without him, she told my father, she was taking her boys and leaving Iran forever. It was 1946. Her brother Aaron was already in America and had sent her a short note from New York: *Hana, come! Bring your family. America is good to Jews.* There was no stopping her now.

For Pop, uprooting was heart-wrenching. In Mashhad, the Aminoff name and legacy commanded multigenerational respect. There, he had once led a regal life surrounded by housekeepers, gardeners, fig trees, lemon groves, and acres of real estate. Even here in Tehran, men strolling the boulevards now tipped their hats, warmly acknowledging him. Why leave it all behind to emigrate to some strange nation where he, invisible and insignificant, might not be able to make a living?

Mom's urges, littered with blind spots, trumped reason and logic. Nevertheless, Pop believed that once she set foot in America, shoved her way through chaotic, kinetic, multiracial crowds, surrounded by indecipherable Anglo-Saxon clamor, she'd panic, feel fear, and beg for home. After six months in *Am-ree-kah*, she'd be yearning for the familiar fragrances, flavors, and people of Persia, he thought. Against his better judgment, he gave a measured nod of approval, agreeing to leave Iran and visit Mom's brother in New York, with hopes of halting further tantrums and returning soon to his homeland.

Layla began begging: "Take me to *Am-ree-kah*. Don't leave me behind." Not knowing what to say, Mom said nothing.

My parents loved Layla. But they also knew she had a problem that would become theirs if they tried to take her with them.

Mom said that in their home in Tehran, down a long narrow corridor, Layla had a dimly lit room of her own—a place for her futon bed, her chadors, her personal belongings crammed into open shelves, an oil lamp, and her *ghelyoon*.[2] Pop had made it very clear

2. *ghelyoon* (Persian/Farsi)—hookah, water pipe

to his sons that "Layla's bedroom is off limits" and forbade them ever to try to enter. He explained that, because she worked very hard, each afternoon between the hours of four and six Layla needed to retreat into her own quarters to rest. Albert and David respected Pop's wishes, and between four and six they stayed out of her way, quietly playing in their room.

Every afternoon, at the start of her private time, Layla went to her bedroom, locked her door, slipped into a cotton nightgown, and placed a mix of opium and tobacco on top of her lit ghelyoon. Holding the water pipe tightly between her lips, she would inhale deeply, each puff soothing tiredness, aches, burns, bruises, and quieting marital memories as she slid into a sedated sleep.

Opium was still legal in 1940s Iran, and its use was widespread. For generations, opium pills, tinctures, teas, had been used by adults and administered to children to treat ailments and promote health. However, policies and attitudes were changing. During World War II, the government had initiated a program to limit availability to registered addicts, but it reached only a fraction of the addicts in the country at the time.

Albert and David's cherished nanny was one of them.

Mom and Pop knew this and did what they could to help her. To ward off her tremors and shakes, Pop visited a particular merchant at the far end of an outdoor market and purchased the opium she needed. Each week, with a bowed head, Layla blessed my father as he handed her the drug that enabled her to work, make a living, and manage from day to day.

Out of her earshot, Mom told Pop, "I worry about Layla. Who will protect her from her husband's burnings and lashings? We must take her with us to *Am-ree-kah*. She's an angel—loyal, loving, self-sacrificing. I can't leave her behind."

There was a long hush as they stood staring at each other.

"We can't," Pop countered. "How will I find opium on the streets of Manhattan? Her needs are too great."

Instead, they agreed they would find her a new employer in Tehran before they left for the United States.

"I cry," my mother told me, as her eyes filled with tears. "I steel cry for Layla."

CHAPTER 12

Queen Esther's Tomb

Before leaving Iran, my mother addressed one more pressing need: her desire for a daughter. She insisted the whole family make a pilgrimage to Queen Esther's tomb in the city of Hamadan, where Mom could make her plea directly to *Esther HaMalkah*[1] and pray for my eventual birth. My mother decided she'd throw herself on top of the buried Queen's tomb, harness Her Majesty's supernatural power, and aim it at her womb—demanding a daughter. A girl she'd name Esther, after her deceased mother—the mother she pined for. This child would complete her, fix what was broken inside, and make her whole again. Mom knew she and this hallowed fourth-century BCE queen had a lot in common: both orphans, both underground Jews, both daring and determined. Who could better understand Hana's lot, feel her pain, and shape her future?

The morning of the pilgrimage, Layla set tea cups and plates on a purple paisley tablecloth. Wearing her red gingham apron, she served Albert and David their favorite breakfast: hot *Nan-e Sangak*[2] smothered with home-churned butter and sprinkled with sugar, alongside soft-boiled eggs plucked minutes earlier from beneath clucking hens. And to quench their thirst, she made plenty of freshly brewed tea. Licking their fingers, the boys ate heartily and chattered excitedly, anticipating a fun-filled car trip to Hamadan.

As my mother entered the kitchen, Layla swung around, placed her brown leathered hands on my mother's waist, and sank to her knees. Hardwired to speak her truth, she pleaded in Farsi.

1. *Esther HaMalkah* (Persian/Farsi)—Queen Esther
2. *Nan-e Sangak* (Persian/Farsi)—coal-oven-baked flatbread

"Take me to *Am-ree-kah*," she once again begged. "*Albairt, Dav-eed*, you and your husband are my family. I don't have children of my own. Your family is my family." She took my mother's hands and kissed her filigree rings. "Take me with you, *Khanum*," she pleaded.

Mom pulled her hands away and stepped back.

"*Layla joon*,[3] you know I love you. You're not only a mother to me but also a mother to my sons. But, remember, you have a husband here. You're Muslim. Iran is your country."

"No, my princess, you are my country. Your religion is mine, your family mine. I'll take good care of all of you for the rest of my life. Don't leave me behind."

Lowering her head, Mom couldn't bear to tell her the truth, and so, again, she said nothing.

I was 15 when Mom told this story during a family dinner. She stopped there, didn't seem to want to say anymore. It was Pop, a man of monkish silence, who insisted on telling the rest of this tale, and told it with wild abandon. My ears widened. Pop, the monstrous monarch, the night stalker, the iron-fisted book-banner, was about to speak. A father who believed he was saving my life with his vetoes and sanctions but in truth was destroying it. This would be my opportunity. If I listened closely to his words, expressions, and inflections, I might glimpse the person who lived behind his prohibitions, his dictatorial dos and don'ts, his explosive "Enough talk!" Was he human? Could I latch onto any part of him? Through his storytelling, I hoped not only to get a peek into Pop, but also better understand my deep ties to my brothers. What had actually happened before my birth?

Pop said he had hired a chauffeur to drive the family from Tehran to Hamadan. He sat up front, next to the driver. Behind him, David was propped on Layla's lap; Mom sat in the middle, holding canteens of water and six spinach-patty sandwiches; and Albert sat to her right, next to the window.

The car dashed full speed through twisting, unpaved, cratered roads that wound over and around dusty mountains. Swerving first to the right, then to the left, fenders rattled loudly as the car streaked over underbrush, wheels crunching gravel and crushing stones, dead snakes and broken branches. Six-year-old Albert sat with his nose pressed against the window, eyes fixed on the browns

3. *joon* (Persian/Farsi)—dear

and grays of the stark, windblown landscape flashing by, mindlessly playing with the backseat door handle.

Rounding another curve, the car shook, the lock unclicked, and Albert's door swung wide open. Panicking, he reached out to grab the handle but couldn't fight the muscular winds. Small and light, Albert shot out like a kite, was lifted high into the air, and flew weightlessly away over rolling hills.

Unaware, the chauffeur kept driving.

Her attention elsewhere, Mom felt a sharp chill, turned, saw the swinging door and her son missing.

"*VASTA! VASTA!*[4]" she shrieked.

The driver quickly responded by slamming the brakes so hard he cracked the heel of his shoe. Mom lurched out onto the dirt road and fell to her knees, wailing hopelessly, banging her head against rocks, yanking out fistfuls of hair. She was certain Albert was dead, his frail body splayed across cold ground somewhere in this godforsaken wilderness.

Clutching David in the back seat, Layla stifled her sobs and clawed her cheeks till they bled. "*Khak bar saram!*[5] I'm to blame!" she cried. "You left *Albairt* in my care. I curse the day I was born."

As Pop was narrating, he feverishly relived this episode, turning it into a quasi-biblical science-fiction epic. He said he darted out of the car and ran through hills and valleys, his short legs never failing, crying through a hot throat, "*Albairt!.....Albairt!.....Albairt!*" Like an eagle he flew, his heart hammering, strategically scouring fields, knowing he wouldn't return without his son. Fueled by a bloodhound drive, he scaled hills, slid down valleys, upturned every mound of rubble, sucking in mountain air, bullhorning: "*Albairt!....Albairt!*"

Instead of a child's whimper, Pop heard howling winds. "It was the voice of faceless thugs who had snatched my son from behind my back, dragging him off, kidnapped, as one of their own."

After hours of searching, running, calling, and trembling, on the cusp of collapse, my father suddenly stumbled upon Albert's seemingly lifeless body half-buried in a mound of mud and twigs. Pop's quivering knees gave out. He sank to the ground, bent over his son, put head in hands, and bawled. Albert's forehead, eyelids, and cheeks were pitted with gravel and shards of rock, his scalp was

4. *Vasta!* (Persian/Farsi)—Stop!
5. *Khak bar saram.* (Persian/Farsi)—I should die.

split and bleeding. Bending closer, Pop suddenly felt the warmth of a faint breath on his own cheek.

Still on his knees, lost in communion, my father chanted *Birkat HaGomel.*[6] Sapped of strength, a divine calm slowly seeped through him. Pressing together his son's bleeding scalp, he slowly gathered Albert in his arms, returned to his feet, and ever-so-quietly carried Albert back to the car.

At this storytelling juncture, Pop shut his eyes. "As I was running in search of Albert," he whispered, "the Lord spoke to me in an audible voice. *Trust me, trust me,* I heard him say. Estaire, I lived pages ripped out from Genesis." Losing his firstborn son, hunting madly through the depths of despair, clinging to faith, and then the miracle of Albert's return.... Pop was certain he had been tested and ultimately blessed just like biblical patriarchs before him, which only deepened his belief in God.

Since it was still a long distance to Hamadan, my father instructed the driver to take them to the nearest village to seek help. Pulling into a shantytown, they caught sight of a beaten-up sign crookedly hanging from a nail: SHOE REPAIR. Pop carried Albert into the shop. A bald-headed, toothless man wearing a black patch over one eye and bearing a deep scar across his left cheek was hammering nails into heels. Pop reached for the thick needle used to sew leather, threaded it, sterilized it over a flame, and with stoic detachment stitched Albert's scalp. Experiencing intolerable pain, Al once again passed out. My mother paced outside the shop, her hair tangled, her face cracked and crooked. She was pushed to the very edge, forced to feel what she couldn't endure.

When they reached Hamadan, Albert was rushed into a dilapidated hospital where, working without anesthetics, a fellow who called himself a doctor removed Pop's temporary stitches and sewed him up. Al, once again, mercifully blacked out.

Later, cradled in Layla's arms, he awoke and softly asked, "Where is David? Is he all right?" She gently kissed his forehead, reassured him David was well, and lullabied Albert into a deep peaceful sleep.

Leaning in, listening closely, I was hit hard. Pop, my sworn enemy, was fully human. I could tell from his voice. I heard passion, dedication, commitment to family. He had been relentless, determined to find and heal his son. Yes—thrumming beneath his hard

6. *Birkat HaGomel* (Hebrew)—Jewish prayer of gratitude recited after surviving a brush with death

surface was a caring, courageous soul. I was struck by how much of his true self he hid and didn't want others to know.

And what I had suspected all along was true. I owed my brothers big time. It was David's burnt earlobe that had set Mom in motion, forcing the family to leave. If not for his scorched ear, I would have been born in Iran, raised behind a chador, unschooled, illiterate, burned, and brutalized—a life I would have had to endure and never been able to escape. And then there was Albert, who flew out of the car and almost died just so Mom could visit Hamadan and pray for a daughter—for my eventual birth. David's seared ear and Albert's split scalp were my foundation, my bedrock. They stood behind my beginnings. My life was built on theirs—a result of their pain and sacrifices.

Owe, owe, owe lapped through my veins as my parents told this story. I felt there was a price to pay for my birth. A huge payback. Should it be full-fledged allegiance to my brothers and parents, now and forever? To their truths and mistruths, deeds and misdeeds? Would I have to numb my brain, say little to avoid havoc? Would it mean shutting down all cylinders and letting Pop determine my future?

My story was lame compared to theirs. I had been born in New York City, in the lap of luxury. On Fridays, I had piano lessons with Mrs. Krall. I spent winter Sundays at Rockefeller Center, ice-skating. My parents and brothers, on the other hand, had suffered and bled, running for their lives.

Did that mean I had less right to mine?

CHAPTER 13

Exodus

Immigration quotas and a flood of refugees made it virtually impossible to leave Iran for America after World War II. Fighting despair, Mom sent Pop to the British Embassy to discuss possibilities. In return for Pop's wartime assistance, the Embassy agreed to offer the family transport by mail truck from Mashhad to Kabul, Afghanistan. From there, they would make their way to Bombay, now known as Mumbai, which was still under British control. In Bombay Pop would have a better chance of obtaining visas from the American Embassy for travel to the U.S.

In 1946, with rolled mattresses, Persian rugs, sacks of clothing, pots, pans, and a large dayereh, my family said a tearful goodbye to Layla and left Tehran for Mashhad, a two-day bus journey. Mom said it was a dusty, wearisome ride interrupted by hourly breakdowns. Days later, riding in the back of an open truck, my parents and brothers bounced atop large sacks of mail as if they, too, were packets en route to a depot in Kabul. Protected by two Afghani guards riding with rifles drawn, the mail truck followed ancient roads passing through hills and mountains rife with Afghani bandits ready to shoot and steal. But after what seemed like endless hours of hard travel, they made it safely to Kabul. From Kabul they traveled by land and train to New Delhi, and then to Bombay.

Listening to my parents tell their story, I was baffled by their courage. Could I have done it? Uproot my family and flee my homeland in this hit-or-miss way? A journey patched together by spit. No airline tickets, no steamship reservations—no guarantors or guarantees. Chancing it from start to finish with a strong possibility of being butchered.

The challenges Mom faced were far greater than mine, and yet, though less treacherous, mine felt more frightening. By now I knew I'd finish high school, since Pop was under the misconception that completing 12th grade was mandatory—a U.S. law—and I wasn't about to correct him. But I wanted more than 12th grade. I wanted to dodge whatever prearranged marriage was awaiting me and sculpt my own life. I wanted to spread my wings and become an astrophysicist, an anthropologist, or perhaps an abstract painter mixing globs of oil paint in some dark, dingy, Greenwich Village garret strewn with palettes. Emperor penguins tugged at my heart. I dreamed of joining a sledging expedition to Antarctica, where I would observe these flightless birds rocketing out of the sea, breeding during seasons of darkness, and study their complex cries. I had read that each penguin's individual call was recognized by its parents, mates, and offspring, always known to its immediate family. Were these calls meaningless sounds, or did they express feelings akin to love and loyalty? Was there infighting, and, if so, over what? Were certain penguins rejected and marginalized for being different? And, if so, how did they cope? I longed to watch for patterns, observe body language, ferret out meaning as they mated, reared their chicks, and traveled back and forth across frozen ice.

Yearnings. I had so many, and hungered to feed them all. What was possible? What was my birthright? And what about ambition? Who was allowed to have it? Would I be able to live out my dreams, or were dreams only meant for men?

I had always feared banishment. After Mom told me about my grandfather's treatment of my father, I understood why. I knew if I defied Pop's wishes, if I became my own person with an agenda of my own, he'd do to me as his father had done to him—cut me out, kill me off, pretend I never existed. Moshe's primal impulses were alive and well in Pop. Choosing my own life, not one my father prescribed, would shame him and cast me into the Siberia of his mind. The dread of being exiled, left homeless, loomed over me.

But Pop had chosen defiance over deference. And both my parents had escaped their homeland. Could I do the same? Did I have their courage? Could I defy them and bolt for the South Pole? As Mom recounted the story of their nerve-racking exodus, I again asked myself: *How much do I owe?*

She said in Bombay they became subtenants of a British woman who lived in a three-room rental a few blocks from the Taj Mahal Hotel. With a dash of stuffiness, their landlady offered to sublet two rooms of her fourth-floor apartment, promising that within a month or two she'd be leaving Bombay and they could then occupy the entire space. Her one requirement was that during the interim she would occupy the center room and the family would have the other two rooms, one at either end. *"Divoone!*[1]*"* Mom screeched. "Why is she planting herself between us?" Pop tried to comfort her by insisting it would only be a temporary arrangement. "At the very most, we will live this way for three months," he said. They had no choice, he reminded her. "Housing is hard to come by."

My father turned the smaller of the two rooms into his office. With hopes of earning an income while trying to obtain their visas, he hired a young Indian typist who not only spoke English but also had a typewriter of his own. A true find. Together they collected addresses and sent hundreds of letters to various Indian tea companies requesting export prices. The family slept, ate, and socialized in the one remaining side room while sharing the kitchen and bathroom with their landlady. In India, during those postwar days, food and water were rationed. Since my parents didn't have ration coupons they bought what was needed on the black market. Water was turned on in their apartment for three hours twice a week. Every available drop was used or stored within this tight window of time. Mom, Pop, Albert, and David bathed rapidly, then hoarded as much water as possible in an assortment of pails, pots, pans, and teacups.

What they thought would be three months in Bombay turned into four, six, eight, then more.... And the landlady, who occupied the center room, never moved out. Pop scraped together a living exporting tea for Bombay's Tata Tea Company, but he couldn't seem to obtain the papers needed to enter the U.S. Mom, a tightly wound coil, was ready to burst. Her moods went from bad to worse, sweating unknowns, living each hour with hopes of leaving. Once again, she viewed Pop as inept and in need of constant prodding.

Several times a day, grabbing Pop by the collar, Mom carped, *"Babai Albairt,* when are we going to *Am-ree-kah?* I never should have let you plan our escape. Your sloppy thinking has brought us here. We are penniless, stuck in this hell with no way out."

1. *divoone* (Persian/Farsi)—crazy

Albert's father dug his teeth into his fist. "*Khanum.* We are waiting for the U.S. Embassy to give us our visitors' visas. Patience! Patience! Every day you criticize and bombard me with complaints. The Children of Israel said the very same to Moses. They, too, beat and battered him with words, forgetting why they left Egypt in the first place. Enough! My hair grows white because of you."

Short on money and long on time, they sparred, taking turns being victim and victimizer.

Bombay, like all of India, was also roiled by strikes and riots, religious, political, and ethnic discord during those years following World War II. The British Raj and British rule were on their way out, and hostilities were boiling over in the run up to independence, with Muslims and Hindus rising up together to throw off British domination and turning on each other over the issue of partition. The Muslim minority wanted its own independent state, and eventually got it, in the country now known as Pakistan, but not before the Muslim League called for "Direct Action" to force the issue, which translated into riots all over the country and thousands of lives lost. There were violent uprisings in Calcutta, on the northeast coast, in mid-February 1946, followed by the anti-British Indian Navy Mutiny in Bombay, on the west coast, just before my family arrived. Another weeklong religious riot in August 1946, now known as the Great Calcutta Killings, left as many as 15,000 dead and 100,000 homeless. It was followed by a series of massacres in other parts of Bengal, including the Noakhali Genocide of October, 1946, when as many as 30,000 Hindus were killed, hundreds of Hindu women were raped, houses and shops were looted and set on fire, and thousands of Hindus were forcibly converted to Islam.

Riots hit Bombay in early September of that year. From their balcony, Albert and David watched militant mobs lunge at nearby railroad stations, pushing cars off their tracks. Violent hordes shook glass soda bottles and flung them like grenades into Hindu crowds. Glass shattered, spraying everywhere, piercing and slicing the bodies and faces of men, women, and children. And that was far from the worst of it. The fighting lasted for days, shutting down parts of the city, killing more than 200 people, and leaving more than 600 injured.

This time, Mom and Pop were outsiders observing. As Jews living in India, they were no longer religious targets. Mom, feeling heartsick, had instant compassion for the afflicted Hindus who were the victims of repeated and horrific organized Muslim attacks. Intolerance, brutality, and compulsory conversions paralleled their own wretched history. Having escaped Iran, seeking religious freedom, my parents were now forced to watch Hindus suffer just as they had.

Each evening, Mom's lengthy bedtime prayers whittled down to one word: *Am-ree-kah.*

For more than a year, they lived in tight quarters with rationed food, rationed water, never knowing when violence might break out again. Listening closely to their story, all I could think was how lucky I was not to have been born yet. As the third and youngest child who always faulted herself, how would I have fared? I imagined myself burying my head between my legs, not wanting to see or be seen. Terrified, blaming myself, wishing myself away. Wanting to shrink. Disappear.

Yet, for Albert and David, India was also enchanting. Gazing down from their fourth-floor balcony, they saw a packed mass of humans unlike any they had ever seen before pass before them. Doe-eyed, mesmerized, they watched women in lush, iridescent saris sail by, homeless urchins begging for money, hawkers singing their wares. They saw flocks of courting, pulsating peacocks, regal elephants, white cows roaming where they pleased. They saw organ-grinders with their noisy monkeys strutting the street and swinging their tails in time to the tune; husky, bare-chested, loin-clothed *málish*[2] brandishing vials of oil, selling their rubs. My brothers watched as men lay flat on the ground, fully greased, legs and chest bare, surrendering themselves to heavy-duty pummeling.

Elephant dung, cow manure, and discarded melon rinds littered dirt roads, baking in the sun. The sticky scent of saffron, curry, and damp earth laced the breeze swirling up to their balcony, intermingling with the smell of fried mangoes, ginger, rose water, and cloves. Hindu music streaming from sitars floated lazily through the thick air as snake charmers roamed alleyways, calling in shrill voices and playing high notes on their *pungis*[3] to herald their arrival, attracting Indian children like pied pipers.

Decades later, Albert recalled the sight of a group of these bearded, barefooted, callous-heeled gypsies. They wore brilliant jewel-toned *lungis*,[4] chandelier earrings, and clusters of shells around their necks. A white turban wrapped around one charmer's head sat lopsided over one ear. Slung over his shoulders was a long bamboo pole, each

2. *málish* (Hindi)—rubber, masseur
3. *pungi* (Hindi)—flute-like instrument made from a gourd
4. *lungi* (Hindi)—sarong or wrap worn around the waist

end bearing a basket filled with slithering snakes. Sitting cross-legged under the buzz of flies, they blew into their pungis, waving them back and forth as cobras slowly emerged from the baskets, extending their hoods, flicking their tongues, swaying to the hypnotic movement and music.

Spellbound, my brothers watched as one of the snake charmers pulled a leashed mongoose out of a bag and set it down in front of one of the cobras, closing the show with a frightful cobra-mongoose brawl. Even monkeys, swinging from trees, stopped to stare. The snake charmer let cobra and mongoose dart and lunge at each other for a while, eliciting gasps and shouts from the children, then yanked the mongoose's leash and put it back in his sack.

Bombay exposed my brothers to a wondrous scope of life, turning the fantastical into everyday occurrences. Aromatic, mythological, India stressed and stretched their seven- and four-year-old minds. They sat cross-legged on *kilims*,[5] sipping tea, sharing their daily discoveries. Months of waiting in this colorful culture whetted their intellectual appetites, nourishing a consciousness and curiosity that burned strong. Albert spent much of his free time constructing shoebox dioramas of Bombay, while David spun fanciful interpretations of all he saw. India gave high wind to imagination and played a large role in Albert's later decision to become an architect and David's love of literature.

Stuck in place for days, weeks, months, some things became routine. Meals turned monotonous. Keeping kosher, Mom steamed rice, alternating the accompanying vegetable for breakfast, lunch, and dinner. It was only on Friday nights, for Shabbat, that my brothers could hope for chicken. In Mashhad, all bar mitzvah boys learned *shechitah*[6] from their elders. After a year of practice, they were awarded a grade—*aleph*[7] or *bet*[8]—based on ability. A bet could slaughter a chicken for himself and others, but only when there was no aleph in sight. At age 13, Pop had been declared a bet. Since alephs weren't roaming the streets of Bombay, Pop became the family *shokhet*.[9] However, killing poultry was not his forte. This wasn't because he lacked the know-how. Rather, it stemmed from his empathy for animals, which got in the way of slitting their throats.

5. kilim (Persian/Farsi)—pileless handwoven rug
6. *shechitah* (Hebrew)—the laws of kosher butchering
7. *aleph* (Hebrew)—the letter A
8. *bet* (Hebrew)—the letter B
9. *shochet* (Hebrew)—kosher butcher

Each Friday afternoon, while wearing a white yarmulke, Pop opened a drawer and, with trembling hands, reached for a small leather case. Inside was a sharp-edged knife and honing stone. Albert and David silently watched as he stood paralyzed for what seemed an eternity before slowly sharpening his blade. In the courtyard, málish were busy oiling and massaging chests and thighs, vendors were noisily selling goods, and snake charmers were playing to dancing snakes. Everything came to a halt when Mom stepped out of the building, holding the legs of a squawking chicken, followed by chain-smoking Pop honing his knife, and their two young sons trailing behind.

"*Zudi, zudi!*[10]" she commanded.

"*Vasta!*" he angrily replied.

A shrill endless back and forth. Finally Pop was ready. No, not yet. He suddenly remembered he had forgotten to pluck its feathers before making the cut. Mom firmly held the wriggling hen while Pop, drenched in perspiration, plucked. Málish, snake charmers, vendors, passersby all stared. After much plucking, and more deliberation, Pop took the chicken, said a *brakhah*,[11] and aimed the blade at bared skin. And froze. Mom furiously screamed out shechitah instructions, and after many shaky false starts the knife did its job. Pop, barely breathing, dripping of sweat, released the fowl only to see it dance about in the outdoor courtyard, blood gushing from its throat. Eventually the bird collapsed, and the courtyard audience loudly applauded.

A successful shechitah meant browned breasts, thighs, and drumsticks for Shabbat.

Finally, on a 1947 April day, beneath a pink sky, Pop hurtled home beaming. The U.S. Embassy had granted the family six-month visitors' visas. Mom, Pop, Albert, and David tore through rooms, laughing, crying, tears coursing down their cheeks, dancing to the beat of Mom's ululating tongue as she whipped out her dayereh for accompaniment. That evening, she celebrated by steaming a large pot of basmati rice, this time with a reckless variety of okra, carrots, tomatoes, potatoes, and artichoke hearts. Dinner was followed by mounds of fleshy ripe mangoes, peeled and sliced—a family favorite. Mango juice ran down their chins as they chewed and laughed. My mother's one-word prayer had been answered: *Am-ree-kah.* 🪬

10. *zudi, zudi* (Persian/Farsi)—quickly, quickly
11. *brakhah* (Hebrew)—blessing

CHAPTER 14

Crossing

My father arranged passage on the *SS Marine Adder*, an American troop transport ship bound for America: a 40-day journey from Bombay to Shanghai to San Francisco.

Unable to read, Mom misheard Adder, the name of a venomous snake, as *Adar*,[1] the sixth month of the Hebrew calendar, and rhapsodized in Farsi over the ship's name.

"The *Marine Adar* has been sent directly to us by the Almighty Lord. He is reassuring us that He will rescue us and take us safely to *Am-ree-kah*. What more proof do we need? Just as it took the Israelites forty years to cross the desert and reach the Promised Land, we, in forty days, will complete our exodus. God bless God!"

Her impassioned prophecy was sown into the hearts of her sons, and, with rapturous awe, they were convinced God would be onboard, steering. Maybe, they'd even get a glimpse of him.

Pop was told by the booking agent that this voyage would include nightly entertainment, which meant every passenger was expected to perform for fellow travelers and crew. Needing to be fully prepared, Pop went to an Indian novelty shop in search of magic tricks, but not just any tricks. Pop sought magic with a moral. Smoke and mirrors, sleight of hand, fooling the eye, were tricks he would use only to turn himself into a high-minded mesmerist imparting some basic truth. Rummaging through baskets, he came across a packet labeled, "A Torn and Restored String—Watch Him Break It, Burn It, Then Pull It Out Whole." This had no meaning. Another read, "A

1. *Adar* (Hebrew)—sixth month of the Hebrew calendar

Coin that Slides Uphill." Too juvenile. He examined "A Mango Seed that Grows Before Your Eyes," and then flipped through batches of flash cards used for hypnosis. They wouldn't do. His one-act show had to combat all logic, leaving shipmates ethically altered for life.

Pop, a man prone to seismic eruptions, suddenly was drawn to a kit containing a packet of powder, which, when placed on the tongue and ignited, would burst into lashing flames. "Tongue On Fire"—now this had meaning and conveyed an urgent and critical message: "Speech is lethal." A truism he swore by. My father bought the kit and hurried home, carrying a packet of pulverized particles wrapped in Hindu newsprint. Once Albert and David heard of his purchase, they couldn't wait to see their fire-breathing father perform.

On a stormy April day, the family headed for the pier. As they boarded the ship, traveling steerage class, they were told all women and young children must sleep in a chamber separate from the men and older boys. The ship's belly had been divided into two cavernous rooms, each filled with rows and rows of hanging hammocks. At night, Pop and Albert were in the male quarters while Mom and David were in the female chamber, each parent cradling a son in a narrow hammock. For 40 days and what felt like 100 nights, they slept swinging in mesh netting, battling seasickness and keeping kosher, eating hard boiled eggs and canned peaches. All the while, hoping *Am-ree-kah*, an unknown destination, was the right decision.

As Pop attended to Mom's persistent nausea, constipation, and temper tantrums, Albert and David explored the enormous *Marine Adder*. The boys poked their heads into every corner of the ship, climbed towering ladders, peered through portholes, hid in secret compartments, and checked out the smokestack and thundering bass horns. With jaws hanging open, they watched passengers playing card games and rolling dice. Men and women prayed, spit, jumped up and down, and chanted "Baby needs a new pair of shoes" before tossing the dice. Then the room erupted in piercing screams and thick laughter. For my brothers, who didn't speak English, these jumbled words and strange behaviors made no sense.

Each night, someone entertained in the dining hall. Every evening, Albert asked Pop if this was the night he'd be performing his magic trick. Pop's response was always the same: "Soon." One evening a tall, lanky Indian holding a pad of paper offered to entertain. He asked volunteers to doodle on his pad and said he'd turn their haphazard markings into art. Albert quickly raised his hand and made a scribble. The artist fancifully added to the lines and created a graceful, long-necked giraffe. Al was impressed but knew his five-foot-tall father was about to become a giant, outshining all other performers. Turning to Pop, he pleaded, "When will you do your trick?" Pop took a lit cigarette out of his mouth, breathed deeply, and with compressed intensity replied, "Soon."

There were nights when women howled opera and nights when men tap danced. My brothers shrieked with laughter. On comedy nights, however, when passengers told jokes in English, Albert and David sat in the front row stone-faced, not understanding a word.

One day the ship's captain announced that the evening's entertainment would instead be held in the afternoon. Told it was a surprise event, Albert and David were certain Pop would be the highly anticipated performer. On this day, every passenger aboard the SS Marine Adder would know that their father with the flaming tongue was a magician of biblical proportion.

Instead, a tall, blond, blue-eyed man entered the room wearing a striped bathrobe and walked to a roped off area in the middle of the floor. My brothers thought this was their cue to laugh out loud, and so they did. The entertainer disrobed, exposing a muscular body clad in loose trunks and etched with all kinds of colorful tattoos.

David pointed to the puffy, oversized, black leather mittens the man wore on both hands and doubled over, slapped his thighs, and roared with laughter. Albert quickly hushed him, whispering, "Don't laugh. Maybe his hands melted into stubs. Maybe he lost his fingers in the war." Then a man who looked like the first man's identical twin pranced into the room, wearing the same mittens and covered even more densely with markings. The men stood in opposite corners of the roped-off square. Unexpectedly, a bell rang, and the brothers rushed into the center, swinging at each other.

Mom yelled at the top of her lungs, "Divoone!" Within minutes the less-tattooed twin fell to the floor, beaten to a pulp, bleeding from nose, mouth, and chin. A bell rang again, and the more heavily inscribed twin raised his arms in the air and marched out of the room with a boastful strut, chest high. As the defeated twin lay unconscious, another man stepped up and poured a huge bucket of cold water on his head. When he opened his eyes, a curvy blonde with huge Bette Davis eyes rushed to his side and covered his bloody mouth with red lipstick kisses.

Albert and David were thoroughly confused.

Never before had the family seen two men slug one another for entertainment. Mom neatly summed it up: "*Hamashun divoone.*[2]" My brothers pulled each other aside, whispered together, and after much deliberation decided: *The denser and scarier the drawings on a man's body, the stronger he becomes. That's why the more heavily tattooed brother won.*

Pop's "soon" never came. On a chilly evening, he stepped out onto the ship's deck and, silhouetted against a full moon, slowly emptied his packet of magic powder into the Pacific Ocean. Albert watched from afar, grasping a thick knotted rope the size of his head, and silently wept. Along with crushed powder, his dreams of a magical father sank to the bottom of the sea. ▧

2. *Hamashun divoone.* (Persian/Farsi)—They are all crazy.

CHAPTER 15

Welcome

The ship docked in San Francisco in late May. From there, a three-day cross-country train shuttled them east. My parents stepped off the train at Manhattan's Grand Central Station, bewildered, clutching eight-year-old Albert, five-year-old David, shouldering futons, rugs, stuffed satchels, and 27 centuries of persecution.

Mom's brother Aaron was there to meet them. Emerging onto the street and tilting their heads back, their eyes climbed enormous buildings so tall their tips seemed to scrape the sky. Shafts of light bounced off glass walls. Streams of buses and cabs honked, belching gray smoke. Pedestrians rushed by like wind-up dolls, people colliding, barely taking notice.

Pop muttered to Mom, "This you call home? Do you smell soil? Nothing here is real. Earth is completely hidden, covered by concrete. This country wants to entice you so it can deceive you. *Khanum*, this is a city of smoke and mirrors."

Mom shrugged. "I don't know where I am, I only know why. The future spreads open before me and I'm stepping right in."

David's roasted earlobe, Albert's split scalp, and my mother's gangbuster will catapulted the family to New York City, where I was born.

There were so many questions that still needed answering. Why didn't they settle in Bombay and stop pushing onward? How could they flee with children in the hull of a ship, across oceans, not knowing where they were going and what lay ahead? Yes, a few relatives had come before them, but America was still a complete unknown. Where did they find the strength? Could I leave my home and never turn back? Did I have the right, after all they had been through? And if I did soar would they sink, leaving me guilt-ridden for the rest of my life? Could I chart my own course while still honoring them? There was no friend, no relative, no teacher to ask. No one I knew had parents like mine. No one could show me the way.

Throughout the telling of their tales, what stood out was their tenacious grit. I paid close attention, knowing there was much more to learn, much more to grasp.

Mom said by 1947 Manhattan's residential rents had spiked. It was right after World War II, with far more demand for apartments than supply. Her brother Aaron and his wife, Millie, took the family in until Mom and Pop could find a place of their own. They had no children, but their apartment in Washington Heights was very small. Pop, thin on cash but in need of a home, searched for months, until he heard of a new rental building at 205 West 95th Street between Broadway and Amsterdam Avenue. Without a job or a cogent plan, not knowing how he'd scrape together the monthly rent, he breathlessly outraced other applicants and snatched a one-bedroom apartment. My parents slept in the congested living room while my brothers camped out in the coveted bedroom. In this pinched space stuffed with Persian futons, borrowed folding tables and chairs, a floral slip-covered couch bursting with orange stargazers, sacks of clothing, colanders, Persian rugs, a dayereh and samovar, they navigated tight aisles, tripping over one another.

Next door lived Mr. and Mrs. Jacobson and their 18-year-old son, Herman, a musical prodigy crippled by polio. They were big-hearted Holocaust survivors who took our immigrant family under their broken wings. With a concentration camp number branded on her left forearm, Mrs. Jacobson compassionately posted a handwritten sign in their building's lobby:

Ring Apt. 3-J: Lovely Persian Lady does hems and alterations.
Also available night and day for babysitting. Very capable and
trustworthy. Please give her a try!

And the doorbell rang.

When I pumped Mom for more details, tears slipped from her eyes. "Dees money pay for meelk, bret, and buttair."

"But rent?" I asked. "If Pop wasn't working, how did you pay your rent?"

"Vee borrow an borrow," she answered, rubbing her white

knuckles and shaking her head. "For two years...vee beg an borrow from my broddair Aaron, from von Aminoff cozeen, from good neighbor Mistair Jacobson... And vee cry."

I t was their first Friday night in Manhattan, and my father was eager to take his young sons to Sabbath services while Mom prepared dinner. After trimming Albert and David's bangs, Mom fussed over her boys, dressing them in newly bought navy blue slacks and sport jackets, stiff-collared white shirts, and flaming red neckties that they couldn't really afford. Pop, wearing one of his British three-piece suits, tightly held each son's hand as all three proudly walked over to an Orthodox temple just down the street.

Here they were, finally in America, free to be Jews, free to pray openly and aboveground. An experience they had never had. Glowing, Pop reminded his sons that they were now safe and would never again be pelted by rocks, called "Dirty Jews," or shoved to the ground with blades pressed against their throats. On this lighthearted, carefree night, all three felt brand new, just like their Sabbath suits.

A *gabbai*[1] wearing a *tallit*[2] was standing outside the entrance, welcoming congregants. As my father and brothers approached, the gabbai greeted them.

"*Shabbat Shalom*.[3] Are you new here?"

Pop smiled broadly. "Yes, thank you."

"Where are you from?" he asked.

"From Persia."

"Are you Jewish?" the gabbai inquired.

"Of course," Pop proudly replied.

The man rattled on in a foreign tongue, then waited for a response.

My father was bewildered. He knew the fellow wasn't speaking English and certainly not Hebrew. "I don't understand what you just said."

The gabbai's tone impatiently sharpened. "What do you mean, you don't understand? You don't understand Yiddish? If Yiddish isn't your mother tongue, you're not Jewish!"

His outstretched arms now blocked the doorway, not allowing my father and brothers to enter. Fighting for breath, Pop loosened his tie, blotted his brow, grabbed his sons' hands, and dashed home.

1. *gabbai* (Hebrew)—synagogue attendant
2. *tallit* (Hebrew)—prayer shawl
3. *Shabbat Shalom.* (Hebrew)—Good Shabbos.

Striking the dinner table with both fists, he shouted, "After all we've lived through! After all we and our ancestors suffered, we now hear we are frauds? In Iran Muslim monsters butchered us for being Jewish, and in *Am-ree-kah* Jews disgrace us and tell us we're not Jewish. I'd rather be beaten for being a Jew then told I'm not one!" He gasped for air. "Didn't I tell you right from the start? *Am-ree-kah* is not for us!"

Crying in three different languages, Mom slapped her full chest with an open hand and spat into her blouse—*teh, teh, teh*—then cursed the gabbai, calling him a mule's ass.

Their long and arduous exodus was thrown into question. In America, they were already viewed as undesirables because they were Iranian—from an unknown country and not quite white in Anglo-Saxon eyes. And now, fellow Jews saw them as counterfeit.

Recovering quickly, Mom brushed off the slight. For her, this was a land of Stars and Stripes, a land of opportunity. It had to be— there was no turning back.

The next morning, she insisted they all get into their Shabbat attire and this time head for Shaare Zedek, a conservative synagogue on West 93rd Street, between Broadway and Amsterdam Avenue. Galvanized by Manhattan's shrill sirens and honking cabs, Mom stubbornly led the way.

Once again they were stopped at a synagogue door.

A gabbai asked, "Are you new here?"

With a creased brow, Pop replied, "Yes."

"Where are you from?"

"Persia," my father answered haughtily.

This gabbai took my father's arm, escorted the family into the building past rows of pews already crowded with worshipers, and sat them in the main sanctuary's front row. Mounting the *bimah*,[4] the gabbai whispered something into the rabbi's ear. When it came time for the rabbi to deliver his sermon, he announced, "I've put aside what I had planned to discuss today. Instead, I want to use this time to warmly welcome our Jewish brethren from the land of Persia."

He asked the family to stand so fellow congregants could see and greet them. Pop translated English into Farsi, and each family member slowly and reluctantly stood. My father muttered to my mother in their now-private language, "Is this a set up? Are we about to be mocked?"

4. *bimah* (Hebrew)—raised platform in a synagogue from which the rabbi leads services

They were not. Honoring these four immigrants, the rabbi, Rabbi Morris Goldberg, spent an entire hour narrating in full detail the story of Purim, Queen Esther, Mordechai, and the Jews of Persia—yoking my family to their rich and resounding past. Mom and Pop were crying so hard they couldn't stop. Never before had they sat in an aboveground synagogue with hundreds of fellow Jews, and never before had they felt so deeply valued for who they were. Shaare Zedek became their house of worship.

CHAPTER 16

Thinking Goats

Aaron and Millie had come to the U.S. in 1945. Fluent in English, acclimated to America, earning a living, they held their heads high. Born in Mashhad and raised in London, Auntie Millie spoke Farsi like an Iranian and English like a true Brit. She helped Mom enroll my brothers in public school and the local Hebrew school. Millie took my mother to kosher butchers and enormous supermarkets, teaching her how to shop American-style. Mom said the first time she set foot in an A&P, she broke down and bawled. Cruising wide aisles, in awe of the assortment of food, she suddenly saw piles of fava beans stacked in clear plastic bags. It flung her back in time to Mashhad, when she was 14, pregnant, and chadored, carrying home sacks of fava beans with Yocheved, viewing the world through eye-slits, breathing through drapes.

"Estaire, I cry in supair-market becauz my face now free—now open, not closed. Open jus like I say I vhant when I fourteen. Amazing meer-a-cal. I real now."

But being real, Mom confessed, was a novel experience that took some getting used to because being *free and open* also left her feeling exposed. Now that her face could be seen, her facial expressions could also be read, which required an adjustment.

Since Auntie Millie and Uncle Aaron didn't have children, Albert and David instantly became theirs. Burly and buoyant, Uncle Aaron showered the boys with laughter and love. Ginger-haired Auntie Millie, picking up on their inquisitive minds, visited her nephews with stacks of model airplane kits. She'd sit by their side with a toothy smile, helping them follow directions, as they each worked with a magnifying glass, tweezers, and glue, putting together their balsa wood aircraft. My brothers relished this problem-solving hobby, which demanded patience, concentration, and precision—traits Auntie Millie nourished.

Albert and David learned English quickly and soon became academic superstars: skipping grades; winning red ribbons, plaques, and medals; acing after-school Hebrew classes. They played baseball, attended Cub Scout meetings, traded comics, and were swiftly embraced by fellow classmates.

For Pop, the first years were harrowing—flat broke, no profession, saddled with young sons and an abrasive wife who made pain and humiliation stick. Jutting out breast and belly, she hit below the belt, blurting, "*Khar*.[1] You're lazy, worthless. You are not a man! Others support their families. Why can't you?"

Under siege, he fired back, "You strangle the life out of me!" and retreated to his bed in search of shelter.

Pop's paternal grandfather, Benyamin Aminoff, had been a successful merchant who invested in a variety of trades. He owned multiple slaughterhouses in Iran's province of Khorasan and exported goods to Germany: Persian lambskin, which was sewn into coats, and pickled cow intestines used for sausage-making. He owned three caravanserais—lucrative roadside inns, where Silk Road traders, traveling Pashtun salesmen, and their camels could eat, sleep, and recover from a long day's journey. One caravanserai was located in Mashhad; the other two were farther northeast in Merv, Russia.

Pop's grandfather also owned a huge farm in Torqabeh, west of Mashhad, and a profitable icehouse that sold blocks of ice cut and packed in winter to keep year-round. There were no refrigerators, and chopped ice was desperately needed by all. In addition, Benyamin grew poppies and harvested heroin, which he exported to pharmaceutical companies in Germany for medicinal use. Since Mashhad lacked a reliable banking system, he invested much of his wealth in real estate in Merv—and lost it all after the Bolshevik Revolution.

Pop walked the streets of Manhattan, clueless. This city of doctors, lawyers, and bankers ran counter to all he knew. He came from a long line of landowners, merchants, traders, and, prior to them, shepherds. How could he earn a living? How could he ever compete?

1. *khar* (Persian/Farsi)—donkey, ass, stupid fool

For five dollars a month, he rented a corner of a furrier's office in Manhattan's Fur District. He had a wooden desk, wooden chair, and his own Murray Hill 4-2548 line hooked up to a black rotary phone. Every day, twisted in knots, he went through the morning drudgery of squeezing himself into rush-hour subways to go to his rented desk, hoping to drum up business, make a deal, repeat his success as a broker and supplier of goods. Weeks, months, a year plodded by and the phone lay dead in its cradle—sitting there, just in case there was a deal to be made. Bitter but unresigned, he conjured up Benyamin, his grandfather, and tried his own hand at selling pickled cow intestines, importing them from Iran and exporting them to Germany. Here and there he sold an odd lot, but not enough to pay the month's rent.

During this dry and dismal time, my father decided to change his last name from Aminoff to Amini. The explanation I was always given was that a few Aminoff cousins with similar-sounding first names who were now also living and working in New York were mistakenly receiving Pop's business mail. By becoming Fatulla Amini, he said, he was creating postal privacy.

This was not a minor matter. Pop came from a highly respected, aristocratic family in Mashhad, and he was hacking the "off" and adding an "i" to prevent mail from going astray? Would a Rockefeller chop off the "feller" and call himself "Rocker" to safeguard his mail? The Aminoff name was an invaluable asset, highly regarded not only in Iran but also throughout the Mashhadi communities in England, Italy, Germany, Israel, and the U.S. Its power and prestige opened doors, commanded respect, and elicited instant trust in business. None of his brothers or his Aminoff cousins would ever consider changing their notable surname. So why trade "off" for the letter "i"? Pop's explanation struck me as odd. But it was the only one he ever gave. Whatever his reasons, I'm certain that altering his ancestral name did not go over well with his father when he got wind of it. Was that the point? Was Pop thumbing his nose at Moshe, silently saying I'm no longer a part of you? Was he showing contempt, disrespect, without uttering a word? Was this a silent payback? If so, it seemed extreme. All his life, my father remained proud to be an Aminoff—even after changing his name.

During this bleak stretch, each night after dinner Pop paced the street outside the apartment, inhaling cartons of Camels, which were pickling his own intestines. Determined to stay in the U.S.,

Mom had become pregnant, knowing that a baby born in America would automatically be a citizen, and, as parents, they too would become official permanent residents. But another baby also meant another mouth to feed. Living with piling bills and thinning self-confidence, Pop's face turned into a palette of beiges, the line between honor and humiliation blurred.

Powerless, he retreated even further into silence—as if to say, *Why waste breath?*—and soothed himself by dipping into his secret stash of memories: the one thing he had plenty of. Dreamily reminiscing, he yearned for the country he wasn't in. He longed for Mashhad and his acres of farmland, where sheep and goats peacefully roamed, grazing side by side, where the whoosh of a fresh gust of wind was sometimes interrupted by the chirp of a blue thrush flitting through clusters of mint leaves, green grapevines, and blackberry bushes. He remembered reclining on a cotton lounge chair, feet up, admiring his cherry trees.

His wandering thoughts returned to goats—gentle Persian goats. Thinking goats, he visualized them bleating, birthing, and began to dwell on the special downy coat which lay beneath their stiff, bristly hair.

One idea led to another. *Why not?* he asked himself. *What do I have to lose?*

After attaining samples of this soft down from Iran, he visited textile mills in New York, New Jersey, and Pennsylvania. Factory after factory turned him away, saying they didn't have proper machinery to weave such fine hair into yarn. Staving off despair, he thumbed through the Yellow Pages and came across Lawson Industries. Pop called and was granted an appointment with Helmut Schultz, founder and chief executive of Lawson.

He arrived at the mill in Pennsylvania, straight and starched in his tight-fitting overcoat, toting a clear plastic sack filled with soft Persian goat's hair. A spindly secretary escorted him into Helmut Schultz's office. Mr. Schultz had the German machinery needed to turn this fluff into yarn and then into fabric, and quickly went to work producing a cloth sample. First weighing, then stroking the sample, Helmut discovered it was light, exceptionally warm, with a rich luxurious feel. Smiling broadly, he shot out his right arm and gave Pop a sturdy Germanic handshake. "Fatulla, you're my man!" he bellowed. "Start sending me bales."

Snugly buttoned into his overcoat, Pop stood numb in his own spotlight. Confounded, he asked himself, *Can this be true? Penni-less for years and now prosperous? How can this be?* He headed home asymmetric, tilting in the direction of this sack—a sack of fleece that had turned to gold. Walking along the frozen Hudson River, hearing plates of floating ice crack, he sobbed convulsively. Swing-ing between disbelief and ecstasy, he dried his eyes.

Pop knew immediately, deep in his bones, that his family's fi-nancial circumstances were about to change, but he didn't know how dramatically. Cashmere was just beginning to become available and popular in the United States when he brought his high-quality samples to Mr. Schultz. Soon, it would become a sensation. Holly-wood stars would be seen draped in creamy cashmeres, turning this supersoft fabric into a symbol of luxury and glamour. Before long, cashmere sweaters, scarves, jackets, and coats would become must-have items for style-conscious men and women across the country.

At home, in a meditative mood, Pop reached for his *siddur*[2] and, through a tidal wave of tears, thanked God. "All I have comes from you. All good fortune comes from you." Overwhelmed by gratitude, he swore he'd never forget God's bounty. In addition to income, his honor and birthright had been returned.

Drawing from the monthly salary he received from Lawson, Pop soon paid back all loans and cleared all bills. On March 1, 1949, in the middle of the night, Mom was awakened by clawing contrac-tions. Leaving ten-year-old Albert to look after David, Pop rushed Mom to Gotham Hospital on East 76th Street, where she was quick-ly sedated. Thirty-seven minutes later, I slipped out. And just like her own mother, I was born two weeks before Purim.

Years later Mom said, "In Mashhad I cry, I scream—I vhant die vhen I give birt. In *Am-ree-kah,* I sleep, vake up, an have you. God blez *Am-ree-kah.*" She then kissed the air.

She'd say Iran burned women while *Am-ree-kah* honored women. This became her constant refrain whenever referencing childbirth, dishwashers, ovens, refrigerators, and washing machines. "Estaire, *Am-ree-kah* love vee-men. So good to vee-men. Always make life eazy for vee-men."

Mom, who came from a land of breastfeeders, was told by her American obstetrician that sticking one's nipple into an infant's mouth was lewd, primitive, unsanitary. She was told that bot-tle-feeding was the healthiest and most enlightened way to mother

2. *siddur* (Hebrew)—Jewish prayer book

one's child. Wanting to catch up with modernity and not appear Third World, she complied.

She straddled the cultural divide by bringing me home tightly swaddled in hand-embroidered Persian paisley scarves, with a bottle dangling from my mouth. Our entry into the living room set off Hebrew incantations from the family members gathered to welcome Mom home. Pop, wearing a white yarmulke, teared up as he chanted from his prayer book. Uncle Aaron, Auntie Millie, and four of Pop's recently arrived Aminoff cousins were all assembled in our home, passing candies as they sang *"Siman Tov u'Mazal Tov.[3]"*

A few weeks later, Mom threw a Persian dinner party to celebrate my arrival—the birth of her long-awaited daughter, the daughter she had prayed desperately for in Hamadan.

After hours of heavy eating and drinking, guests clapped, sang, and danced to the beat of the dayereh. Mom, deliriously happy, sang the loudest, danced the hardest, as women in flouncy, tiered skirts followed her lead, swishing across our living room. A night of celebration that spilled past midnight into early morning hours. ◪

3. *Siman Tov u' Mazal Tov* (Hebrew)—Hebrew celebration song

Benyamin Aminoff, Esther's paternal great-grandfather, successful merchant and trader who owned caravansaries along the Silk Route.

Tuti and Moshe Aminoff, Esther's paternal grandparents, married when Tuti was nine years old.

David Levi (right), Esther's maternal grandfather, who died when Esther's mother, Hana, was two.

Esther Levi (right), Esther's maternal grandmother, married to David Levi at age 12; she died giving birth to Esther's mother, Hana.

Fatulla Nissan Aminoff, Esther's father, at around age 17, at boarding school in London.

Hana Levi, 14, and Fatulla Aminoff, 34: Esther's parents as newlyweds.

Esther's parents, Fatulla and Hana, in Mashhad soon after their marriage.

Esther's mother, Hana, wearing a chador, passing for Muslim in Mashhad while secretly living as a Jew.

Hana's stepmother, Yocheved (second from left), at her son Solomon's wedding.

PART THREE

OLD WORLD
MEETS NEW

CHAPTER 17

Showering with Mom

By 1950, there were six Mashhadi families linked by blood or marriage living in New York City, all looking to buy their first home. Given their deep ties, they succumbed to the psychic pull of Iran, their fierce sense of interpersonal responsibility, and sought a single neighborhood where all could settle. Six heads of household, including my father, spent Sundays checking out various neighborhoods in Queens. They needed to find a community with a synagogue, Hebrew school, kosher butcher, *mikvah*,[1] and a direct subway line into Manhattan. These six men looked for an area where houses were affordable; while some were already doing well, they kept in mind others, like Pop, who were only beginning to make a living. For my parents, these caring and concerned families were the belt around their waists, holding them up.

Meshing all variables, the six families chose Kew Gardens and bought houses just blocks from one another. I was two years old when Pop purchased our home and moved us from Manhattan to Queens.

For seven years Iranian merchants steadily shipped bales of goat hair from Iran to New Jersey docks, where Pop inspected all shipments before sending them off to Lawson's mills. Seven years of plenty. Seven years of prosperity. A win-win for all.

However, in the eighth year my father learned that Western winds of commerce were not only mercurial but duplicitous. Bales of goat hair sent from Iran were now arriving at the pier but by-

---

1. *mikvah* (Hebrew)—bathing facility used for ritual immersion

passing Pop. Lawson's cashmere-spinning looms continued to hum with or without him. In 1958, Helmut Schultz went straight to Pop's suppliers and began importing directly, eliminating the middleman, my father. Pop was erased, discarded, the American way.

My father was neither legal-minded nor strategic. He hadn't imagined the inevitable, much less looked for ways to forestall it. He had never insisted on lawyers or contracts and hadn't even known to do so. Pop came from a corner of the world where a handshake was all you needed, and that's what he relied on for seven years—a firm Germanic handshake. In Iran, Persian merchants formed trusted relationships that lasted lifetimes, passed them on to children and grandchildren, with only a verbal agreement. A man's word was his honor. *Aberu*[2]—face, reputation—was one's contract and currency. Who would think a man would want to tarnish his own name, jeopardize trust? In Iran, hacking off limbs, slicing throats, would be the consequence. A pragmatist, Pop felt no ill will toward his suppliers. He knew they also had to make a living and couldn't afford to turn buyers away.

Pop left Lawson Industries, shooting Schultz a cutting stare.

My father, a self-made man, was now unmade, and family survival was once again at risk. Paralyzed by fear and distrust, Pop returned to what he knew best: pickled cow intestines—importing and exporting, which somehow seemed to keep us afloat.

Pop never said a word to me about those seven good years. It wasn't until I opened a basement closet at age 15 and discovered burlap bags filled with bolts of cashmere fabric that I had reason to question Mom. Sadly, she relayed the entire tale behind these rolls and remnants, the painful reminders of my father's sudden rise and sharp fall.

At 15, I downplayed loss, extracted one fact and prized it: My immigrant father, who struggled to feed and clothe his family, had helped dress our entire nation in cashmere. Be it luck, sheer perseverance, or stroke of genius, it made no difference: He was heroic, and so I pocketed my pride.

My day-to-day life from age two to nine remained the same. If Pop soared and then took a financial hit, I never felt it. I didn't sense euphoria or a crashing downfall. But the unwavering message I did get from him throughout those years was: *You must learn how*

2. *aberu* (Persian/Farsi)—face, honor, reputation

to tend to husband and family. Soon you'll be running your own home, so watch your mother and learn from her.

In this way, I too would preserve aberu—the family's and my own.

And my mother always seemed to be setting the standard, teaching me lessons, showing me how.

At the end of one long, meat-grinding, floor-waxing day, Mom was sitting in the den, darning socks, shortening hems, and crocheting the colorful cotton *leefs*[3] we used as washcloths. These woven leefs had accompanied her across oceans and continents. As a nine-year-old, I took them for granted as merely functional items, but, for her, they maintained webs of connection to her early years in Iran and the visits to Persian *hammams*[4] that had once brightened her life. Each week she and her girlfriends would meet at a hammam to both bathe and party, bringing their handmade leefs along with picnic baskets and tambourines. Here in Queens, she continued churning out batches at a time, in festive, carnival colors—violet, canary yellow, orange, lime—always handing me the hot pinks. On this night, a hot pink was already nested in the stack.

Bone-tired, Mom rested her thick ankles on a footstool as her long fingers rapidly moved in and out, manically crocheting. With one eye fixed on the crochet hook and the other fastened on the TV, my mother was learning English by watching *Father Knows Best*. This pose captured an ever-present split that confused and divided me: Mom, thoroughly Iranian, embracing life in America.

"Estaire, vhat means *jinko-lo-vinski*? Tell me Farsi verd."

Awww, hell. Not another annoying question. Not another annoying back-and-forth between Farsi and English. "Ma, what are you talking about?"

"Vhen I leesen, fadder know bess say to Bud, you *jinko-lo-vinski*."

My lips sprayed laughter. "Do you mean juvenile delinquent?"

Unfazed, she nodded.

After translating, I insisted she enunciate after me, "Ju–ven–ile de–lin–quent."

Mom caught onto meanings but not to thickets of syllables. From then on, whenever she spotted tattooed hoodlums on street corners, twirling switchblades, she pointed and roared, "*Jinko-lo-vinski!*" hoping shame would reform them. Holding my breath, I'd

3. *leef* (Persian/Farsi)—crocheted rectangular wash cloth or bath mitt
4. *hammam* (Persian/Farsi)—Persian bath house

squeeze my eyes shut, envisioning switchblades pressed against our throats while we were gang-raped. Instead, muscular hoods looked at her blankly, certain she was speaking some foreign tongue. Thanks to Mom's mangled English in need of English translation, our lives were spared.

Once, standing on a subway platform, she took note of a nearby tattooed bicep and asked, "Vie day have 'MOM' on mus-ceel?"

I answered, "Some guys who really love their mothers have the word MOM put on their arms."

"No good! Torah say no tattoo. Body holy. Estaire, even you loave me—nevair burn MOM on skeen."

"I'll remember that," I said sarcastically.

It was the late 1950s, and Russia's nuclear threat loomed large. In preparation for the next war, my mother filled our basement closets with stacks of leefs, toilet paper, Ivory soap, Iranian rice, saffron, apple juice, matzos, Del Monte tomato sauce, cling peaches, castor oil, and milk of magnesia. A proto-prepper for annihilation, Mom was a model, as if she had been training for the End of Days her entire life. She had me convinced our basement closets would also serve as fallout shelters, keeping us safe from the onslaught of Russian bombs.

Public School 99 also anticipated atomic warfare and made sure we practiced monthly duck-and-cover drills under our two-foot-by-two-foot wooden desks. As soon as we fourth graders heard the piercing sirens, we dropped to our knees, crawled under our desks, tucked our heads between our elbows, laced our fingers over the back of our heads, and prayed that Russia's hydrogen bomb wasn't targeting Room 404. Night after night, I had sweaty nightmares of America, New York, Queens, Kew Gardens, our house shelled—an Armageddon—while I, panic-stricken, sooty-faced, ran through war-ravaged streets, climbing over rubble, bawling, in search of my family.

Nine-year-old Cathy Storch lived in the house next door. She, pretty, all-American-looking with pale blue eyes and long, red curly hair, wasn't having nightmares. She wasn't preparing for the next holocaust. Unlike me, she spoke her mind, never wavering, never second-guessing herself. Jumping rope, the soles of her shoes slapped the pavement with confidence. As a child of Iranian immigrants, an inferior species, I walked, and jumped, tentatively, never certain I belonged. From supermarkets to synagogues, there were people who looked at my family, scrunched up their faces,

and said, "Yuck—you Arabs. Go back to where you came from!"
We weren't Arabs.

Cathy traced her family lineage back to the Mayflower. Bug-eyed, I listened as she sketched out her future plans. She was being groomed for Radcliffe, her mother's alma mater, and expected to graduate magna cum laude with multiple PhDs. I, on the other hand, came from strictly kosher, Mashhadi parents who were dead set on marrying me off by my 16th birthday. I thought it best not to bring up my nomadic shepherd ancestors.

All the same, once Cathy's freckled nose got a whiff of the aromas wafting from our Persian kitchen, she chose me as her *best friend*. I also chose her, after taking a good hard look at her mother. Each morning, at the same time that Cathy and I left for school, her mom, a red-haired anthropology instructor at Marymount College, glided out the door in horn-rimmed glasses, carrying an overstuffed leather briefcase, with a freshly lit cigarette dangling from her lower lip. If my brain could have drooled, it would have. Mrs. Storch never chopped bales of dill and parsley, and wouldn't be caught dead sweating over pots of Persian stew. Quite the contrary, she was a hardcore thinker—a type of female I had never known. Ashamed of my mother, I didn't tell Cathy mine was illiterate, and I made sure Mom never uttered *jinko-lo-vinski* in her presence. I also made sure Cathy came over only when Pop was nowhere in sight.

Cathy loved spending time at my house. After school, sharply dressed in a prep school blazer and houndstooth plaid kilt, she'd climb over the low wooden fence dividing our yards, rush in through our back door, flit past me, and tackle Mom with hugs and kisses, which Mom, for some reason, tolerated. Sitting at the kitchen table, she let out lip-smacking "oohs" and "aahs" while devouring freshly baked Nan-e Taftuns and guzzling chilled chocolate milk. Mom and Cathy were tight.

"Your home smells sweet—like cotton candy." Her braces glistened as she smiled.

I rolled my eyes. Mom was wedded to her stove; Mrs. Storch, to Marymount College. While I taught Mom the alphabet, Mrs. Storch taught Cathy Proust. Cathy, with her waist-length spiral curls, stood tall on her mother's shoulders. Mom stood on mine. I felt gypped.

"Mrs. Amini, pretend you love me," she crooned between long sighs.

"Vhat? Cat-tee sveetee, I NO pretend." Admiring Cathy's ginger-colored hair Mom said, "I loave Cat-tee!"

I entered a deep freeze and looked the other way. *Cathy loves anyone who'll feed her.*

Alone with me in my bedroom she let it out. "Es, you have the coolest comic book collection and the greatest mom, baking and feeding us Persian cakes and oven-roasted nuts. She's always home, opening the door with a huge smile and..."

My face twisted. "Who cares? That doesn't make her great. You can buy cakes, cookies, and cream puffs at our local bakery."

"Let's trade moms. I want yours. Mine's a tight-ass."

Cathy hadn't lived through pots and pans crashing into kitchen walls, hadn't been caught in the crossfire of Persian curses or stood helpless as Mom dashed out of the house, running away from Pop and gone for days. She also never asked why I bit my nails. She only smelled the cake.

Cathy complained that in her home comic books were forbidden. "Mom says they trash minds and impede intellectual growth." I admired Cathy for knowing lots of big words and being unafraid of using them. After looking up "impede" and "intellectual," I sank into sadness, grieving the damage I'd done to my mind by having already consumed hundreds of *Archies*, *Jugheads*, and *Betty and Veronicas*.

Cathy kept coming over for cakes and comics and I indulged her, providing she brought me books her mother sanctioned. My primary goal was brain repair. One afternoon she lugged over Darwin's *On the Origin of Species*, Mead's *Coming of Age in Samoa*, and Dostoyevsky's *Crime and Punishment*. We were swapping mothers.

It was a full year before Cathy invited me to her home, and when she did, she insisted I bring along a fresh stash of *Archies*. This was living life a bit too dangerously. If caught red-handed, I was convinced her mother would never allow me to set foot in her house again; she'd accuse me of poisoning her daughter's brain. Didn't Cathy realize bringing over printed materials that "impede intellectual growth" would cost us our friendship? Why couldn't she, in the safety of my bedroom, break the law? That wasn't good enough. Cathy craved the rush of thrill-filled sin.

Stealthily, under my raincoat, I snuck in what her mother forbade and was relieved to discover her parents weren't home. Titillated, Cathy ripped open my bags and carpeted her bedroom floor with comics. In shorts and tank tops we lay flat on our stomachs, swinging our feet in the air, ponytails bobbing, as I read what was hers and she read what was mine. Her bedroom was subtly decorated, color-coordinated in shades of white and heather blue. Mrs. Storch's anthropology, archaeology, sociology, philosophy, and psychology texts lined all four walls. Beside Cathy's canopied bed hung a framed print of Picasso's *Guernica*. I'd never seen anything like it. Using her mother's words she explained, "Picasso is accessing the subconscious and depicting the horrors of war." Memorizing "subconscious," I reached for a dictionary. She reached for the turntable, replacing Vivaldi with Rosemary Clooney. As Clooney sang a jazzy "Come On-A My House," we leapt to our feet, swung our hips rip-roaringly free, swayed our boney arms in the air, and squealed with laughter.

This was ultimate freedom—having the run of her home as a parent-free zone, without a single adult in sight. We went down to the kitchen. Cathy opened an empty refrigerator, searching for snacks, then nimbly climbed onto a kitchen counter, reached into a cabinet, and brought down two stale Hershey bars.

"They aren't Nan-e Taftuns," she said sadly, lowering her head to hide sudden tears.

I bit into my Hershey's. "I'll take chocolate over Nan-e Taftuns any day."

After drying her eyes with the back of her hands she gave me a tight squeeze.

Later, stepping into her bathroom, I noticed that her tub was leef-less. Slung over her shower handle was a tattered, terry cloth rag.

"Cathy, what's this?"

"A washcloth. Haven't you ever seen one? My mom buys packs of them from Woolworth's. Why, what do you use?"

Her dust-filled home smelled smart, like old books—much brainier-smelling than the thick scent of Persian stews. Her empty refrigerator looked modern and enlightened. But a rag called a washcloth seemed peculiar. Mom's leefs, knotted in thick cotton, were tough and abrasive, somewhat like her. Even in the shower, when I thought I was finally alone, I wasn't. Scouring myself with a hot-pink leef, frenetically scrubbing my back until it practically bled, I could feel Mom hovering, making sure I didn't take short cuts, making sure I stepped out brutally clean.

Cathy's cloth looked cheap, drab, lifeless. Mrs. Storch wasn't in the shower with her—maybe she didn't care how Cathy washed, or if she did. Stark naked as water smacked her head, Cathy was all alone.

While Cathy's latchkey childhood was about *not enough*, mine felt strangled by *too many* and *too much*. And while Cathy's parents fed her mind, mine wished I didn't have one. ◈

CHAPTER 18

Neet

Thankfully, my brothers reversed my fate, offering options. They cranked up expectations: living loudly, airing strong opinions, intellectually omnivorous, questioning, refuting, inclined toward doubt, betting that best brains win.

Once docked in America, Albert and David carried the weight of family on their young shoulders. As child translators they dealt with utility companies, exterminators, house painters, plumbers; they mediated family feuds, and later, as adults, would come to Mom and Pop's financial rescue, each growing at a rapid pace, parenting parents. Fortunately, they were endowed with sparkling wit and vigorous pluck.

Mom attributed their smarts to hemoglobin. Unlike all other Mashhadi couples, my parents were not related to one another. With a staggering level of pride, my mother boasted in Farsi: "Mashhadis are stupid and crazy because they all married their first cousins. My children are brilliant because their blood is fresh, not stale."

Dazzled by Al and Dave, I liked to think of myself as the third and youngest brother as we biked through Flushing Meadow Park, smacked tennis balls against schoolyard walls, and watched *Alfred Hitchcock Presents* with me sandwiched between them, peering through my shaky, laced fingers. Late at night in Al's bedroom, I'd lean in close, smelling their sibling scent as they leaned toward their homemade crystal radio, listening to WOR's Jean Shepherd. When I was seven, Shepherd's detailed narrations of bygone days, like snatches of Swahili, flew over my head. But it didn't matter that I couldn't follow his lengthy trains of thought since, for me, it was less about hearing a live radio broadcast and more about inhaling, breath after breath, what my brothers exhaled.

We always had a ping-pong table tucked in our basement. It was a must, like having a bed or lamp—an absolute necessity. On Friday nights after Shabbat dinner, we three submarined downstairs to play hot sweaty rounds. Al and Dave were as swift as any Chinese pro, having perfected their slams during the long, hot afternoons of Bombay. They whacked ping-pong balls from one tip of our green table to the opposite edge at the speed of light. Transfixed, I hero-worshipped.

Thoroughly drenched after hours of volleying, they'd hand over a wooden paddle, show me the proper grip, and mentor the flick of my wrist as I switched from forehand to backhand. "Stay agile," David said. "Light on the tips of your toes so you can run fast from side to side." In time, I, too, mastered ping-pong, relishing spinning serves and unreturnable slams, just like a third brother.

They were equally strong in academics and relished dinner table debates, which served as a boot camp for my female Persian-American brain. As third in line, I gained. I was neither the firstborn nor the middle child, but the last—well buffered. Ten years younger than Albert and seven years behind David, I lived in the bleachers, studying cause and effect without being directly affected. At times I grumbled under my breath or over it, pining for options never meant for me. But I didn't jockey for position. Whether sitting on my tail or wagging it, I simply watched, reveling in their company.

Mom's blistering drive to be *a somebody* was funneled into her two sons. While American mothers helped their children with reading, writing, math, history, science, my mother, every evening after dinner, did what she could do. Mom rushed upstairs with three bowls of fruit. Each bowl contained an apple, an orange, and a banana, with a fruit knife carefully squeezed between them. Proudly, she'd place a bowl on each of my brothers' desks as tutorial assistance. For them, her fruit praised, chanted songs of support: "Keep studying, my brilliant sons. You are the smartest and will someday conquer the world." The bowl she brought to my room dully hummed, "Eat and go to sleep." But I outwitted her, secretly changing my fruit's message to theirs.

Albert attended high school at academically elite Brooklyn Tech and spent evenings hunched over a makeshift drafting table, measuring, drawing, and right-angling. He had rulers of every shape and size push-pinned to a cork board; 30 or 40 hung over his head—round, semicircular, triangular, and square. When I was seven, I'd follow him into his bedroom and watch with awe as he drew. The rulers and my brother seemed one and the same. He measured winding spaces that spilled open, sunlight bouncing off walls, and the length and breadth of complicated shadows. Museums, concert halls, stadiums, bridges, highways burst from his penciled lines. His dream was to become an architect and sculpt space in ways that had never been done before.

Pop preferred to see Al become a Persian rug dealer. Now that had prestige. According to my father, drawing buildings wasn't a trade. Mom, on the other hand, wanted educated sons. She licked her lips as she boasted to her butcher, "My son vhant be ar-kee-tect," not quite knowing what it meant but enjoying the sound of its hard consonants.

When I was eight, Al was awarded a full scholarship to Cornell University's College of Architecture. With shoulders thrown back and blueprints in hand, he left for Ithaca. I cried for weeks, sorely missing him. Al worried about me. As eager as he had been to escape our war-waging parents, he was also fearful of leaving me behind, less shielded, with only one brother to protect me.

Every other day after Al left, I received a postcard from Cornell. On the back would be a cartoon drawn in pencil. If he knew I had an upcoming dental appointment, he would draw me happily seated in the dentist's chair with a comical comment bubbling out of the dentist's mouth. If he caught a cold, I'd receive a sketch of Albert in bed with a lopsided hot water bottle on his head, a huge thermometer in his mouth, his hair tangled crazily, and one big toe sticking out from under his blanket. One card had me seated in class, wearing my new red-framed glasses as I stared happily at the blackboard. This was his way of saying, *I'm still with you.* Some of my friends collected Topps baseball cards, packaged with a flat pink slab of bubble gum. I collected stacks of stamped postcards cartooned by Al.

Before each college break and visit home, Al would instruct me to make lists of all my problems, large and small, so that, in the quiet of my bedroom, we could discuss and solve them. And so I did. When Al returned home, he'd lie flat on my bed with his knees drawn up, sit me atop them, and one by one, with open ears, listen to and discuss my worries. I tried my best to speak. But more importantly, raised high by his knees, I knew I mattered.

When I turned 11, Al noticed that my breasts were budding. He never said so, just casually asked if my sixth-grade classmates were wearing bras.

I was amazed. "Al, how did you know? Yeah, in fact Walter Gonzales likes to sneak up from behind and twang bra straps. The girls act real annoyed, but they love it."

"What makes you think they love it?" he asked.

"Oh, I can tell. It makes them feel sexy."

"Es, what do you say we go shopping and get you some training bras? We'll find a saleslady to help us out."

Albert had spotted my breasts? I didn't think anyone was aware of them but me. Mom hadn't noticed, and I kind of hoped she wouldn't. I knew the more my body changed and turned into a woman's, the harder Pop would push for marriage. If I had to go bra-shopping with anyone, I was glad it was Al.

The very next day we hightailed over to Queens Boulevard and sauntered, hand-in-hand, through Alexander's department store. Eyeing a triple-chinned, buxom saleswoman standing near the lingerie counter, Albert whispered, "She looks like that British actress Margaret Rutherford. I get a good feeling. Let's ask her."

With a solid voice, far beyond his 21 years, he began: "This is my sister and she's never worn a bra. Do you think—"

Before he could finish, the saleswoman gripped my wrist and whisked me into the dressing room. As if fulfilling her life's purpose, she measured length, width, breadth, slipping me in and out of styles that fit my bust. Her gray and white jumbo curls bounced as her nimble fingers snapped and unsnapped hooks, rapidly chattering like a Mary Poppins. At one point, standing behind me, she unexpectedly wrapped her arms around my skinny waist and, with tearing eyes, gave me a tight squeeze. I figured she thought I was motherless. Why else would a brother be buying bras for his kid sister?

Margaret Rutherford, looking scrubbed and scoured, ruled out transparency, stretchy beginner bras that flattened my chest, and bras that wouldn't hold up after multiple washings. Settling on thick white cotton without itchy lace, we returned to Al, who was waiting by the counter. With a generous smile he opened his wallet and bought me five. Glamorized by bras, I felt I had entered womanhood.

All the way home, swinging a shopping bag filled with wrapped-up lingerie, I mused: *Will Walter snap my bra straps now?*

A few weeks later, Albert came home carrying a small brown paper bag and asked me to follow him into my bathroom. Steeped in silence, he sat on the lidded toilet with his upper lip weighed down by worry.

"Es, I've been thinking about your legs."

"You have?" I groped for words. "What about them?"

"You're going to start wearing stockings soon, and I want you to look really great. So I asked around and found out: You should never use a razor. It will make your hair shoot up fast and thick."

I threw up my arms and let out a sigh. "Thank goodness I'm not using razors!"

My brother rolled up his khaki slacks, placed one leg in the tub, opened a tube of Neet and smeared a strong-smelling pink cream all over his bushy shin.

I broke out laughing a younger sibling's laugh. "Al, you're crazy! What are you doing?"

"This is a test run. I picked this up for you, but first I want to make sure it won't sting or burn your skin."

After waiting the prescribed ten minutes, he rinsed his leg. My mouth fell open as I watched clumps of coarse black hair wash off and spin down the drain.

"Perfect!" he winked. "It doesn't hurt one bit."

I reached over, stroked his silky-smooth leg, and cackled uncontrollably.

"Okay, Es. Now it's your turn."

Following his example, I coated my legs from ankles to knees with thick pink paste. During our ten waiting minutes, he said my legs were beautiful and reassured me "hair-free they'll be even more gorgeous." It all sounded pretty good to me.

A few months later, Al knocked on my bedroom door, clutching a human anatomy textbook. We sat on the floor as he flipped to pre-tabbed pages. In a flat and factual tone, he said he needed to inform me.

"When you hit twelve or maybe thirteen, you're going to begin to ovulate."

"Ovulate" sounded awfully close to salivate and mutilate. Acid dripped into the pit of my stomach. Thinking hard and fast, I suspected "ovulate" was some kind of teenage crime I might soon commit... he did say between ages 12 and 13. He was forewarning me to make sure I didn't screw up.

"Al, I'm scared." I ripped off a nail. "Tell me what I'm about to do that I shouldn't."

My brother turned to colored illustrations of womb, ovaries, eggs, and explained why and how females ovulate and menstruate. I sat stunned. Who knew a nest was growing inside me?

In this thoughtful way Al filled in for Mom, knowing she couldn't take it on, surely not the way he'd want her to—not the way some American mothers might.

I didn't know if my mother knew that Al was preparing me for womanhood. If so, she gave no indication, and I didn't ask. Everything I learned about my body came from Al, until I started high school and grew bold enough to talk over such matters with my closest friend, Bernadette. She and I shared a friendship of secrets, one of which was menstruation. Every high school girl who hadn't yet gotten her period was obsessed with it: When will it come? What does it feel like? What will it look like? And what do I do when it does show up? Should I buy sanitary napkins now, carry them in my pocket for a year or two, just in case? Or do I do nothing, just wait to be stained? Should I buy tampons? If so, don't I need to know where they go? The girls who had gotten their periods weren't talking. It was as if they had all joined some exclusive club. I couldn't discuss any of this with my mother; nor could Bernie with hers. Bernie did some research and found out that we have a narrow road inside us that leads to an inner room, but neither of us knew where this road was.

One afternoon, she brought over a box of Tampax and behind shut doors unfolded the diagramed pamphlet.

"Wow," we both sighed.

"Mom makes me feel like what I know is there just isn't," I told Bernie. "I may think I have a uterus, but she acts like I don't. Only Mom determines what's real, even if it isn't. A total brain-blitz."

"Es, that's nuts."

"But I have Al...." 🔲

CHAPTER 19

Cornell

When I was ten, Al persuaded our parents to let me visit him in Ithaca. Since Pop was clueless when it came to college and campus life, his only reservation was the flight and letting me travel all by myself. Accustomed to fathering our father and allaying his fears, Albert guaranteed my safety. He promised to meet me at the airport when the plane landed and drive me everywhere in the red 1953 Morgan convertible he had recently purchased. He pledged to take good care of me and send me home safe and sound. Because of Al's dogged persistence, Pop finally gave in and allowed me to fly.

Sporting a red Cornell sweatshirt, baggy blue jeans, braided pigtails, I fancied myself an Ivy Leaguer as all ten years of me climbed aboard a Mohawk Airlines twin-engine plane at Idlewild on a Thursday morning in October, tightly clutching my much-needed diary. Never before had I sat in a plane, much less flown in one alone. Flying solo to Ithaca was like blasting off to Mars—the stardust height of my preteen life.

From my seat by a window, I looked around the plane and counted male passengers, all in three-piece suits, either rummaging through attaché cases or burrowed behind *The New York Times*. Feeling real grown up and real scared, I latched my seat belt, unlocked my pink plastic diary, and wrote:

Dear Diary,
This plane is wobbly. It's rolling down the runway groaning, belching, jerking from side to side—but I don't care.

It's a jailbreak. I've escaped. When Myra Merkin called me last night, I picked up Mom's bedroom phone and heard Pop's heavy breathing on the kitchen line. I was Spooked. He's crazy. This time he didn't shout, "Estaire is not home!" Instead, he secretly spied. Don't know what I'll see and do in Ithaca—just know Pop won't be there.

I feel footloose and jittery, all rolled in one. Pop grunted when I waved goodbye, as if I was up to no good, as if I was no good, as if I was running away. I am, for four whole days. What if I never return? Yes!

Earth looked so different from up above. I rolled up one sleeve and smelled my bare arm, double-checking it was me hurtling through silver clouds. Craning my neck, I noticed no two clouds were alike and jotted that down along with my needling worries.

Hope Al will be at the other end. What if he forgot? What if he gets a flat tire on his way to the airport? He's driving his 1953 Morgan. Al's reliable but his red convertible isn't.

A high-heeled, uniformed stewardess wearing a platinum bob walked over. She smiled. A pin on her navy blue lapel read *Betty.*

"Honey, everything all right?" Morning light bounced off her rubbery face.

I shrugged, avoiding her happy eyes. I wasn't sure what was right or wrong high up here in the sky. I knew that airlines required stewardesses to be single and fired them if they married. Mohawk had made news the year before for hiring the first African-American stewardess and then letting her go six months later because she got married. I felt I kind of understood the no-marriage rule. If Betty had a husband, he wouldn't let her leave him in Brooklyn to go fly. He'd be afraid she wouldn't return after seeing Rome and Paris. I figured Mohawk was smart, making sure marriage never got in the way of takeoffs.

Betty's red nails reached for my hand. "Would you like to meet the pilot? I can take you up to the cockpit."

I didn't like the sound of this word. I didn't know what a cockpit was and didn't want to find out. Besides, why would I want to talk to the pilot? He needed to keep his eyes glued to sky highways and just keep flying.

"No, thanks," I prudently answered, using a tiny key to lock my diary.

When the plane hit the ground with all kinds of metallic bumps and jumps, landing in an open field in Ithaca, I clattered down steep metal steps, suitcase in hand, red-framed glasses circling my eyes, and searched wildly for my brother. The Ithaca Tompkins Regional Airport looked nothing like Idlewild. Here, there was no sprawling terminal crowded with planes, just empty fields and windy wide-open space.

In the far distance, I spotted a lone, low building. Since it was the only one in sight and other passengers were walking toward it, I tentatively followed, squinting and searching. Skittish, queasy, and dizzy, feeling lost and forgotten, I choked back a boulder-like lump. The same feeling I had when Mom ran away, leaving me behind, totally erased. Racked with fear, I began hyperventilating. My messy mind had reached its tipping point. I scrambled in my pockets for change, hoping to find a pay phone inside that matchbox terminal.

Then I noticed a tiny figure, a speck of a person, standing on the terminal's roof deck. Quickening my pace, he came into focus. I burst into tears. It was Al, waving, motioning me toward him. Found! I was found!

After long tight bear hugs, we jumped into his red convertible and slowly chugged toward campus with puffs of exhaust streaming from behind. As Al steered, pointing out sights, we munched on his homemade tuna on rye, neatly resting on white waxed paper. He drove by athletic fields, research labs, residence halls, libraries, the Cornell Plantations, fraternity and sorority houses, eateries, natural waterfalls, gorges, and academic buildings, all the while teaching me the difference between Gothic, Victorian, and Neoclassical architecture.

"Why are so many students driving cars and riding bikes on campus?"

"It's the only way they can get to their next class on time. Academic buildings are spread far apart, over hundreds of acres."

It was 1959. In a wide-open field, flocks of students sat on the grass strumming guitars. Frisbees floated in the air as footballs whistled by. Standing on East Hill, overlooking the toy-like town and sparkling Cayuga Lake, I heard the wind purr.

Albert wanted me to attend all of his classes. We sped off to the first one, where thin, spry students with rolled-up flannel sleeves were sculpting plaster models. Some clenched cigarettes between their teeth, others roughly chewed gum, all deeply absorbed. Al said the assignment was for each student to draft and then build a habitat for a specific animal. Together, as a class of architects, they were designing and constructing a huge municipal zoo. To make sure each residence suited its tenant, students first had to learn about their assigned animals: their eating, sleeping, mating habits, as well as their need for warmth, light, and shade. "Each animal is different," Albert said. "We have to be well-informed, so they can thrive in captivity."

I was blown away.

"Do some live in silence, while others crave noise? Do some need locked doors while others want open passageways?"

"Sure. Now you're catching on."

I thought of Mom and Pop, both mammals but with opposing needs, and reached my own conclusion: housing different members of the same species in a shared space doesn't always work.

Shy, I shadowed Al as he went from table to table, introducing me to his fellow students, asking them to show me what they were working on. Feeling I knew nothing, I said nothing. Through blueprints and intricate models, I visited new enclosures for gorillas, flamingos, butterflies, giraffes, and even snakes.

My brother was designing an elephant house. His streamlined, humpbacked, gray plaster structure mimicked the shape and bulk of elephants. Each aspiring architect had a transistor radio softly playing, so quietly that only he or she could hear the music. Some drafted to jazz, others to rock 'n' roll, others to Bach, Beethoven, and Mozart. Instead of a radio, Albert worked with a tape recorder by his side, sketching, measuring, and sculpting to the hypnotic harmonics of Gregorian chants, his favorite. Tucked away in the back of the room sat a white-haired, bow-tied professor calmly puffing a pipe. This alternate universe was astounding to me—nothing like dull, drab P.S. 99.

With a slide rule in his left hand, Albert drew with his right. "It's a competition," he said. "When we finish each habitat, we'll be judged, and the best architectural solution will win."

"How cool is that?" I sighed. "Al, I hope *you* win."

One month later, Albert's elephant house won first prize.

Studio Art was his next class. Following Al, I walked in on a scrawny girl, buck-naked, sprawled out on a Hawaiian-print tablecloth. Students stood behind easels painting her curves as if she were some green vegetable in a grocery store. No one looked shy or embarrassed—not even the model. I refused to act the part of the uneasy, bumbling kid sister, too young for nudity and college.

Instead, gliding through aisles with a puffed chest, my message was: *I see this all the time.*

My brother shared a tiny off-campus apartment with a room-mate named Ed, an aspiring veterinarian. Al had told me, way in advance, he was going to invite his friends over so I could meet them. On Saturday night, I unpacked my black velvet skirt, white turtleneck, and black patent leather Mary Janes, getting myself ready for Al's party. I figured a skirt made me look womanly, especially since I had built-in drawbacks: short, flat-chested, and only in fifth grade. Hoping to blend in with Cornell girls, I combed a center part and wore my thick chestnut hair loose and long.

By 9:30 p.m., Al's tiny apartment was crowded with future archi-tects, poets, lawyers, engineers, Judaic scholars, and dentists. There were bareheaded friends and friends wearing turbans, yarmulkes, baseball caps, even fezzes. Those pulling all-nighters popped by for a short study break; others came to stay, carrying chips, beer, pizza, wine, and soda. Young guys and girls introduced themselves, asked how I liked Cornell, chitchatted, laughed, and mixed easily with one another. A stack of 45s stood high on the turntable, dropping one at a time: Bobby Darin, Connie Francis, Fabian, Elvis Presley, Dion, Ricky Nelson....

Expecting to have a bit part in Albert's Saturday night bash, I practically backflipped when he introduced me as his Guest of Hon-or. His friends clapped. Buff Mike, twice my age, grabbed my hands, swung me around and sang, "Honey, I'm a grungy geezer. Can you overlook it and give me this dance?"

I gave him a sarcastic roll of my eyes. "You're much too old for me!" And leapt into his arms. Shimmying my frail frame, I was on a hot streak, free-form dancing to "Jailhouse Rock," "A Teenager in Love," "Lipstick on Your Collar," and "Turn Me Loose."

Feeling weightless, filled with helium, I danced with each of Al's pals—who were now all mine. A newborn feeling. Blasting music, flooding the apartment, spilled out onto the street through open windows. The room flamed with life—legs kicking, green couch wobbling, lampshades jiggling—all to the rocking beat of Fabian singing "Like a Tiger." Swapping partners, trading wisecracks, bor-ders opened wide. Game for anything. My dancing feet weren't given a minute's rest as my voice reached high octaves, laughing with delight. And feeling so free: certain that none of these college men were thinking of me as a future wife, that not a single guy had thoughts of matrimony, of taking me as his child bride. Words didn't come easily to me, but far from home, they suddenly did. It was as if I had been mute my entire life, then opened my mouth and released a full-throated cantata.

Clasping a hot pan with singed potholders, Al came out of the kitchen with a sheet cake he had baked in my honor. Celebrating me as if I were their college campus queen.

Rocking 'n' rolling, I spun and swayed, my mind outpacing my feet as little voices in my head dictated diary entries—deliriously happy, adrenalin-rich entries.

When the party ended at around 2:00 a.m., Al placed his hands on my shoulders and asked if I had had a good time. With peals of laughter, I answered, "No."

He goaded. "Essie, tell me what it was like for you."

I shook my head and looked up at him. "I can't even talk, Al. I'm stuffing this night into a jar and sealing it forever. Get it? Tonight was a night I'll never forget."

Thrilled, he grinned, then stretched out on the creaky couch and fell fast asleep, snoring.

Wearing pink cotton pajamas with an Eiffel Towers print, I crawled into bed and reached for my diary. My pen grew hot as I scribbled out thoughts. I had told Al I couldn't speak, I didn't have the language, but now that he was asleep and I was alone, words poured out. As the hours passed, I frenetically wrote, stuffing the night into the jar of my journal—every sound, sight, and smell—and preserving it forever in dark blue ink. Guarding privacy, I locked the diary, hid the key in my suitcase, and fell asleep with all lights on.

The next morning we climbed gorges, crossed the Triphammer Foot Bridge, and hunted Iroquois Indian arrowheads. By Sunday afternoon, my pockets were bulging.

Maybe it was listening to Gregorian chants, or watching students design a collaborative zoo, or dancing to Fabian's "Turn Me Loose," or filling my pockets with arrowheads. Maybe all that and more led me to question: *Who am I?* In Queens, I lived concealed behind walls, under the control of parents enmeshed with Mashhad. Caught between Pop's wiretapping and Mom's kamikaze meltdowns, I was gasping for air, air too thin to breathe, and I was about to return to that very same place. I now knew I had to go to college, one way or another. It was my only way out. The only way to figure out me.

Listening to chants on his tape recorder, Al would hit pause, think, then replay certain melodic passages. Returning home, feeling poised and petulant, I did the same. I rewound the weekend and pressed pause, freezing moments, holding them in place, thinking and writing in my diary. When I replayed the weekend, I examined it closely, each frame offering exhilarating alternatives. Alternatives to life in Queens, in our Mashhadi community, and in my home.

CHAPTER 20

Friday Night Cleavage

The lavish parties Mom and Pop gave when I was ten were entirely different from the one in Albert's apartment. It seemed Pop's business had grown and he was now doing well again, importing and exporting pickled cow intestines. On Friday nights, our dining room swelled with Persian merchants, jewelers, newlyweds straight off the boat, grieving widows and widowers, and Iranian students headed for colleges across the nation. Mom, drawn to homeless countrymen, anointed herself a one-person welcoming committee. As soon as she heard that some rootless Iranian immigrants had set foot in Queens, the hapless transplants were hauled in for a Shabbat dinner. They brought with them hearty appetites, fond memories of Mashhad, Tehran, Shiraz, Isfahan, as well as respect for and distrust of Anglo-Saxon America. While men expressed gratitude for the chance at prosperity this country offered, they also, through their male gaze, found fault with American women, deeming them unnatural, masculine, loud, and much too free.

My mother would knot my hair in a bun, dab my cheeks with rouge, and seat me sandwiched between college-bound bachelors. I was on exhibit for the young, eligible, Iranian men—and cast as a potential bride. It didn't matter that I was ten and they 20. Didn't Tuti marry at nine, Mom at 14? And wasn't Pop 20 years her senior? Mom's unspoken goal butted heads with mine. Stifling horror, sending telepathic messages, my eyes drilled into hers: *These goons come from a foreign planet. I don't like the way they smell. They smell like Iran. And, remember, I'm pulling As, so I don't have to marry*—a deal I had made with myself.

The Iranian students on either side of me avoided my jutting elbows just as I avoided theirs, and we never talked to one another, mutually fearing benign conversation would be misread as: "I want you." Matrimony was a leaden cloud hanging over my head. When Pop's eyes caught mine, they sternly advised I stay quiet. He believed the less a female said, the more likely a man would fall in love with her. He drew from his own experience. Didn't he fall hard for Mom and quickly decide to marry her before he even heard the sound of her voice? He'd seen her holding court, making other women laugh, but he'd never heard her speak, knew nothing of her sharp tongue. *Crazy,* I told myself, rejecting his belief, never suspecting that, one day, it would become my own.

Every Friday night, Mom's bosom was served alongside platters of roasted chicken thighs, saffron rice, and Persian sweet-and-sour meatballs. Her plunging necklines revealed endless cleavage propped up by a padded cone-shaped brassiere that lifted her breasts to eye level. And each Friday night, Pop's jagged brows scrunched together, pointed at her exposed bosom. He'd glare at her with burning fury, only to be met by icy indifference as she leaned over a pot of stuffed cabbage. I felt stinging shame. The shame she lacked. Looking down at my twisted napkin, I would redden, as if Mom's indecent exposure were mine. As if my ten-year-old flat chest had suddenly sprouted meringues that were leaping out of *my* dress.

I didn't understand Mom's breasts. Unclothed, they were half their public size, so what I was seeing and cringing over wasn't even completely hers. She had a talent for showing too much, creating something out of nothing, fooling everyone and loving it. As a child I wondered, *Is that what women do? Do they create something out of nothing? Is that what men want? Falsies? What if I never grow plump breasts? Will I wear falsies?* I shuddered at the thought of becoming Mom and swore I'd choose flat over false any day.

Mom's obvious aversion to romance, sex, and men made her exposed bosom even more bewildering. Under her breath she frequently warned, "Pee-nis, no good." For her, it was an unruly, lethal beast with an impulsive, unpredictable will of its own, to be avoided at all cost. Since she didn't like holding hands or being hugged, and jerked away from being touched, I didn't know why she coquettishly showcased Sophia Loren breasts. A brain-boggler. *If her homemade cleavage wasn't a call for lovers, what was it for?*

With the passage of time, it became clear: Tightly contoured dresses accented by sinful cleavage helped her maintain her status as Queen Bee, insuring that all eyes were locked on her. She did whatever it took to eclipse every other woman. Occupying center stage, she sought attention, filling the room with rip-roaring humor, prickly sarcasm, and hot Friday night cleavage.

Fair-skinned and delicately featured, my mother was a Persian beauty. For Shabbat, she wore her raven hair swept into a cornucopia of hills and valleys, culminating above her neck in a French twist. This voluminous hairdo, held together by hundreds of hairpins, was her matriarchal headdress. Dark eyeliner outlined her light brown eyes. A shock of pomegranate-red filled her full lips. She penciled a perfectly round, black beauty mark just above the right corner of her mouth, suggestive of 1950s Hollywood sirens. Before bounding down the steps to greet dinner guests, her earlobes, cleavage, wrists, ankles, back of the knees, were all bathed in Chanel No. 5, Mom's signature scent.

Every Friday night, Persian love songs crooned from our tape recorder as Mom shuffled out of the kitchen in her red-velvet mules with platters of Ghormeh Sabzi, *Polo Shevid,*[1] *gonteveh,*[2] *Khoresht Nokhod,*[3] and beef kabob. Tubs of *flanken*[4] cooked with parsley, dill, scallions, mint leaves, and hand-chopped meatballs were placed single file on the dining table, along with bowls of fried eggplant, beef, and chickpeas smothered in thick tomato sauce. Beefy stews simmering in sweet and sour plums, peaches, apples, and rhubarb emerged from the kitchen. And, of course, there were mountains of white rice crowned by golden saffron. Deserving of a drum roll, *Tahdig*[5] made its long-awaited appearance: thinly sliced potatoes slathered in corn oil, covered with rice and cooked until crackled to a thick crisp. Mom used her copper *kafgir*[6] to scrape each sumptuous slice of Tahdig off the bottom of her pot. In 1947, when she emigrated to the States, she made sure to bring along her kafgir, since the thought of living in America without Tahdig was unbearable.

1. *Polo Shevid* (Persian/Farsi)—Persian rice with dill
2. *Gonteveh* (Persian/Farsi)—Persian hamburgers
3. *Khoresht Nokhod* (Persian/Farsi)—Persian stew made with tomatoes, tomato sauce, beef, chickpeas, and onions
4. *flanken* (Yiddish)—short ribs
5. *Tahdig* (Persian/Farsi)—Persian rice steamed in a pot with a bottom layer of crispy fried potatoes
6. *kafgir* (Persian/Farsi)—perforated metal skimmer used for cooking

One Friday night, broad-chested rug dealers and jewelers sat around our table exchanging tales of financial coups.

"I just shipped one hundred and fifty bales of *khaneh mandehs* to Los Angeles," one dealer said proudly, using the colloquial term for old maids to describe merchandise he was stuck with and couldn't sell. "Los Angeles will never sell those rugs," he said, glistening with sweat.

"If they don't sell, won't it cost you?" another guest asked. "Won't you have to pay for their return shipment?"

"*Neh*," he replied, mopping his brow. "There are no returns. I was paid upfront. The check cleared before I shipped the bales."

The other men whistled and clapped.

Sterling silver nutcrackers passed from hand to hand as tales of mercantile success were punctuated by the sound of walnuts being cracked wide open. Mom drove the night with free-flowing cognac. Rug merchants and jewelers threw back their heads, downing drinks, reliving negotiations, purchases, sales, all to the background clatter of cutlery and clinking glasses.

Not everyone was impressed. To David, my 17-year-old brother, Iranians obsessed with stockpiling money were loathsome. After listening to the men boast, his teenage hormones and righteous anger burst through.

"Your preoccupation with money sickens me," he said. "You're hollow, fraudulent, and totally immoral."

Albert, visiting from college, joined in. Going after everything these businessmen believed in, he discredited their stance on capitalism, communism, Judaism, Catholicism, and American culture. As our guests grumbled, then raged, David jumped in to support his sib.

I sat on the edge of my seat, convinced I had gods for brothers, and felt so proud to be their sister. For me, the multicourse homemade meal was excessive: too abundant, too loud, too pungent, too room-filling, causing me to lose my appetite. Instead of eating, I fed off of Albert and David's courage.

Being the youngest of three, the only American-born, and a female no less, I conveniently remained invisible. In such Persian company, no thought, opinion, or question was expected from a girl my age. I was to sit in silence and show respect. This suited me just fine. Seated among boastful merchants, combative brothers, a mother flaunting her cooking and cleavage, I found safety in hiding. No one thought to include me, and I couldn't include myself. Even if I had been asked, "Estaire, what do you think?" my tongue would have withered in my mouth. I felt tiny, empty, with nothing to say, nothing to offer. Wordless. All that I had gained from my weekend at Cornell vanished. Al and Dave had theories, viewpoints, convictions. I didn't. I told myself, *They're speaking on my behalf. What they think is what I would think. What they say is what I would say. They have big ideas, complex concepts, and easy access to all kinds of words. They're verbal. I'm not.*

As my brothers' attacks and counterattacks became more pointed and heated, Pop's eyeballs, as if wired to springs, jutted out of their sockets. With beef kabob stuck in the pocket of his left cheek, he stomped his foot, slammed his hands on the table, and jumped from his seat.

"Enough! Change subject!"

Mom turned to her sons and widely smiled. "Albairt and Daveed vairy smart. Talk eez good!" Encouraged by her quick nod of approval, my brothers carried on. Until it was Mom's turn.

"You're a delicate rose," she said brusquely in Farsi to a newlywed at the table named Reena, "but your husband, Khosrow, is a cow." Turning to Khosrow, she embellished: "You don't worship your wife, you worship your stomach. Reena should have consulted me before marrying you. I would have stopped her." She shook her head disapprovingly. "Reena *joon*, your life is burnt!"

Mom reached for a chicken thigh and bit into it with gusto, as if nothing had happened while everyone at the table fell silent. She chastised women who weren't two-fisted and disliked those who were. I slunk down in my chair, keeping a casualty count.

Mom's culinary skills were in a class of their own: incomparable, leaving every other Persian housewife in the dust. Jewish Mashhadi men valued women who were exceptionally beautiful, wizards in the kitchen, and wholeheartedly deferential. When it came to beauty and cooking, Mom was off the charts. As to deference, she was a total and proud failure.

A few years later, a silver-framed, 11x14 photo of my mother shaking hands with the Shah of Iran assumed place of honor inside our glass cabinet. In the picture, she is wearing an elegant evening gown and smiling broadly, as if to say, *This is where I truly belong. This is my rightful station in life—in the company of the King.* The photo was taken at the Waldorf Astoria, at a reception and dinner honoring Shah Pahlavi of Iran and his wife, Empress Farah Diba, during an official visit to the United States in April 1962. My mother said the King invited almost all the Iranians living in New York City to this banquet with the intent of wooing them back to their homeland. During the gala, she dismissed his speech and instead made note of certain decorative touches on the tables, and from then on made sure our table was set the same way. Every Friday night, the centerpiece would be a large tree of celery stalks with black olives nestled in the leaves. Halved grapefruit was served with a plump red grape in the center, and dinner napkins were twirled and inserted into water glasses—all linking us to the Shah and the glory of his reign. ▨

CHAPTER 21

Protégé

With Al away at Cornell, David became my in-house counsel. Attending Columbia, he lived at home during my neediest stretch: adolescence. Feeling possessed by parents for too many years, my mission had now become self-possession.

David's bedroom was lined from floor to ceiling with books: American, British, Russian, German, French, Scandinavian, Spanish, and South American novelists, playwrights, and poets. Western European writers dominated—with no hint or trace of his Iranian heritage.

Nosing through his collection, I came across female authors who broke down barriers and gained their freedom by reading and writing. There was George Eliot, the Victorian novelist, who hid behind a male pen name to ensure her books would be taken seriously. Charlotte, Emily, and Anne Brontë, like many of their female contemporaries, first published as men, using Currer, Ellis, and Acton Bell as their names. Louisa May Alcott, best known for *Little Women*, used the androgynous pen name A.M. Barnard on her "unladylike" gothic thrillers. Circumventing gender bias, they each wore a mask in order to be seen. They each spoke through stories, through literary characters, in order to be heard. They weren't afraid. They didn't hold their tongues. I still had an uneven relationship with spoken words but had been writing in my diary faithfully for years. Now, the power and possibility of written language became an even more invigorating thought.

Tucked in his book-laden second-floor room, wedged between shelves of spines, reading and defiantly smoking cigarettes, David would call out through our shared bedroom wall, "Esther, get over here!" In soundless socks I'd rush to hear him recite T.S. Eliot, William Wordsworth, Gerard Manley Hopkins, and Dylan Thomas. Together we'd pick apart the syllables. Mark Twain's *Adventures of Huckleberry Finn* was his American Bible. Tenderly flipping through it, he'd stop at carefully penciled Huck and Jim dialogues, reading them out loud like a Talmudic scholar, savoring sentences, practically tasting them in his mouth. His love for the written word replaced both female and male friends. He turned Thoreau, O'Neill, James, Freud, Joyce, Dostoyevsky, and Mann into bedfellows. We sat together interpreting passages, lost in our reading.

But as soon as we heard Pop's footsteps on the stairs, the climate changed. Imperiled, I'd slam shut all books and look up with studied innocence.

"Go to your room! Why are you here? Quickly! Go back to your own room!"

Books were the enemy. Pop was convinced that by exposing me to published words David was turning me into a man, not a desirable woman. According to my father, the brain was a male organ, so developing mine would alter my gender, making me masculine and totally unappealing to prospective husbands.

David's vast record collection also fanned my quest for self-possession. He often knocked on my bedroom door and whispered, "You've got to hear what I just bought." Eager to hear anything Pop outlawed, I tiptoed over to listen to Lead Belly moan over women, liquor, and prison in his tobacco-cured voice while strumming on a 12-string guitar. Stacked near David's turntable were recordings by John Cage, Ravi Shankar, and Dylan Thomas reading "Do Not Go Gentle Into That Good Night."

Hand in hand, we took long walks. David pondered everything from the miraculous to the mundane. "Writers," he told me, "are the greatest psychoanalysts, delving into the mysteries of God, love, hate, birth, and death. Shakespeare anticipated Freud by three hundred years. He recognized the subconscious—the buried parts in each of us." His inquisitive mind stretched mine, taking me beyond anything I had learned in school.

Quirky queries were now saved for Dave. During one of our walks, twirling a white dandelion about to release its seeds, I scratched my head and asked, "Persian men with pencil-thin mustaches love busty, brainless women. Don't they ever want to marry fascinating women with interesting ideas—thoughts they hadn't had on their own? Isn't that a turn-on?"

"No," was his flat reply. "Not for pencil-thin mustaches. They want a different skill set." He chuckled.

My shoulders drooped. "I don't get it." I tried once more. "If a man is with a really smart woman, does it lower his testosterone?"

David didn't answer immediately. "They're all morons," he finally said. "Forget those downstairs characters. Forget Mom's dinner parties. You're different. Don't ever plan on becoming one of them."

I didn't want to, but I thought that meant something was wrong with me. I needed someone to say it was all right to be different. Dave gave me that—permission not to be them.

One day when I was 13, during a stroll through Forest Hills Gardens, David quoted George Orwell. "Saints should always be judged guilty until they are proved innocent." He asked what I thought. My cognitive functioning felt limited. I hesitated. He pushed. I came up with a long list of Hebrew-school teachers I felt were downright evil. "They act like they're real holy. They teach kindness and then embarrass us when we don't know the right answer. They're hypocrites! It also makes me think of Mom and Pop. Pop sneaking around the house, spying, listening in on my phone calls, and Mom with her meltdowns, running off, leaving us for days, and always twisting the truth. Just because they're adults doesn't mean they're trustworthy. Is that what Orwell means?"

He nodded.

Once a month David and I rode the E train to Fifth Avenue and 53rd Street, heading for the Museum of Modern Art, David's stomping ground. I was 12 when he first convinced me to come with him, promising a fun-filled afternoon topped by chocolate cake and chocolate milk in the museum's café. It didn't sound so fun-filled to me. I still spent many Sundays in my room, painting with the oils Albert had introduced me to years before, but the idea of visiting an art museum seemed boring. And it was at first. Hair in braids, wearing my favorite buckskin fringed jacket and cowboy boots, I followed David as we aimlessly wandered, checking out Chamberlain's crushed car parts, Picasso's "She-Goat," Giacometti's "Tall Figure,"and Miró's collages. I had trouble taking it in.

At the end of each visit, we would rest a while in MoMA's Sculpture Garden, sitting opposite Maillol's "The River," a massive naked woman tumbling sideways, her hair dipping into a gurgling pool.

"Why is she called a river?" David prodded one day. "Go ahead. Think with your eyes."

Letting his question spin, I stared at the sculpture while asking myself what a river—running water—had to do with a naked lady. What was the connection? Light bulbs flickered. "Everyone comes out of a woman. She's the source. Life runs through her like a river. Is that it?"

"Not bad," he said.

At first, I agreed to these interborough journeys only for the chocolate cake. Later, I passed on cake. Looking at art, answering Dave's questions, and asking some of my own became the draw.

"David, I overheard a lady on the bus say she fell in love with her husband watching him clean squid. Could I fall in love with a squid-cleaning man?"

My brother arched back, laughed so hard he hiccupped.

"Can I hate and adore in equal proportion?"

"Sure. It's called ambivalence."

"How truthful are polygraphs? Can't they be conned? What if I'm a born liar? Can they tell?"

"Good question."

Broodingly I asked, "Dave, I could never trust a man wearing an iridescent polyester sports jacket. Could you?"

He went to pieces. "You know who you are? You're Phoebe, Holden Caulfield's little sister."

I felt thrilled. There was no greater compliment. Having just read Salinger's *Catcher in the Rye*, I knew how much Holden loved Phoebe.

David became my confidante and advisor, taking me from victim to victor, boosting my energy and blunting my pain—the pain of being matched with parents I never asked for and yet felt bound to. Parents who couldn't hear or answer any of my questions.

Mom loved cholesterol, Pop loved fear, and David loved to think. He didn't bash domesticity. Quite the contrary, his Persian male genes thoroughly won out when it came to enjoying hot, homemade meals prepared by Mom. But he had a rare mix of traits: curiosity and comfort with ambiguity as he mined for meaning—latent, manifest, or anything in-between.

My brothers certainly had a hand in raising me, but I often wondered: Who raised them?

Once again, Pop caught me in David's room. Baring knuckles, he blasted with imperial force, "Estaire! Enough books! You must marry young. You have agreeable features. A woman quickly blooms and then loses all her petals. Your clock is counting down." Standing on fallen arches, Pop leaned over me and pressed his wristwatch against my ear, pushing the time angle.

David angrily interjected, "Forget clocks! Do you want to evolve or devolve? Which side are you on? Choose!"

Eidgah was nipping at my heels. I didn't want to become some Persian mail-order bride, so I continued orbiting my brother.

One Friday morning, when I was 14, Dave insisted I cut school and join him at Columbia. Remembering how much I had loved visiting Al at Cornell, I didn't need persuading. Feeling self-conscious, I sat beside him in classes taught by Lionel Trilling, Quentin Anderson, and Kenneth Koch, some of the most influential thinkers in their fields. College students madly scribbled every word uttered by these English Lit professors. Holy reverence filled each lecture hall. Never before had I witnessed such worship. At Russell Sage Junior High, teachers were boring and, with luck, forgettable.

Since David was fostering my interest in painting and sculpture, he made sure that we also audited a lecture by art historian Meyer Shapiro, one of Columbia's crown jewels. In the packed auditorium, grungy guys and gritty Barnard girls stood in silent awe, as if in God's presence. Here, in Morningside Heights, I encountered a breed who lived to think—not to eat, shop, or amass money, but to obsessively think, even turning it into a career. On our way home, David muttered, "Es, create a mind you want to live with."

The next summer, high on Shakespeare, David decided the time had come to introduce Mom and me to *Othello*. On a dank summer evening, he eagerly brought us to Central Park's Delacorte Theater to see the Free Shakespeare in the Park production. James Earl Jones, an up-and-coming star, had the title role. Taking me felt right. Taking Mom seemed insane. Given how much she struggled with English, misinterpreting and often butchering simple, straightforward phrases, I knew there was no way she would understand 16th-century Elizabethan English. But Mom was eager to come.

We sat in the crowded open-air amphitheater with Mom between us. She wore her hair in an old-fashioned feathered bouffant stiffened by hairspray and was dressed in a bronze brocade suit, Persian chandelier earrings, and gold spiked heels. Her coloring was heightened by rouge. People way behind us, in the very last row, could smell her Chanel No. 5, I was sure. One might think she was attending some gala 900-guest Persian wedding at the Plaza Hotel. But for Mom, this was much more important than a Persian wedding. David, a son she intensely adored, had invited her into his inner sanctum. She, looking proud, had dressed up for him, and wanted him to feel extraordinarily proud of her.

As a golden sunset darkened to evening with stars constellating in the sky, the actors delivered their lines. Mom periodically tugged on David's sleeve, jabbing an elbow into his ribs. *"Chi mige? Chi mige?[1]"* she asked in higher and higher registers, unabashedly as loud as Desdemona. But so what if she didn't understand a word—a mere technicality. Tonight she was living off proceeds—an educated son and his unintelligible Shakespeare.

At one point, while she concentrated on the stage, I tapped her arm. She turned.

"Don't you want *me* to understand *Othello*?" I asked her in Farsi. "Don't you want *me* to have more than you did? Education! A daughter who can stand on her own two feet, strong, self-sufficient, independent, just like your two sons?"

Mom looked at me blankly and said, "Huh?" ◈

1. *Chi mige?* (Persian/Farsi)—What is he saying?

CHAPTER 22

Kitchen Confidential

Just before I entered junior high, my parents sold their Kew Gardens house and bought a larger one in genteel Forest Hills Gardens. The previous owner had tiled the kitchen walls red and painted the wooden cabinets white. Mom had the cabinets repainted in glossy hot pink. We now had fire engine red tiles alongside blindingly pink cupboards. The kitchen was Mom—pure dissonance.

Every home has its own smell. In some, it's the smell of dogs or cats. In others, it's plants, books, or cigars. In our home it was flanken, meatballs, kohlrabi, cardamom, saffron, and rose water. As juices thickened in their pots, steamy aromas escaped from under the lids and spooled high and low, into every room. Throughout my high school years, our stove's twin doors and eight burners were birthing Nan-e Taftuns, Nan-e Berenji, and *Loze,*[1] as well as rice puddings and grainy porridges from the days of Omar Khayyam. Pounding her Persian pestle, my mother crushed saffron, chickpeas, and pistachios, while always mindful of all eight baking cakes.

Albert and David loved her cooking and ate with gusto when they were home. Pop wasn't an eater. He picked at the feasts Mom prepared and lived mostly on toast, tea, boiled chicken, and canned cling peaches. According to Mom, by rejecting her food, Pop was rejecting her. As a child, wanting to please her, I chewed in place of him, but once I reached my teens I couldn't quite separate Mom from her cakes, cookies, and thick stews. When I ate her food, I felt I was swallowing her, and since she was hard to swallow, so much

1. *Loze* (Persian/Farsi)—Persian marzipan

more than I could digest, the thought of eating became repugnant. I played with my fork, poked, separated, and squished food on my plate, hoping it would look eaten, consuming enough to dodge her attention, but that was all.

Nothing stopped her from cooking. Home was a beehive on Sunday afternoons: baking day in Mom's kitchen. Persian wives filed into our kitchen in click-clacking heels, cotton stockings rolled halfway up their calves, sleeveless house dresses revealing fleshy upper arms, all the while buzzing in Farsi. Each member of Mom's platoon tossed on a neck-to-knee yellow apron she supplied and dutifully stuffed her coiffure into a black hairnet. Every woman was swift and meticulous, taking great pride in her assigned task. Some threw their weight on top of wooden rolling pins, flattening dough tissue-thin. Others used pastry wheels to cut sheets of dough into diamond-shaped patterns and tossed the cut-outs, one by one, into sizzling oil. Using kafgirs, designated women scooped out the fried *Goosh-e Fil*,[2] while others rapidly sprinkled them with powdered sugar. Once our oven hit 400°F, walnut, plum, and cinnamon cakes and trays of Persian macaroons slid in and out.

For Mom and her kitchen brigade, it was a reliving of what they loved and missed most about Mashhad: leaving husbands behind, gathering under one roof, communally baking, and allowing tongues to wag fast and furious. These steamy afternoons were an odd mixture of juicy chunks of gossip and heartbreaking tears, as women baked, fried, talked, laughed, and cried.

At some point, in need of a study break, I'd come downstairs, perch on a corner kitchen stool, and eavesdrop. I learned fairly quickly that these wives were of one voice, one heart, with identical gripes, and, seemingly, married to the same Persian man.

"He's selfish, hot-tempered, I'm sick of him!" portly Sarah, pregnant with twins, confessed.

"Sleep, sleep, sleep," Rakhel tacked on. "When he's home from work, all he wants is to eat and sleep." She raised her mannish eyebrows and scratched her whiskered chin.

"Home cooking. He only wants to eat what I make with my own two hands," said Leah, in a tone of infinite weariness. Her fingers looked pot-scrubbing dry; her fingernails, cracked and chipped. "I'm tired of cooking. I say, 'Let's go out for dinner.' 'Sure, sure,' he

---

2. *Goosh-e Fil* (Persian/Farsi)—thin-dough pastry shaped like an elephant's ear, deep-fried, and sprinkled with powdered sugar

answers. That day never comes. Then, as if I had never complained, he asks, 'When are you making more of your *gontevehs?*' I'm his *gonteveh* machine." Twenty bakers, with flour-smudged cheeks, moaned in agreement.

"He doesn't talk to me," growled henna-haired Talia, looking tigerish. "Every night after dinner, he hides behind his paper. When it comes to me, he has nothing to say. After thirty years of marriage, I need talk. I need appreciation." Her double chin jostled like jello. "Nothing! I get nothing back."

Oven-roasted cheeks bobbed in sympathy as the sweet scent of burnt oil and fury filled the room. I smelled their pain—pain that specifically belonged to married Mashhadi women in Queens.

This *shared husband*, after bathing, left behind oily bathtub rings. He also shed like a bear while towel-drying his hairy back, leaving piles of curly fur on the bathroom floor. Propping my elbows on my knees and cradling my chin, I caught every lament, learning that these husbands mistook their wives for servants: cooks and cleaning ladies. Understanding Farsi had finally paid off. Inoculated against marriage, I told myself, *Stick with school, choose a profession, pay your own bills, and stay clear of marriage.* I'd marry myself, thank you, not piles of curly black fur.

By the time we moved to Forest Hills, it was also home to a growing community of Boukharian Jews who began arriving from Afghanistan after World War II as increasing anti-Semitism and So-viet repression drove them from their lands. Like the Aminoffs, many Boukharians were merchants and traders whose great grand-fathers plied the ancient Silk Road, traveling back and forth between Afghanistan and Mashhad. The ties between the two communities went back generations and remained strong. So on alternate Sun-days, Boukharian housewives stormed into my mother's kitchen to bake. Bawling in Boukhori, a Persian dialect, these ladies brought their own set of marital grievances, further stoking my dread of matrimony. They, too, were married to the same man.

Husbands never changed, was what I learned. What changed were the quality and size of the jewels they offered their wives to make up for their infidelities and other serious transgressions. On special occasions, these women's earlobes, necks, wrists, and all ten fingers were heavily laden with rocks the size of fists. Matrimonial bribery. Men paid their wives to look the other way, and they did, or at least pretended to. Their stories convinced me of what I had already suspected: Marriage was one of life's cruel circumstances. But what could they do? They felt cuffed and chained, totally trapped. Their luxurious homes filled with antique rugs and French tapestries weren't palaces but prisons. Unhappy, unseen, unheard by their husbands, they stood crying and complaining in our steamy kitchen: a room full of sore hearts.

During one Sunday baking session, Mom suddenly brought a woman's sob story to a full stop when, in a thunderous voice like that of Moses on Mount Sinai, she bellowed in Farsi: "Empty the swine's bank accounts! Change front and back door locks! Kick him out stark naked on his herpetic ass! You're chained to a filthy pig!" The room went silent. Mom sucked in more air. "You live in *Am-ree-kah*. Divorce the swine!"

Stunned, the women caught their breaths: She was championing anarchy—overthrowing the ruling class. But they had been raised to live with their lot, not chuck it. With eyes smudged by mascara, the women exchanged glances, and each wife seemed more alarmed by Mom's battle cry than by her own husband's offenses.

I, too, did a double take and looked at Mom with heightened clarity. She wasn't just a gurgling pot of Persian porridge but, rather, a woman way ahead of her Mashhadi and Boukhari sisters.

Beneath the hairnet, behind the apron, Mom was a militant, battle-axe feminist, urging other wives to stand up for themselves. Here in our Forest Hills kitchen, she was once again ripping off chadors and setting them on fire. *Self-govern*, was her dictate. *Take charge of your life! You're in America!*

I felt proud of Mom. It was a good and unfamiliar feeling. But I also knew enough not to wholeheartedly trust her. Right now in her kitchen, she was the activist, hailing female self-empowerment, condemning capitulation to men. Yet, on other Sundays, when she insisted I come down to the kitchen, I knew her wish that I learn to bake was directly linked to landing me a husband. While she ordered housewives to kick their spouses out, she was telling me to master the art of baking so I could get one.

Returning to my bedroom, I thought, *Mom is gutsy, but also false and two-faced.*

CHAPTER 23

Lady Liberty

Mom, the dayereh-slapper, best Persian cook, keeper of Iranian customs and ritual, had fallen hard for America the moment she stepped off the boat. She kept a Crisco-stained copy of the *Declaration of Independence* scotch-taped to the refrigerator, even though she couldn't read it, and became a full-fledged citizen when I was about eight, as soon as she knew enough spoken English to pass the oral test.

Pop was totally against her decision to become an American. He was certain it would cause problems when they returned home to Iran, which he believed was only a matter of time. But he knew no matter what he said she wouldn't listen. For Mom, America was home, and there was no going back.

Albert was away at Cornell by then, so David helped her prepare by teaching her some basic American history and civics. I watched him sit with her at the dining table, just as I had in first grade, quizzing her and helping her memorize answers to the questions she might be asked. She still couldn't read or write, but she had a phenomenal memory and was determined to do well.

As was her wont, Mom went by herself to her interview. She passed and soon after received a letter in the mail telling her when and where to show up to take the oath of citizenship. For Mom, this was huge. We didn't celebrate. But once she took her oath and received her papers, she walked with a new sense of pride and seemed to loom even larger over Pop. She always felt entitled, but now she felt invulnerable. She had rights: She was an American citizen.

My mother had also fallen hard for the Statue of Liberty. Each summer, when the weather warmed, she would take me on at least one ferry trip from Battery Park to visit The Lady and her Torch. She would gasp in awe from afar, gazing up at Lady Liberty as the ferry approached, and gasp for breath inside, as we climbed the narrow, steep, spiral, metal staircase, 162 steps from the pedestal, to peer out over New York Harbor through the Statue's windowed crown.

I often wondered if the Statue of Liberty had now replaced Queen Esther of Hamadan in my mother's pantheon, offering Mom a strong, liberated, larger-than-life, free-standing, torch-bearing heroine instead of the dead queen horizontal in her crypt.

Sometimes Mom rode the ferry by herself, and sometimes she led a pack of Iranians visiting the United States. I remember her charging out to lead one such tour group dressed in a sulfur-yellow silk blouse, string of pearls, black pencil skirt, and Ferragamo pumps. She returned looking like a public monument, with wind-blown hair framing her broad, neatly powdered face. Dabbing the corners of her mouth with a lace handkerchief, her lips and nails painted the same vivid red, she said, "Nex time, Estaire, you cum veet me. Verrie gooood treep."

Standing together at the rail during one outing, she caught me studying her as we approached the Statue, watching her face light up as it always did. She threw back her head.

"Feel it all—deeply," she said in Farsi. Mom lived life knowing it had an expiration date.

CHAPTER 24

About Face

One Saturday afternoon, offering *chai*[1] to Pop, Albert, David, and our Shabbat guests, I approached a group of men seated in the upper half of our living room, interrupting a heated discussion on the shifting price of Persian rugs. Reaching for tongs, they helped themselves to three, sometimes four lumps of sugar. Then, with a cube clamped between their front teeth, they slowly sipped their steaming hot chai before resuming their conversation.

Persian men didn't spend Shabbat afternoons discussing sports, travel, the latest Hollywood films. Nor was the "advancement of women" ever touched upon. Instead they agonized over the loose morals and lack of ethics rampant in American business and politics, the stunning disregard for aberu. Seated among them, Pop sealed his lips and frowned, taking no chances, since he believed silence was safest, words were dangerous, people talked much too much. They said more than they should, costing them their self-respect as well as their family's honor. Pop often said, "Speech is the cause of all maladies." Driving the point home, he would add, "The best way to safeguard *aberu* is by not talking at all."

I lingered and listened to the men grumble. Their Iranian obsession with *saving face* felt both gripping and repugnant, having nothing to do with my American high school life.

In a thigh-high floral miniskirt, sandals, my hair down to my waist, I went from guest to guest, balancing 20 small glasses of tea on a silver tray handcrafted in Isfahan. Pop, with his burning gaze,

---

1. *chai* (Persian/Farsi)—Persian tea

stared at my bare legs, practically searing the flesh off my thighs. His wiry eyebrows crisscrossed into an X. I was the X. X-rated. He was losing me to heathens. *"Aberu darim,[2]"* he messaged through his glare. "We have face, honor, a reputation to uphold. Go upstairs and change your clothing, right now. Cover those legs!"

"One lump or two?" I asked a seated guest, turning a blind eye to Pop, this time making *him* feel *he* wasn't present, even if he was. This time treating Pop as if *he* were invisible, even if he was right by my side. *I can do it to him now*, I thought, remembering that humiliating day when Gwendolyn had rung our doorbell and all the times he had made me feel unseen. Now, I wanted to erase Pop, obliterate him, and not care how I made him feel.

Pop, with drum-tight lips, stared at my short skirt. Erupting in a cold sweat, he reached for his chin and rapidly plucked out whiskers. I knew what he was thinking: *Esther looks like a whore. No decent, eligible Mashhadi bachelor will want her now. She'll live under my roof for the rest of my life, become an old maid, and only bring shame to our family name.* In response, I told myself: *You want the title role in a life you can call your own. Don't buckle.*

I was tired of pleasing him, of always considering his aberu. At 15, I called my younger self a wimp and wanted to throttle that compliant child who wouldn't allow herself to be real. On slow burn, I blamed me. It was my own deferential bent that rankled me most. Keeping a sharp eye out for old behaviors, I was determined not to slip back to being the timid child I once had been.

At home, aberu was the thick air I breathed. I had cheered John Glenn orbiting the earth, wept over Kennedy's assassination, and watched the Beatles on *The Ed Sullivan Show*, all to the background murmur of *"Aberu mon raft[3]"* and *"Aberu rizi.[4]"* All-pervasive and invasive aberu, with its endless dos and don'ts, was the strangling companion I had to dump.

There isn't an equivalent Anglo-Saxon word that accurately conveys aberu's weight and power. A tenet of daily Persian life. *Ab* (water) and *ru* (face) translate into purifying water streaming over one's face. To Persians, it means honor, standing, reputation, status, all rolled into one. Accumulating and maintaining aberu is centrally important. If your great-grandfather, grandfather, and father lived honest and ethical lives, lives of integrity,

2. *Aberu darim.* (Persian/Farsi)—We have honor and reputation to protect.
3. *Aberu mon raft.* (Persian/Farsi)—We have lost face.
4. *Aberu rizi.* (Persian/Farsi)—We are disgraced.

wisdom, and proper social conduct, then when you're born, you inherit their honor. Aberu, a respected face, becomes your social currency, wealth, even a credit line, unless lost through missteps. In Iran, ill-conduct didn't just damage one's own social status; it had lasting multigenerational effects, tainting the reputation and prospects of future descendants. If parents lost face, they couldn't marry off daughters or find suitable wives for their sons. Aberu, both inherited and earned, came with built-in incentives to live up to what was passed down and accumulate more for future generations.

Perhaps my grandfather lost aberu when Pop returned from London after mismanaging his father's money. Did Moshe once again lose aberu when Pop broke from tradition and married Mom, and later compounded the crime by naming his firstborn son after Prince Albert? As I grew older, I wondered more and more why Pop changed our name from Aminoff to Amini, consequently throwing off generations of acquired aberu. I'll never really know.

I do know that, at age 15, lifting the hood of aberu, I didn't like what I saw. I called it daily asphyxia. For me, saving face meant losing self, a trade-off that left too much of me behind. I had always found it hard to speak, to use my words, and now aberu was wielding its power, also corking me up. What if I let it be known that, thanks to my brothers, I had marched in an anti-Vietnam War demonstration, I had attended a Beatles concert, and I was now reading Arthur Miller? Maybe future generations would be proud. How could the Persian community know how my great-grandchildren would feel? Aberu struck me as one huge lie. Yes, it could inspire one to live an honorable life, but it also was used to bend wills and lock them in place. Drawing from Orwell, I thought, aberu "should always be judged guilty until proved innocent."

According to traditional Mashhadi male values, Mom both enhanced and tarnished our family's aberu. She was physically striking, an extraordinary cook, and she kept a spotless home—all plusses. Within our Iranian community, however, Mom was deemed *porru*,[5] *bi haya*,[6] and *bi aberu*.[7] Back-talking, uncensored, provocative, and flirtatious, Mom boasted characteristics earning her all three labels. She didn't flinch. To her, they were badges of courage, sending a tingle down her spine.

5. *porru* (Persian/Farsi)—cocky, sassy, arrogant
6. *bi haya* (Persian/Farsi)—shameless
7. *bi aberu* (Persian/Farsi)—without face

After our guests left, I stood in the kitchen with Mom, multi-tasking. My right eye made sure I rinsed lipstick-stained tea glasses while the left shadowed Pop. With balled fists he thundered at Mom, "Why do you allow Estaire to dress this way? She looked like a *jendeh*. Modest! You must buy her modest clothing. We have a reputation to uphold."

Mom didn't respond. She loved fashion and enjoyed seeing me wearing the latest teenage trends. Letting me dress as I wished was one of the ways she gave herself the American adolescence she had never had, and that was fine with me.

Pop rubbed his temples. "*Khanum, khejalat bekesh.* And why did you call my aunt *bi dast u pa?*[8]"

Clad in chartreuse, Mom walloped back in Farsi, "Because her *Khoresht Nokhod* is always too salty, her rice dry, and her cheap cut of meat undercooked. I speak the truth. I don't care about her or your *aberu.*"

Fixated on the shell of a dead fly trapped in a screened window, I kept rinsing.

With pouty lips and widening eyes, she ramped it up, honking her nose. It was tunnel-vision tribal war, each in grass skirt with spear and shield in hand, lunging. Hardwired to a fault, Mom threw caution to the wind, refusing to be shackled by shame or face.

Without uttering a word, I sided with her.

Mom told me that once, when I was little, she pressured Pop into joining fellow Iranians at Manhattan's Copacabana nightclub. "Vee never go out. I go myself. You cum or no?" His marrow-deep commitment to aberu ruled. How could he allow her to go to a nightclub without him? What would the Mashhadi community think and say behind their backs? He shoved a pair of earplugs into his coat pocket and, with a tortured expression, followed her out the door.

Carmen Miranda, the Brazilian bombshell, was the main attraction: singing, dancing, entertaining under her enormous fruit-laden hat. At one point during the evening, a tall, dark stranger stepped up to their table and asked one of the married Iranian women in the group to dance. Her husband was in the men's room, so she jumped to her feet and merrily samba'd to the hot beat of the Copa's Latin band. When the music stopped, her dance partner chaperoned her back to the table and vanished. Her husband was livid. Mom said

8. *bi dast u pa* (Persian/Farsi)—incompetent

Pop insisted that whatever aberu this couple and their ancestors had amassed over generations had been hot-footedly forfeited right then and there. All for a samba.

When a distant cousin, visiting from Israel, slipped a Parliament between her lips and puffed, hand-wringing Pop called her bi aberu.

When an elderly aunt laughed at a high pitch, Pop critiqued: bi aberu.

Whenever a woman chose to sit on the male side of the living room during Saturday afternoon gatherings and engage in conversation with men: bi aberu.

And when a young woman in our community named Shoshana broke off her three-month engagement to a young man named Ephraim: bi aberu. Her, not him.

Over time it became clear that bi aberu applied more to women than to men. The more women leaned toward equality, the more they behaved as a man's equal, the more face they lost. A gnawing thought sent me into a tailspin: observing the rules of aberu required that I limit myself and lower my rank.

Worn thin by Pop and his antiquated credos, I griped to high school friends, those I thought most broad-minded. On a patch of green in a nearby park, surrounded by our coolers and blankets, one friend listened intently as I vented, looked at me with a crinkled forehead, and said, "If your dad was mine, I'd lock myself in the bathroom with a bottle of gin." I felt deeply understood.

Obligations to ancestors and descendants were values my long-haired, bell-bottomed generation rejected. But even though I told myself the traditions of aberu and *khejalat*[9] were ancient and obsolete, they took root deep inside my nagging conscience. When I stormed out of the house in indigo denim, a la Joan Baez, I heard voices judging me as bi aberu. I couldn't go to a rock concert without looking over my shoulder, feeling indecent. I couldn't stroll through Central Park's Sheep Meadow, with its sunbathers and hippies, without feeling I was humiliating my father, sullying his aberu. Freedom and guilt melded together. Deep, deep down, I felt I *was* the delinquent daughter destroying thousands of years of accrued aberu. Under layers of reasoning, I felt I was wrong and he was right.

But Mom had no such qualms. She was beyond bi aberu—way beyond.

---

9. *khejalat* (Persian/Farsi)—shame

On another Saturday afternoon, 20 Iranian men and women were seated in our living room, sipping tea, chewing cakes, and exchanging gossip. As a 16-year-old daughter, it was my job to carry a heavily stacked fruit tray from person to person, first offering and then insisting each guest take. In keeping with the Persian custom of *taarof*,[10] guests graciously declined when in truth wanting. I had been taught the ceremonial protocol: Insist three times and don't take *no* for an answer, since a Persian *no* often means *yes*, especially when it comes to food. As I went from guest to guest and my load of pineapples, watermelon, and cantaloupes lightened, I heard Mom's booming voice.

The room grew silent as she informed our guests of what she was in great need of and wasn't getting in her bedroom: penile engorgement. Seated on the couch, she announced she was a *bad-bakht*,[11]—stuck with a boring, antisocial husband and his lifeless penis. She merrily carried on, ridiculing and impersonating the length, width, and nature of my father's limp appendage. She likened it to a dead rat. Mom's neurotransmitters had clearly spiked, gone into overdrive; the switch had been thrown. Her mouth was off and running, knowing no bounds. My brothers got up and left the room. Shocked, not knowing how to respond, some guests nervously laughed with her—and at her. The harder they laughed, the more graphic her words became. Ripping into Pop was a blood sport at which she excelled.

As I listened, the hair on my arms shot up, my skin prickled, my mouth dried. Was she downright evil or simply mad?

Seated in a champagne-colored French Provençal armchair, Pop's face turned mustard green. He stared at his trembling hands, knowing her tongue could not be tamed. She lacked filter, conscience, hitting below the belt whenever she felt the need. On this Saturday afternoon, I burned from inside out, loathing her. As she publicly humiliated my father, I felt an urge to smack her. No one stopped her, no one challenged her—perhaps fearing she'd turn on them.

After our guests left, Pop let her have it. With a foaming mouth, he called her *bi aberu, jendeh*, and verbally skewered her until she bled. Bawling, she ran upstairs and locked herself in their bedroom.

No one had parents like mine, not remotely close. None of my Iranian friends had a father who sanctified silence or a mother who

10. *taarof* (Persian/Farsi)—complex form of Persian civility
11. *bad-bakht* (Persian/Farsi)—ill-fated, unfortunate

regaled her guests by publicly castrating her husband. She impersonated him, mimicked him, and publicly satirized his comatose penis. When my father could no longer restrain himself, he erupted in earthquaking curses. She, the instigator, retaliated, slicing him with a serrated tongue. Pop never laid an angry hand on her, not even when she was at her worst, but she laid many hands on him: whacking him with her stilettos when he came after me, and beating him with frying pans, cookware, and umbrellas when they fought. But sandwiched between *jendeh, pedaer sag,* and the physical blows, I always heard *Khanum* and *Babai Albairt.* Throughout their 55 years of wartorn marriage, Pop always called Mom *Khanum,* and she called him *Babai Albairt.* They never once used each other's first name.

Visiting other Persian homes as a child, I listened closely to how spouses addressed each other. First names—Faradjullah, Mairvory, Khosroe, Sarah, and Eli—rolled off their tongues. I soon discovered it was normal, natural, and culturally appropriate for spouses to call each other by their names. Why wouldn't Mom and Pop? Did they think it was smutty or coarse? Their fights certainly were.

In the throes of adolescence, all heated up, discovering my voice, I found the courage to confront them. I felt it was time they took a good hard look at themselves and made some changes. Battling the part of me that said, *Shush, be quiet, say nothing,* I stepped forward and spoke.

"Mom, it's crazy that you call Pop *Babai Albairt,*" I said one day as we were sitting at the kitchen table sorting rice. "He's your husband, not just the father of your firstborn son. Don't you think it's weird that you never use his first name, especially when lampooning him? Call him by his Muslim name, Fatulla, or his Hebrew name, Nissan."

She listened without interrupting.

"Day in and day out, I hear 'Albert's father,'" I continued. "Didn't you give birth to three children? Pop is also David's father and my father. Which means he's *Babai Albairt, Babai Daveed* and *Babai Estaire.* What a mouthful. Try rattling all that off at once."

Mom clutched her midriff and squealed in laughter.

"Okay, Estaire... Now I call Fatulla...Fatty. You happy?" She pretended to call out, using a sing-songy voice. "F—a—t—t—y....vhair are you?" Tear-stained black mascara ran down her cheeks as she let out lusty laughs and multiple snorts. Springing out of her seat, Mom thanked me for entertaining her and walked out of the kitchen.

The next day I cornered my father sitting in the den. "Pop, cut out this *Khanum* nonsense. Your wife isn't a stranger. Just call her Hana. That's her name. People use names."

Pop stroked his chin, raised one brow and gave me a piercing look that told me I had trespassed, crossed the line. Picking up a newspaper, saying nothing, he quickly dismissed my foolishness.

No one budged.

Perhaps these impersonal labels stemmed from the fact that Pop, at 34, had robbed the cradle, marrying his 14-year-old captive against her will. Theirs was more a father-daughter relationship than husband-wife: Pop, the prohibiting, condemning father; Mom, the foul-mouthed adolescent daughter.

Perhaps *Babai Albairt* became her name for him at age 15, when, screaming in pain and fearing her own death, Mom pushed out her firstborn son—a trauma that branded Pop "Albert's father" for life.

Could calling her *Khanum* be another one of his daydreams—a wish that by repeating the label often enough he could magically transform his petulant child-wife into a refined lady?

Or perhaps calling each other *Khanum* and *Babai Albairt* was their way of maintaining a certain distance between them, serving as reminders that though they shared a room, they slept in separate beds.

Regardless of what I said, calmly or shrilly, Mom and Pop clung to their titles for each other. They didn't change, but I did. Their once mute daughter was finally using the tongue she had kept fenced behind her teeth. Instead of keeping silent, I became a silence-breaker, alive with an electricity that pulsed. 🔲

CHAPTER 25

Origins

My father once said, quite nervously, "When you see random gore, your neighbors butchered, you're forever changed and never the same." Then, in a more somber tone, he added, "Better you don't know."

But I needed to know. By age 16, I was trying to understand how living as crypto-Jews, secret Jews, had molded my parents, because I was keenly aware their trauma was snaking its way toward me.

I wanted to know more about my family history, but really I needed to know if I, as their daughter, was already doomed.

Researching my origins, I learned that my ancestors had lived in Persia for more than 2,700 years. The first Jewish diaspora arrived in 722 BCE, when the Assyrian King Shalmaneser V conquered the Northern Kingdom of Israel and sent ten of the Twelve Tribes (the Ten Lost Tribes) into captivity at Khorasan, a northeast region of Persia. Later, in 586 BCE, the Babylonians expelled Jews from Judea, forcing large numbers to once again flee to Persia. Throughout the land, Jews, Christians, and Zoroastrians were called *dhimmis*[1]: inferior subjects of the Islamic empire. From 634 to 1255 A.D. dhimmis were prohibited from bearing arms, riding horses, and testifying in court against or on behalf of a Muslim. All this ensured that Jews remained captives of a corrupt and brutal society. Denied the right to self-defense, controlled and muzzled, they were held hostage.

I feverishly wrote it all down in my journal, as precisely as I could, recording what I discovered and listing all I was up against.

1. *dhimmis* (Persian/Farsi)—inferior non-Muslim subjects of the Islamic empire

Pop wanted *me* controlled, contained, muzzled. I was his dhimmi; he was my Mashhad.

Researching further, I discovered that around 1502, when Shah Isma'il I founded the Safavid dynasty, uniting independent Iranian states into one Iranian empire, Shi'a Islam became the official state religion. Shi'a placed great emphasis on ritual purity—*tahara*.[2] Anyone who wasn't a Muslim was deemed ritually unclean—*najis*.[3] Jews, proclaimed impure, were now expected to take on dirty jobs like dyeing and cleaning excrement. All forms of the performing arts were also considered dirty. They were no longer allowed to enter public baths, and were forbidden to step outside their homes when it rained or snowed for fear their impurity might wash off them and contaminate a Muslim walking down the street.

Reading this, I felt instant skin-to-skin closeness with my ancestors, linked to a people and place I didn't even know. I couldn't help imagine: *What if there was some unexpected emergency while it was raining? What if a pregnant woman suddenly needed a midwife, or a child was deathly ill? What if someone's house went up in flames? Even dogs and cats wander in wet weather.*

To this day, whenever it rains or snows, I remember and shudder.

Under the reign of Shah Abbas I (1588-1629), Jews were forced to stitch a distinctive badge onto their clothing and headgear. This "Jew patch," declaring them "Jewish and Impure," predated the Nazi's yellow star by more than 300 years.

I came across the 19th-century historian Israel Joseph Benjamin, who wrote about a visit he paid to Persian Jews in 1850: "If a Jew enters a shop for anything, he is forbidden to inspect the goods... Should his hand incautiously touch the goods, he must take them at any price the seller chooses to ask for them." In contrast, he noted: "Sometimes the Persians intrude into the dwellings of the Jews and take possession of whatever pleases them. Should the owner make the least opposition in defense of his property, he incurs the danger of atoning for it with his life."

My body temperature dropped. "Diabolical logic," I wrote in my journal. Weren't these self-righteous pilferers touching and taking what they themselves had deemed "impure" goods? Or didn't this doctrine apply when pillaging?

I learned that these and countless other forms of persecution

2. *tahara* (Persian/Farsi)—ritual purity
3. *najis* (Persian/Farsi)—impure, unclean

were lived truths in my own family's history, and I suspected centuries of being judged unworthy and unclean had trickled down to me in some way, coloring my feelings about my growing body. My father told me that even in 20th-century Iran, when making a purchase in a store, he had to place his coins in a washbasin filled with water and let the storeowner pluck them out. This Islamic custom was practiced throughout the provinces, he said, as a ritual cleansing of all currency coming from the pockets and hands of Jews, otherwise known as infidels—even those, like my father, who masqueraded in public as Muslims.

"Pop, this is outrageous," I said. "Weren't you furious? You were demonized—treated like a deadly contagious disease." Surely, I thought, he would have lots to say now that he no longer had to fear consequences. I waited to hear the blow by blow, granular details of his life. I waited for his anger, for the booming baritone voice he so often unleashed. But my father, who viewed life through censorious prisms, only shrugged as his cheeks sunk into his face.

I thought of Mom, labeled an infidel and raised not to touch. Here in America, she did the very opposite. She not only touched but seized all that wasn't meant to be hers—Santa Claus, Oscar de la Renta, a driver's license, Idlewild Airport.... As if to say: *Don't you dare tell me who I am and what I can or cannot have.* Was this Mom's latter-day payback?

But then again, it was she who didn't like to be touched. She'd pull away, as if an outstretched hand was dirty, distasteful, in some way dishonest. Was this connected to having to place her coins in a shopkeeper's washbasin? Did it have anything to do with being called a Dirty Jew? An Infidel? It was a mystery.

Digging deeper, I came upon Charles Willis's 1886 book about living and working as a medical officer with the British Telegraph Department in Persia from 1866 to 1881. Among the things he witnessed: "At every public festival—even at the royal salaam, before the King's face—the Jews are collected, and a number of them are flung into the hauz or tank, that the King and mob may be amused by seeing them crawl out half-drowned and covered with mud. The same kindly ceremony is witnessed whenever a provincial governor holds high festival: there are fireworks and Jews."

Reading this, my bitterness grew. Since Jews were subjected throughout Persia to humiliations and never-ending persecution, I wondered how my ancestors had come to live in the holy city of Mashhad, the most religiously fanatical Islamic city in all Iran, where ninth-century Imam Reza, the eighth Imam, was buried. Of all places on earth, how did they end up smack in the center of a Holy Mecca that millions of Shi'ite Muslims from around the world visit each year, where Jews were especially despised and debased?

The answer, I learned, lay with an 18th-century Persian king's desire to protect his power and riches. Nader Shah, often referred to as the Napoleon of Persia, rose to power as the Safavid dynasty was crumbling and the Persian empire was coming apart. After repelling invaders, reuniting the empire, and having himself declared king, Nader Shah went on to invade India in 1739. A military genius, he crushed an army many times larger than his and was given the keys to the royal treasury as incentive to withdraw. Nader's troops hauled away treasures worth hundreds of millions of rupees on the backs of thousands of elephants, horses, and camels. His war trophies included the *Kooh-i-Noor*[4] (a 186-carat white diamond he is said to have named), the *Darya-ye-Noor*[5] (a 186-carat pink diamond), and the jeweled Peacock Throne.

In 1746, Nader Shah built a treasury outside Mashhad to store his plunder. Mashhadi Jewish lore and tradition hold that he then ordered leaders of the Jewish community in the city of Kazvin, northwest of Tehran, to select 40 families to move to Mashhad, and that these families, known for their integrity and social vulnerability, were instructed to guard his treasury and protect his wealth. Other accounts hold that Nader Shah moved many families to Mashhad and not all were Jewish.

In 1747 my ancestors on both my mother's and father's side were among the Jewish families selected to move from Kazvin to Mashhad. And so they began their long hard trek by foot, camel, and donkey across Iran, from west to east: men with wives, elderly parents, children all in tow. Just as these families settled inside the gates of Mashhad, Nader Shah, by then a cruel despot, was assassinated by one of his own captains. His rule was overthrown, and his empire came apart.

The *chosen* were now the *cursed*. Ill-fated, these Jews found themselves stuck in Mashhad. Unprotected by the ruler who had brought them there, they fell prey to even greater persecution.

---

4. *Kooh-i-Noor* (Persian/Farsi)—Mountain of Light
5. *Darya-ye-Noor* (Persian/Farsi)—Sea of Light

Anti-Semitism—a repeated trope—erupted into mob violence in 1839, when a Jewish woman was accused of desecrating a Muslim holy day by slaughtering a dog. The entire Jewish community was charged with making a mockery of Islam, and this blood libel led to the devastating pogrom now known as Allah Daad. Some Jews were sentenced to death by 1,000 lashes. Others were decapitated in public squares. Young women were abducted and sexually assaulted. Mobs broke into the Jewish quarter, burned the synagogue, destroyed Torah scrolls, and slaughtered an estimated 36 Jews. The rest were given an ultimatum: Convert to Islam or die. Many fled to other parts of Iran or across the Afghan border to Herat, leaving their possessions behind. An estimated 300 families agreed to convert and became Jadid al-Islam.

So began the practice of secretly observing Judaism—the practice into which my parents were born. For the next 100 years, into the mid-20th century, these crypto-Jews artfully balanced dual identities. Mom said that, each year, prior to Passover, women gathered in Yocheved's basement and surreptitiously, by candlelight, baked matzos. Men, posing as Muslim, chanted from the Koran in public squares alongside their Muslim neighbors while at home in their basements they taught their young sons Hebrew and fervently studied Torah.

There was a science to the streets. Mom would buy meat from a Muslim butcher only to hand it out to street beggars, leaving some behind in back alleys for stray dogs scavenging for scraps. Jews had their designated underground shochet who discreetly distributed kosher chickens to Jewish families.

Posing as Muslim while living as underground Jews, these Mashhadi families had a singular mission: Ensure Jewish continuity. Communal loyalty and mutual responsibility deepened. Back then, it was never each man for himself, but, rather, each man for the collective whole. The tougher life was aboveground, the more cohesive they grew underground. Staunchly against marrying outside their faith, they were also opposed to marrying outside their own Mashhadi community. To this day, Jews from Tehran, Isfahan, Shiraz, Kerman, Kashan, and other parts of Iran speak of Mashhadi Jews as a distinct community: devoutly religious, deeply ethical, and extremely insular.

After learning more of the history, I went back to my father and asked him again how he had survived this purgatory—how he had endured the barbarism, the daily cruelty. I kept asking, boiling each of my questions down to its tar, until, finally, he answered.

"Estaire, anti-Semitism, like poison ivy, is deeply rooted and swiftly spreads. We turned to the Torah. It bound us together. The more we were cursed, beaten, and hung, the more we studied Torah."

I wasn't satisfied. I was sure Pop had dodged my question. But it was all he would say.

The Mashhadi Jews were the fringes of the fringe. Persecution was never eradicated, just postponed. They were powerless, with no judicial system or police force to turn to and no one to shield them from abuse and injustice. So, of course, there were no push-backs: no sit-down strikes or demonstrations, no hired guns, and definitely no way to alter the balance of power or rearrange the religious hierarchies.

What was in the sealed minds of these full-time Jews, part-time Muslims who lived in daily fear of reprisal just for being who they were? Did they dream? If so, of what? Or didn't they dare?

And what about the women? Were there women with large ideas, unconventional wishes and aspirations? Did some want to write, or simply think out loud? Were they imploding? My mother certainly was. That much I knew.

Vivid in the minds and hearts of my parents was their historical memory. Their veins throbbed with secrecy and multiple identities. Fearful, they lived as prey waiting for the next wave of predators.

The more I researched my family's history, the more I felt its weight pressing down on me, pushing me back millennia. For women, especially, the underground Jewish ghetto in the city of Mashhad was a culture of clipped wings: forced marriages, child brides, children birthing children, illiteracy, and fear of the outside world—a legacy I wanted no part of.

Mom and Pop had immigrated to America, leaving behind the black chador, but the Iranian drive to keep women veiled still prevailed.

Now I knew for certain: Like Mom, if I wanted to escape, I would have to fight.

PART FOUR

BREAKING AWAY

CHAPTER 26

Behind Bars

My father was convinced infiltrators were trying to enter our home and destroy our family, and the horizontal mail slot in our front door was one possible gateway. As mailmen pushed personal letters and copies of *Reader's Digest*, *National Geographic*, and *TV Guide* through this opening, Pop dashed down the hallway and tried to catch them before they hit the floor. As if intercepting enemy communiqués, he scrutinized each sealed envelope, opened everyone's mail, and discarded whatever he chose, keeping unwanted words outside the home, all in the name of familial protection. I labeled him paranoid.

My 16-year-old self practiced acceptance. I couldn't get bent out of shape over everything he did. I told myself to hold back, look the other way, and fend off my utter outrage.

Mom and I spent a lot of time that particular summer at Rockaway Beach, back-floating, jumping waves, and deepening our suntans. In the evenings, curled up on my bed, I read and corresponded with friends touring Europe and my Aunt Mina, living in Japan. Corresponding meant writing in script with chunky fountain pens on personalized stationery and then walking over to the Forest Hills post office to have letters weighed, stamped, and mailed.

On a steamy Wednesday afternoon, with mail in hand, I stood on line for stamps. When I got to the window, a tall, blond, male teller with perfectly straight white teeth greeted me with a smile. He was much older than I. Maybe twice my age.

"You look lovely," he said as I slipped my batch of envelopes under the iron bars of his window. "Wow! Such a dark, rich tan. A c-r-e-a-m-y shade of caramel." *Creamy* rolled around slowly in his mouth as he weighed each letter and counted stamps. "Where have you been?" His lagoon-blue eyes dove straight into mine.

My armpits dampened. No male, young or old, had every spoken to me this way. He was looking at *me*, telling *me* he actually liked what he saw.

"I just came back from the beach," I replied, haltingly.

Bill—his nametag was pinned on his chest—found me *creamy*.

The following Wednesday I handed him a letter destined for Kobe. Bill softly asked, "Who in Japan are you corresponding with?" No one was standing behind me, so I answered.

"I have this cool aunt who lives in Kobe. My uncle exports pearls, and she studies Japanese flower arrangement. I like to think of myself as the daughter Auntie Mina never had." I tested out a giggle. "We write every week and our letters crisscross."

"How wonderful! Esther, you're remarkable! Beautiful and so bright." Bill's eyes sparkled.

How did he know my name? He must have read my return address. I blushed and rapidly paid for the stamps.

Flying home, my feet never touched the sunny sidewalk. I replayed the moment—his eyes, words, and silky voice—as the outside world hummed. *Beautiful and so bright.* Next Wednesday couldn't come fast enough.

The following week, Bill said, "You must be chased every day by dozens of men. You're irresistible. Tell me, do you have a boyfriend?"

Irresistible. Looking into my purse, I choked, "No." I didn't tell him I had never had a boyfriend. I didn't say: *I'm a worm—a bookworm. I don't always have a caramel-colored suntan. In fact, in the winter I grow pale, rather sickly looking.*

Lying on my bed, hyperventilating, I decided Bill was my *beshert.*[1] *He loves me and I love him.* Goosebumps crawled up and down my arms. Clearly, he wasn't Jewish, but that didn't matter. *He'll convert,* I reassured myself.

Writing led me to the post office, which then led to Bill. Auntie Mina and my other pen pals had no clue why they were being bombarded by mail that summer. But I needed legitimate postal reasons for visiting my clerk. I couldn't just walk over to gab; I had to show Bill I had serious business to attend to, other than him.

---

1. *beshert* (Hebrew)—preordained, life partner

Having my own secret felt womanly—sexy—and I made sure not to share it with Auntie Mina, my brothers, or any of my girlfriends. This secret was private and belonged only to me. Smiling to myself in my bedroom at night, I remembered how I had thought this summer would be a total washout. Pop, as always, just wanted to be left alone. Albert and David had their own lives. That left me with Mom. Each day, I was sure, would be just like the last: lying flat on the beach with Mom by my side. Didn't people say, *Do what you love and you'll meet your beshert*? Some people went bowling, others went skiing—and then there were those of us who corresponded internationally and had to buy stamps.

Forbidden to date, I had brilliantly found my way around Pop. Wednesdays at four o'clock became my designated once-a-week, highly romantic rendezvous time. Hours before, I showered, washed, and blow-dried my long, thick hair. Finding the perfect blouse took thought and effort. Flipping tops over my shoulder, I emptied drawers, looking for a subtle blouse that highlighted my tan. Behind bars he couldn't see my bottom half, so that half didn't matter. I focused on waist up, only what was visible to Bill.

When I stepped up to his window he was all mine. He flirted. I blushed. He told me he missed me. I blushed. I liked having him behind bars, caged, contained, and waiting. This way I didn't have to deal with all that happens when men are free to roam. I didn't know how to handle an uncaged man. Bill couldn't touch, grab, or kiss. He couldn't stand me up or walk out. And he was so easy to find. I did the comings and goings while he stood still. Always behind bars.

I had found true love, totally on my own, without any interference from my Persian matchmaking father. Bill wasn't real like volcanic Pop, or self-centered, mood-swinging Mom; instead he was adorably unreal, just like the black-and-white Cary Grant poster hanging over my bed. I could stare at his perfect features and turn the rest of him into whatever I needed at the time. When frightened, I imagined him brave; when enraged, he comforted me; and when I needed time alone, he simply evaporated, always there to serve and please.

Wanting my marriage to be nothing like Mom's, I chose Bill and skipped over unnecessary details such as his full name, his age, his family history, his likes and dislikes. Didn't he radiate *najabat*?[2] What more did I need to know? Pop believed the less a woman said, the more a man would fall for her. Only in our case, the less Bill and

2. *najabat* (Persian/Farsi)—kindness, gentleness, generosity, nobility

I both said, the more deeply we fell in love. I just knew we were cut from the same cloth and we didn't need words.

Since Bill was the ideal husband, I, for the first time, fantasized marriage. He smiled, was good-humored, and made no demands. Bill even told me everything I said and did delighted him—I was "simply perfect."

Then, one Wednesday, as my fingers slid envelopes under the bars, Bill placed his hand heavily on mine. "When can we get together?" he asked.

Get together? I thought that's what we were doing.

His 30-year-old, square, warm palm massively sat on top of my teen fingers, triggering waves of fear. This caged pet of mine had crossed the line and had broken an unspoken rule. He was to keep his paws contained, on his side of the bars, and never touch.

"Oh, Bill, you're such a flirt," I said, pulling my hand out from under.

That night, sprawled on my bed, I harmonized with Paul Anka's "Puppy Love" cooing from my record player. Moonstruck, I stared at the ceiling, dreaming of Bill.

Suddenly, Pop barged into my room and yanked me by my arm into the den.

"Estaire! I forbid you to ever go to the post office again!"

I went numb. What the hell was he talking about? How did he know what I was doing on Wednesdays at four? He never came home before five.

"I told that man Bill I will kill him with my bare hands if he ever contacts, sees, or speaks to you again."

I stopped breathing. Bill? How did Gestapo Pop know his name? Did he pretend to go to work but really spend his days shadowing me?

With clenched teeth, Pop continued. "Bill is evil. He *belongs* behind bars."

What was he saying? Who was evil? Pop was the one who belonged behind bars—in a dungeon, gagged and bound.

Against my will, tears poured down my face. "What are you talking about?" I hollered. "Are you stark raving mad?"

He stamped his foot. "Estaire! Bill is a bad man. He wrote you a letter and I opened it."

"Give it to me right now!" I cried. "I want to read what he wrote!"

"I burned it!"

"What? You burned it? It was addressed to me! It was *my* letter! You had no right to burn what's mine!" I was now way past tears and wanted to wield an ax. "Don't I have rights?" I yelled. "Rights to privacy? Is nothing mine? I hate you!"

"No. You're my daughter. My responsibility is to protect. Your job is to obey. I am your father and you still live under my roof. Bill said things that should not be said to a sixteen-year-old girl."

With nerves snapping and firing, I could have knifed him right then and there.

Pop stared me down. "I went to the post office and found this Bill. '*Pedaer sag!*' I yelled into his face. 'I am Fatulla Amini, Estaire's father. If you write, call, or talk to her, I'll kill you with my bare hands.'" Pop's fingers grew large as he reached in mid-air for Bill's throat.

"I forbid you to ever see him again."

Pop stood before me stiffly erect, loyal to centuries of his Persian-Jewish ancestors. No daughter of his would date. No daughter of his would be abducted. Not through our front door mail slot and not through postal bars.

I ran out of the den and up to my bedroom, slammed doors, cursed out loud, and buried my head under pillows. Once again I was humiliated by this madman I called my father. I ached, thinking of Bill. *What did Pop accuse him of? Oh, God....* I shook at the thought.

Now, instead of Mom, it was I who wasn't speaking to my father. I avoided him, making sure we weren't in the same room at the same time. I ate dinner early, way before he came home, and then locked myself in my bedroom for the rest of the evening.

The following Wednesday I slunk over to the post office, stood on a long line that led to Bill's window, and hid behind the woman in front of me to make sure he didn't see me. When it was my turn to step up to his cage, his face paled.

Trembling, I forced words out. "Bill, I came to apologize for my father's outrageous behavior."

As I looked into Bill's eyes, I couldn't find *him*. Instead, I saw blue ice.

"Don't come back."

My cheeks reddened. "Bill, I never read your letter. My father screens our mail and got to it before I did. What did you write?"

He squirmed, lowering his voice. "I asked you out. A day in the woods. I just asked if you want to spend..." he stammered, "...a day in the woods with me."

He stopped short, gritting his teeth. "Go home. Stay away from me. Don't come back." He then called out to the woman standing behind me. "Next person, step up."

A day in the woods? Did he really mean a day in the park? Was he asking me to join him for a picnic lunch, with straw basket, French bread, cheese, and wine, sitting on a red checkered blanket next to other young, smiling couples? Of course, Central Park. That's what he meant.

CHAPTER 27

Booklegger

Feeling defiled, disgraced, I was sure my wounds would never heal and I'd never be able to forgive my father. I couldn't see that Pop had probably rescued me.

Rescue was what he was best at: a realization that took many years to form. The evidence mounted bit by bit, with painful slowness.

Pop's love hovered from afar, preferring distance to close range. However, the childhood illnesses that always sent my mother running drew my father closer. Some of my most treasured memories are of being securely held in the crook of his arm when I vomited. As my knees buckled, he'd swoop my tiny body off the bathroom floor, wrap his right arm around my waist and place his left palm on my clammy forehead.

"Estaire, let your weight fall on me. I am here. Don't be afraid. Close your eyes. Let it all come out. I will be your legs." His short, crisp directives were just what my near-lifeless self needed.

As I let myself go limp, somehow I shrank and all five feet of Pop grew. Salty tears stung my eyes and convulsive retching scooped out my stomach. While I was mortified that I was making a mess in the bathroom, Pop's grip only tightened. In his arms, I would bawl as I purged, feeling shame and fear. In Farsi Pop would whisper, "Estaire, don't be ashamed. You're not bad. Everyone gets sick. You will recover." How did this nonverbal, Stone-Age father of mine know I felt I was bad and incurable? Somehow he did, and with sweet calm, he'd nurse me back to health.

When faced with my stomach-clutching cramps, broken bones, gushing blood, my father was steady and competent. Nursing me through mumps, measles, chicken pox, gall stones, tonsillitis, appendicitis, and thermometer-shattering fevers, Pop was unruffled. Beneath his belching warrior cries and saber-rattling paranoia lived an inexhaustible source of reassurance...whenever I was ill. What threw him off balance, what terrified him most, were my strong, bold, healthy days.

One evening, as he was intently watching a PBS *Wild Kingdom* episode on the jungles of Africa, I asked if he had ever dreamt of becoming a doctor. Pop softly looked at my curious 16-year-old face. I sensed he had never been asked such a question. With gratitude he reached for my hand, as if to say, *You truly care. You want to know me.*

In a hushed tone he answered, "I love Africa."

I wanted to slip right in and tour his mind. "Do you wish you lived there?"

He bit his thumb. "If I could have done anything I wanted, I would have worked with Albert Schweitzer in the deepest jungles of Africa."

"Who's Albert Schweitzer?"

Pop took off his black-framed glasses and through a liquid gaze replied, "Estaire, he was a great, great man. Albert Schweitzer was a doctor. He went into African jungles and cured sick natives with Western medicine. He used his education to save lives."

Suddenly, with a sharp jerk of the head, Pop clammed up. Inserting his index fingers into his ears he shouted, "Enough!" A steely expression clamped down. He had told me more than he had intended.

My father slipped his glasses back on, turned away, and focused on the fleeting cheetahs, lumbering water buffaloes, rhinoceroses, and orangutans swinging across our screen. I was accustomed to his abrupt starts and stops, his split-second retreats. Much of my childhood was spent chasing disjointed fragments of information, piecing them together, trying to know a father who didn't want to be known.

Later, consulting the *Encyclopedia Britannica*, I found Albert Schweitzer and learned that, armed with a doctorate in theology and a medical degree, he had built a small hospital on a riverbank in Gabon, where he and his wife devoted themselves to providing medical care to the local tribes, treating heart disease, tropical dysentery, malaria, leprosy, strangulated hernias, and jungle fever. Next to the lengthy text was a black-and-white snapshot of Schweitzer. Oddly enough, he strongly resembled my father. They could have been fraternal twins, sharing an ample forehead, prominent nose, square jaw, and silver-white hair.

It seemed to me Pop was a closeted Iranian Schweitzer and my various maladies were his diseases in the African jungle. From then on, whenever Pop sat next to me as I was roasting with fever, I imagined him clad in khaki shorts, short-sleeve shirt, a wide-brimmed Safari helmet, swinging a machete through thickets with the sole wish to heal. My wide array of ailments unlocked Pop's Schweitzer-esque side, and so I welcomed loss of health, knowing illness brought him closer to me.

Pop's natural instinct to rescue and heal extended to wildlife. When squirrels found their way into our basement, Pop rolled up his sleeves and slipped on gardening gloves. Equipped with nets, shovels, burlap bags, he methodically trapped and caught trembling invaders and freed them unharmed. When fledglings fell down our chimney and were caught in the chute, peeping, he reached up through the fireplace, cupped these panicked birds in his hands, and carefully released them in our backyard.

Broken-winged pigeons, lost and hungry kittens spoke to his noblest impulse and, like me, were tenderly nursed back to health. But there were limits to his empathy for other creatures. He would march up to our attic and enthusiastically set mousetraps, bat traps, courageously safeguarding our home. With Iranian virility, he'd slap misguided mosquitoes on our bedroom walls. If not for family, I sometimes thought, he would have made a good snake charmer, a lion tamer, or a male Jane Goodall, studying chimpanzees in Tanzania. I imagined him cradling Flo, Goodall's bulbous-nosed female chimp, rocking her in his arms, singing Persian lullabies.

One Saturday afternoon that same year, I entered my parents' bedroom, looking for my mother, and found Pop in his favorite position: in bed, blanketed, sipping tea, munching matzos, studying a tattered book.

"Pop, what are you reading?"

He remained silent. But I knew. My father was most content left to himself, hermetically sealed in his Art Deco sleigh bed, dressed in gray flannel pajamas, lying under virgin wool blankets, reading his frayed *Chumash*[1] translated in Farsi, with a steamy glass of Swee-Touch-Nee tea and a plate of matzos by his side. This combination of bed, tea, matzos, and Torah satisfied all his wants. Pop had no

---

1. *Chumash* (Hebrew)—Torah, Old Testament

need for companionship, vacation, or vocation. Horizontal in bed, he found refuge, enjoying quiet in his own underground.

"I'm reading the Chumash," he finally answered. "God teaches us to never reach into a nest and take freshly laid eggs in the presence of a mother bird. Shoo her away, spare her the pain, and then take what you must." Pop's voice cracked as his eyes filmed with tears. "God tells us to be sensitive even to the mother bird, and if you are such a caring person, then your days on earth will be lengthened."

He shook his head in awe. "The Torah commands us not to give grief even to a mother bird. How much more careful must we be when it comes to our fellow man?"

My father spent his life reading and rereading the Torah, but he never quoted Abraham, Isaac, Jacob, or Moses. Instead he cited Deuteronomy 22:6, a passage that spoke to him like no other—centering on birds.

Pop's interpretation of this particular verse revealed his soft spot. I treasured these scraps of insight because he and I didn't have heart-to-hearts, and we never discussed longings, anxieties, and hurt. I suspect his enormous terror and distrust of people stood in the way. Glaring, he'd stare down my girlfriends, letting them know they were not welcome in our home. When the phone rang, he'd pick up the receiver, shout, "She's not here!" and slam it right back into its cradle. For Pop, this was not "giving grief to his fellow man." Instead, he was being an exemplary father, protecting his young. At the time, I didn't know who the hell he was protecting me from since all my girlfriends were wholesome and all of my phone calls were homework-related. Only later did it occur to me that maybe he was protecting *himself* from what was too much: the outside world.

I minimized Pop's coarser paranoid impulses by conjuring up Albert Schweitzer—my father's alter ego—and the Pop that longed to walk the open plains of Africa, befriending a stately giraffe or perhaps wondrously stumbling upon an aardvark crossing the road.

I respected his hidden longings because I, too, had mine.

Way back in first grade, I had started forging Pop's signature on every report card—not because I did poorly in school but because I did well. As I traveled up the grades, through elementary school and junior high, Fatulla's signature markedly improved. It wasn't until I reached high school that my father demanded to see my grades. My stomach cramped as he slowly read out loud each subject with its shimmering A. Pop's veined eyes bulged as he cursed the day he stepped foot in America. It was as if he had discovered I was a drug addict, mainlining heroin, and all of my As were discarded needles. His face reddening, pulling at his thick white hair, he swore that his one and only daughter would never reach her desired destination: America's brothel—college.

"In Iran we suffered anti-Semitism," he admonished. "We escaped and immigrated to America, to live freely and openly as Jews—not as Americans. Not to end up cursed with a daughter who wants school."

I decided he was certifiably insane. If this was his way of looking after me, then his urge to protect and rescue be damned. I couldn't turn to Mom. She was completely indifferent when it came to my schooling. My brothers had encouraged me, sharing their passions and introducing me to museums and lecture halls. But they had their own lives now. Albert was out of the house, working as an architect. David still lived at home and taught English literature at a local college. I couldn't ask them to take on this fight. Outraged, feeling totally wronged, I knew this was an injustice I'd have to battle on my own.

Pop despised bookcases jam-packed with volumes of words, thoughts, and opinions that hadn't first passed his inspection. Certain they were subversive, he believed they were designed to undermine the law and order he had firmly established in our home.

Every night after house patrol, Pop would march into my bedroom and find me reading in bed. He'd grab the text out of my hands, bellow, "Enough books!" and flick off my lights before slamming the door. Pop thought by turning off all lights he was turning me off. He didn't know I was a booklegger, hiding stacks of contraband under my pillows. After he darkened the room and shut the door, I'd reach for my flashlight, another book, and dive under the sheets—feeling both stymied and challenged. Beneath layers of bedding, my breathing labored, I'd squint until my eyes adjusted to the circle of light, and read under the covers, soundlessly turning pages. Every so often, I'd surface for a deep inhale of fresh air and then slide back beneath the sheets.

The more I read the voice of others, the more I had an urge to use mine.

For generations my ancestors hid who they were to survive. Now I found myself doing the same. Burrowing under sheets, I hid not from the Muslims of Mashhad but from my own parents. I also lived a double life. There was the aboveground revealed daughter they saw, and the concealed one who hungered for what they condemned.

In the 1960s, as high school girls teased their hair into beehives and applied hair-spray hourly for reinforcement, I wore my hair long and natural, and concentrated on raking in As. Stellar grades were my lifeline to the outside world. Yet, while I busted my chops over algebra and physics, my father was praying I'd become a high school dropout. The more I read, the more he felt kicked in the face.

Rapping his knuckles on our dinner table, Pop barked, "America is not good. It's a wild country. There is too much liberty here. Just look at the nasty, loose girls walking the streets. They all take drugs, wear short skirts, wanting you to look up and see everything when they cross their legs. American girls are *jendehs*—a syphilis-soaked race! It is my responsibility as your father to protect you from Americans and not allow you to become one."

Nonsense, I told myself. *I wear miniskirts. That doesn't make me a jendeh. Or is he saying I am one?*

"As a result of education," he continued, "American women squeeze themselves into subway cars, carry attaché cases, smoke cigarettes, and sleep around, as if they too are men."

Memories of my childhood friend Cathy Storch and her anthropologist mother came barreling through, spurring me on. I imagined Cathy now shooting for top-tier schools, not allowing anyone to get in her way, and took my cues from her.

Chasing what I wanted, I secretly sent out college applications. In 1967, the elite Ivy League schools only accepted male students, so I couldn't apply to Harvard, Columbia, Yale, or Princeton. Instead, I applied to Radcliffe (Harvard's sister school), Barnard (Columbia's sister school), Brandeis, and Hunter College. Radcliffe was my first choice, but even if I was accepted, I would need my father to sign forms, and I was certain he never would. I could forge his name, but I couldn't pay for four years of college. What was I thinking? I wasn't. I blocked out those thoughts.

My most immediate concern was college interviews. How to get myself to them? Once again, David became my accomplice, my Kee-mo-sah-bee, as we relived our Lone Ranger and Tonto days, this time switching roles. He offered to smuggle me out of Forest Hills behind our parents' backs and drive me to Massachusetts for my Radcliffe and Brandeis interviews, which I had scheduled for the same Friday—one in the morning, one in the afternoon. It meant we would have to slip away at 4:30 a.m., accomplish our mission, and return home before dark.

The night before our great escape, I laid out a navy blue plaid skirt with a white starched shirt. My black penny loafers were slickly polished and lined up, ready for our run. College forms, maps, driving directions, two cream cheese sandwiches, and two cans of apple juice were snugly packed in a tote bag. My bathroom shared a wall with my parents' bedroom, so for weeks I had been practicing washing my face and brushing my teeth noiselessly. David and I agreed that we would not use our toilets on our runaway morning because the flushing would wake up Pop.

After setting the alarm clock for 4:00 a.m., I tucked it under my pillow so only I would feel and hear its vibrating ring. Since Pop lived in perpetual fear that someone would break into our home, he slept with ears cocked and one eye open. This did not work in my favor. I was certain that if he heard the floor creak, he'd jump out of bed and charge down the staircase.

At 4:00 a.m. the next morning, the alarm clock, gagged and vibrating, woke me. David and I had agreed to meet at 4:30 by the kitchen door. I washed my face and brushed my teeth in well-practiced silence, dressed, then tiptoed down the long mahogany staircase—penny loafers in one hand, tote bag in the other—and made it to the kitchen without waking Pop. My brother placed a polite, handwritten note on the breakfast table telling our parents we were taking a car trip, not to worry, and to expect us home in time for dinner. *David is brilliant*, I told myself. Assuring my parents that we'd see them at dinner made us sound conscientious, obedient, respectful, and would prevent them from thinking we were juvenile delinquents, stealing the family car and running off.

Having mastered the art of soundlessly opening and closing the kitchen door, my brother skillfully unlocked it and gently shut it behind us. I now knew that if I ever decided to rob a bank, David was my man.

We entered the garage through a side door, and my brother slipped into the driver's seat of our family's red Valiant. The plan was that David would switch on the engine and put the car in reverse while I raised the garage door. There would be no time to yank it back down. Our only possible glitch was the sound of rusty chains as I did the heavy lifting. If we were well-coordinated and swift, we could make our escape before Pop reached the driveway.

David turned the ignition key. The engine groaned. We had only seconds to disappear. I quickly raised the door. It let out a piercing screech. I jumped into the front seat. David hit the gas and was speeding out backward when suddenly Pop's face flashed in front of the windshield. Barefoot, in gray flannel pajamas, his thick white hair spiked upwards, he tried, with flailing arms, to wave us down and block our escape.

We sped off with the nerve-racking energy of a jailbreak. ◈

CHAPTER 28

Risky Move

My father began his hunger strike. He stopped working, stopped eating, and no longer shaved. Each day I came home from Barnard College to find him in the same flat, horizontal position in bed, growing thinner, weaker, with no desire for food, speech, or life. An unkempt white beard had spread over his face. I wrestled with strangling guilt. *Am I killing my father?*

"Outbluff his bluff," my friend Christine Buckley advised. "Just move out. He's manipulating you."

"You don't know him, Chris. You don't understand the Persian Mashhadi culture he comes from. Iran is not Iowa. A Mashhadi daughter only leaves her father's home to enter her husband's. She doesn't move into a college dorm. He's killing himself all because of me. The fact that I made it this far—that I'm a student at Barnard—is a miracle. I can't push it any further."

"Change rarely comes without a fight. Give it all you've got. I promise, he won't die. You have to outwit him."

"And, Chris, if he does die, what then?"

With unshakeable certainty she repeated, "He won't kill himself," and planted a kiss on my cheek.

I wasn't so sure.

Christine was my cool and detached college confidante. She had a keen analytic mind and was always deciphering the indecipherable, but she had never met Pop. After living with my father for two whole decades, I couldn't predict his next confounding move. How could she? She was a blonde, blue-eyed, 20-year-old Wasp from

Greenwich, Connecticut, the daughter of a charismatic, sailboat-racing, martini-drinking dad who was refined and rational. Hers talked. Mine didn't. Hers didn't go on suicidal hunger strikes. Mine did. How could she think she knew my Iranian father better than I?

This had all started in 1967 when Barnard sent me an acceptance letter. Drunk with joy, I clutched it to my heart, dreaming of the coveted Morningside Heights lecture halls. Not only was I the first female in my family to go to elementary, junior high, and high school; now I'd be the first woman to pioneer my way through college.

But once Pop got a whiff of my euphoria and learned the reason for it, he hollered, "Rip that letter up! I will never pay for college. You will not go!"

Blood drained from my face. I stood before him, chalk-white, terrified.

David, now 25 and working, leapt between us and threatened to take out bank loans. If Pop refused to pay, my brother said, *he* would.

With that one swift blow, David dethroned our father, knocking the jeweled crown off his regal head, securely placing it on his own. Pop heard the subtext: *Now, I will be her father.* A mounting coup.

My father's face shattered. We had twisted a dagger into his heart. He had always believed that America was a melting pot of thieves, hoodlums, gangsters, rude children. Weren't we the living examples?

He was right: America did encourage children to reject their parents' teachings and replace them with *college.*

Outmuscled and humiliated, Pop knew he could no longer protect me from the evils of education, from the Ivy League brothels of America. Shamefaced, clutching his head, my father fell silent.

"Pop," I sputtered, "you have nothing to worry about. I'll be going to Columbia University, in Manhattan, where David went. I'll live at home like David did and commute each day to school. I'll be home every night, every weekend, and still sleep under your roof. You'll know where I am each day and see me each evening—it'll feel like I never left high school. Pop, I promise. You have nothing to be afraid of. And if you give me this, I'll never ask you for anything ever again."

With head bent, hands jammed in his pockets, he brushed past me into his bedroom, dragging his feet. Days later, fearful of losing his patriarchal power in the family, he agreed to pay my tuition bill. But it was David's threat that made him do it.

I entered Barnard in September 1967, on the eve of explosive student protests and demonstrations on the Columbia-Barnard campus. Sit-ins and teach-ins. Rallies against the Vietnam War, military recruiters on campus, the University's involvement in Defense Department research. Opposition to the construction of a new gymnasium in Morningside Park that would allow only limited access to residents of the black and Hispanic community—a project protestors dubbed "Gym Crow."

In the spring of 1968, less than three weeks after the assassination of the Rev. Dr. Martin Luther King, student rallies swelled into a weeklong occupation of five campus buildings, including Columbia University President Grayson Kirk's offices in Low Library and acting dean Henry S. Coleman's office in Hamilton Hall, where he was detained for 24 hours. After a week of student sit-ins and campus demonstrations, President Kirk called in the police to empty the buildings and clear the campus. Violence ensued, and students organized a strike in response. Members of Students for a Democratic Society (SDS) and other groups reoccupied buildings a few week later. President Kirk once again called in the police, who unleashed even more violence, and the student strike lasted the rest of the semester.

Many participated. I didn't. Mob mentality scared me, and I knew why. It allowed for only one right answer. I stood to one side, watching, learning about the issues but saying nothing, drawing from Pop's teachings: *Silence is safest.* My mind leapt back to stories Mom told of vicious mobs attacking Jews in Mashhad and rabble-rousing crowds throwing hand grenades in Bombay. Even though student rallies were peaceful, I kept my distance, expecting bloodshed. It was as if I were living in Eidgah, seized with a deep need to hide behind thick black cloth. The urge to be veiled felt hereditary—a search for safety. That's where campus unrest took me—to a Mashhad I hadn't known but felt I had lived.

As demonstrations, sit-ins, protests, and rallies swirled around me, I kept my word to Pop, studying in college libraries late into the night and returning home to sleep. For the entire school year, I commuted from Forest Hills to Broadway and 116th Street, just as I had promised. Sabbaths and weekends were diligently spent with my parents, as pledged.

Things had quieted down on campus by the start of my sophomore year. President Kirk stepped down during the summer, and the

University took steps to sever its ties with the Defense Department. Increased student and faculty input had brought gym construction to a halt, and the administration made other important concessions to student demands. I started to feel more relaxed strolling the campus, more able to breathe and enjoy my studies. But by the end of the first semester of my sophomore year, I had grown weary of subways and begun pining for the full college experience—dorm life.

Mustering courage, one morning I slunk into Barnard's Housing Office and explored options. I was told there would be half of a double room available in a three-bedroom dorm unit the following semester and that a student by the name of Carmen Grazzia occupied the other half. Sight unseen, I said, "I'll take the room and roommate."

Riding home on the F train, I rehearsed my monologue. Once I stepped foot into our kitchen, the words shot out:

"Mom and Pop, I must tell you. This long subway commute back and forth to college is wearing me down. For one and a half years I've been attending classes, studying in the Columbia libraries, and at the end of each day returning to Forest Hills, way past midnight. This is too difficult. To make my life less stressful, I registered for a room in a single sex, *all female* Barnard dormitory."

Pop jumped out of his chair, charged up the staircase, ripped off his three-piece suit, threw on pajamas, and collapsed horizontal in bed. He had officially begun his hunger strike. His face a graveyard.

As the last days of the first semester of my sophomore year creaked by, Mom told me daily I was murdering my father. She made it very clear that I would be the cause of his upcoming heart attack and imminent death. Day after day he lay in bed, not going to the office, refusing to see or speak to me, rejecting food, occasionally sipping water, hoping his body would eat itself away in despair. My wish to experience dorm life felt lame. Was I trading my father for a dorm bed? How infantile, selfish, shortsighted of me. What if he suddenly died? Could I continue to live my life knowing I had killed him?

For Pop, sleeping in a Barnard Residence Hall meant rejecting his protection, his values, his moral codes, and he was convinced that college girls spent all their after-school hours engaged in sex— often for money. They were loose, wild, amoral women who would corrupt me. According to my father, I was leaving home to become a slut and would end up selling sex on street corners.

These twisted thoughts, products of his grotesque imagination, were insulting. I, straight-laced, intensely studious, never having had a boyfriend, was intent on remaining a virgin. I had never had a sexual affair, much less engaged in prostitution. Why didn't he have faith in me? Why was he so certain that if I slept in a bed outside of his home, that bed would overflow with naked men?

There were days when I wanted to murder him. But as my fury deepened, so did my guilt. And as my guilt deepened, so did my resolve. I didn't know if Pop would relent and pay my dorm fees, but I knew if I succumbed to the fear that this innocent wish to live on campus was going to cost him his life, I would never be able to live mine.

On a Sunday evening, the tenth night of my father's hunger strike, I clung to Christine's words and asked David to drive me with my belongings to Barnard. We packed my books and clothing into the trunk of the Valiant. Mom, ordinarily very loud, became silent. To her credit, she didn't protest. Instead, she announced that she was coming along to check out this place I had chosen far from home.

Chris's words echoed in my ears: *He won't kill himself. He won't kill himself.*

I climbed into the car next to David. Mom, tight-lipped, sat behind me. We backed out of the garage and were starting up the street when, suddenly, as if escaping from a sweaty nightmare, Pop appeared, his face stricken and unshaven, disheveled in his flapping flannel pajamas and slippers, running after us. David stopped the car. Pushing Mom to one side, my father squeezed in next to her. He had come to witness the loss and ruin of Estaire, his only daughter.

The four of us rode in silence all the way from Forest Hills, Queens, to Broadway and 116th Street. With windows sealed, Pop's stale breath filled the car with the sour smell of bile. Crossing the Queensboro Bridge, my head pounded and my hands grew sweaty. As we arrived in front of the building, a parking spot unexpectedly opened up—nothing short of an urban miracle. *This is an omen*, I reassured myself. *This parking spot is God's work. He's watching over me. He's in my corner. God wants me to move in—and He will make sure Pop survives.*

At the front desk, in the lobby and hallways, girls stopped and gaped as my father passed. They had never before seen such a grizzly, Neolithic caveman father. Waves of guilt, hate, shame churned inside me as Pop followed me up to my third-floor suite. We moved along in single file, passing students with hanging jaws. I rushed forward, hiding my burning face behind a coat sleeve. My father stomped down the hall in slippered feet, gray flannel pajamas, with the popped, predatory eyes of an alligator. His long white hair was thickly tangled. Ready for warfare. Fatulla Nissan Amini had come to see for himself the depraved life his American daughter had defiantly chosen.

We entered the common area of my suite and, as quickly as I could, I found my room. The door was locked. While turning the key I told myself, *If he has to be here, humiliating me, at least he'll see this dorm room is just like my bedroom at home. It'll have a desk and chair so I can study. He'll return home feeling ashamed, knowing he made a fool of himself.*

Pop, straight from hinterland Mashhad, craned his neck as I slowly opened the door. Mom and David were directly behind him, carrying suitcases and cartons of books.

We walked into a large dark room. I switched on the light. To the right was my bed and desk. To the left lay a young woman I assumed to be my roommate, Carmen Grazzia, naked in bed.

Sexually intertwined with a man.

CHAPTER 29

Change Subject!

Punched in the gut, Pop bolted out of the suite, mouth foaming, cursing in Farsi. With bones crushed and spirit spent, he left, destroyed. Mom and David dropped all they were carrying and ran after him. I quickly left the bedroom, shut the door behind me, and sank into a hallway chair.

As far as my father was concerned, he had been proven right: Education and spread legs were a package deal. Having just seen naked Carmen, his hyperactive imagination had *me* in bed—feet, arms, torso entangled with Columbia men of all ages, races, and religions. I had joined a smutty demimonde, enrolled as a live-in whore, and Barnard was the facilitating pimp. Pop was certain college professors, standing erect, gripping podiums, were instructing virgins to give it all away. Libraries were stuffed with books that preached: "Defy your father. Kill him slowly, torturously, drawing out pain, disgrace, and humiliation." And with a college degree tucked under my belt, he knew I'd in no time graduate from hooker to brothel-keeper.

A sheet of boiling water sank into my stomach as I imagined Pop's heavy Iranian hand coming down, obliterating me. Would he sit shiva, mourn my death, erase me from memory, tell himself he had never had a daughter? As a youngster, I had been afraid of Mom's Medusa-like strength and didn't want to be near her. But on this day, at this mind-scrambling moment, I summoned her strength, drew from her ore, extracted her obstinance, accessed her inner outlaw, making myself more similar than dissimilar. Unadulterated *will* traveled from Mom to me as I plugged into our point of connection: disobedience.

I had sought after college, fought for college, worked too hard to get here—and I was hell-bent on staying.

After Carmen's paramour fled, wrapped in a robe, she threw open the door, pulled me into our bedroom, and tightly hugged me.

"Esther! I had no idea you were moving in tonight! I was sure you were coming tomorrow! If I had known, I would *never* have let Jason stay over. *Oh, shit!* And for your parents to see me this way. What must they think? I'm so embarrassed." She started crying. "Can you ever forgive me?"

Since she was the one sobbing, I sat beside her on her bed and tried to comfort her.

"There's nothing to forgive, Carmen. You didn't know I was coming."

Sitting cross-legged, she listened attentively as I told her about my family: beginning with my parents' early years as underground Jews in Mashhad, explaining my father's peculiar views on college-educated women, and concluding with his recent hunger strike. The more she heard, the more caring she became: not an ounce of mockery; just pure compassion. She was tall, willowy, with curly blond hair and large green eyes. We couldn't have been more different, but I instantly knew Carmen and I would become lifelong friends.

Pop, in contrast, was not what you'd call a big-time conversationalist. I had learned long ago how to translate a flickering smile or barely visible nod into wordy paragraphs. He was a silent film, and I added the subtitles. When he gave me his brittle back as he darted out of my dorm room, I supplied the words: "For me, you are dead!"

Afraid of losing the only father I had, I came home every Friday and stayed through the Sabbath, exhibiting allegiance to mother, father, and Judaism, wanting to show Pop that living in a dorm had done no damage, college hadn't made a dent: I hadn't learned a thing, I was unchanged—I was still his. Sitting around our dinner table those first few Friday nights, pretending we hadn't had a falling out, I racked my brain in search of cordial conversation, trying to sidestep hot button topics, making sure to avoid the two most flammable subjects: college and dorms. I was super excited about my art history courses but knew not to speak about classes or anything I was reading.

Cooking, I thought, watching Mom pass platters of food. *Maybe I should ask Mom for some of her recipes. That would make her happy and show Pop I cared about becoming a good homemaker someday. No. Bad idea. He'd envision me cooking in a strange man's kitchen.* If I brought up movies, he'd take it to mean I went out at night with drunken, lustful rogues and came home at all hours of the morning—or worse yet, didn't come home at all. I couldn't talk about my girlfriends because Pop would turn them all into the young woman he had walked in on the night of my move—a no-go zone. On Friday nights, shushed and shunned by his short seething back, I ate in silence as he nursed his fury.

Mom, on the other hand, took the opposite approach. Braving husband, community, and Mashhadi mores, refusing to follow the Aminoff tradition of severing familial ties, she nonchalantly suggested one Friday that we start meeting for lunch on Tuesdays at Barnard, between my scheduled classes. I immediately agreed, feeling surprised and secretly thrilled. When Al was at Cornell, Mom would visit him every month, riding the Greyhound bus with a platter of Nan-e Taftuns wrapped in dish cloths on her lap, intent on feeding him and all his college friends—reminding him of his roots, where he came from, and who fed him best. Albert was, after all, her firstborn son, whose ambition and drive made her proud. "My son vhant be ar-kee-tect." But I didn't think she'd ever want to visit me.

On that first Tuesday, she appeared at my dorm room an hour early carrying tins filled with warm, freshly-made Nan-e Taftuns and a variety of other treats she had baked, grilled, and pan-fried that morning.

"Vhair your roommate? I vhant all girlfriend eat my *Nan-e Taftuns.*" Her broad cheeks flushed as she unpacked saffroned and rose-watered scones.

I shared the three-bedroom suite with five other girls. Making her rounds beneath a disco ball hanging from the center of the ceiling, Mom worked every room and on her very first visit won over all my suitemates. From then on, whenever Carmen, Francesca, Bridgette, Chloe, and Suzanne heard Mom's voice, they pranced out of their bedrooms in bras and undies eager to give her welcoming hugs.

During her first visit, as we all sat eating Mom's homemade delicacies, the girls asked her about her life in Mashhad, and how she felt having to wear a chador.

"Chador do no-ting. Man is problome, not voomen. Man mus control tinking. He tink sex, he vhant sex. He see preetty girl—he blame girl. Man mus control tinking."

I rushed in to translate. "My mother is saying face coverings do nothing. Men must govern their thoughts, not mask their women. If a man is aroused seeing a pretty girl, that's his problem—not hers. He has to control his thoughts, not conceal her looks."

All five cheered, jabbing feminist fists in the air. Differences in age, dress, nationality vanished. Mom was now one of them.

It was the early days of the women's movement, and my suite-mates were drawn moth-like to Mom. They loved her pluck, her straight-from-the-oven baked goods, and adored her chopped-up English. They each privately pulled me aside and said, "I wish she was mine"—a wish I had often heard expressed by girlfriends, dating back to Cathy Storch.

"She's vibrant and vigorous," was Bridgette's summation. "Feisty. Devilishly fun."

"Saucy, she's just so saucy—outspoken and irreverent," Chloe said, chugging down an ice-cold beer. "I love her. She's where head meets heart, you know what I mean?"

I smiled and nodded agreement. I was glad they all liked Mom. But they hadn't lifted her veil and weren't privy to the full view: her erratic, often frightening contours—her self-pity, and legend-ary tantrums.

On Tuesdays, when my suitemates knew Mom was coming to visit, they delayed leaving the dorm and hung around instead, wait-ing for their Iranian Auntie Mame to arrive. Chomping on Nan-e Taftuns and homemade marzipan dusted with crushed pistachio, they chatted and laughed with her, before flying off to their classes in physics, astronomy, chemistry, economics, and Byzantine art.

I, too, looked forward to Mom's visits. She entered my new home away from home with cinematic richness, poised, dressed in one of her Oscar de la Renta suits, hair styled, gold chains draped around her neck, lips cherry-red, exuberantly carrying care packages, all with a Persian bounce to her gait.

After she handed out her aromatic delicacies to each of my suitemates, we'd stroll arm in arm in lockstep down Broadway, past Chock Full O'Nuts, and into a nearby café for lunch. Mom would order pancakes, waffles, French toast, scrambled eggs, French fries, insisting I eat all. Every week our smorgasbord meal was topped with dense cheesecake and multiple cups of coffee. Each Tuesday, I ate for 12, enough to carry me over to the following Tuesday, as Mom brought me up to date on her latest Saks Fifth Avenue finds, her Weight Watchers weigh-ins, unfolding scandals in our Persian community, and, with a heavy heart, her matrimonial strife, which always included cantankerous scenes of Mom hurling kitchen crockery.

During one of our lunches, she told me that a niece in Tel Aviv had recently married and moved with her husband to our Queens neighborhood.

"She sad. She cry. She mees muddair, foddair, broddair, sistairs. I vhant she no tink of dem. Vee go to Alexander's for shopping. Delancey Street to buy towel, sheet. To Statue Lee-bair-tee for fresh air.... I vhant she no tink about muddair. Tink about *Am-ree-kah* instead."

Mom said she understood her niece and knew how it felt to long for a mother. Seeking instant relief from sorrow, she suggested they go to the theater and be distracted by a happy Hollywood film.

Walking along Jamaica Avenue, they came across a string of movie houses. One marquee advertised a film all about mothers, Mom said. In Farsi, she told her niece: "This is about maternal love. You'll learn all about American mothers—how they live, cook, clean, treat their husbands, and raise their children. Perfect for you. It will warm your heart." They bought tickets, popcorn, soda, and seated themselves in the front row, waiting to be uplifted and entertained.

Mom cocked her head, gestured to my cheesecake, indicating I should keep eating as she finished her story.

She said as soon as the film began, wolves howled, coffins flew open, monsters dripping in black tar ran across the screen wrapped in bandages. Stabbing knives, flying bats, dense cobwebs, and bloodcurdling shrieks all sent electric jolts down their spines. Mom and my cousin ducked their heads and ran out, pushing through swinging doors into sunlight, gasping for breath.

My mother gave me an exasperated look and in Farsi said, "All Americans are demented. This, they call *Mommy*?"

I burst out laughing so hard I almost teetered off my chair. Tears rolling down my cheeks, I hooted, "Ma, you were watching a horror film. The film was called *The Mummy*, not *The Mommy*. A mummy is a dead body. Your movie was about an embalmed corpse that returns to life—a mummy, not a mommy's love."

Mom's eyes went wide and we both exploded with laughter.

"*Va-veylah!*[1] I vhant make her happy. I make her verse." Coffee squirted through our cheesecake-coated lips as we tried to stifle our howls.

After each lunch, Mom would slip me a $20 bill and say, "Jus case you see sumting you vhant to buy." With misty eyes I air-kissed both her cheeks and headed for class.

While studying Greek mythology, I had read of Hercules wrestling Antaeus, son of the earth goddess. Each time Hercules threw Antaeus to the ground, he was strengthened by his mother's touch. Now a sophomore in college, shunned by my father and touched each week by my mother, I understood the myth of Antaeus in ways I never had before.

Balancing my wish for the full college experience and my need for Pop's approval wasn't easy. He insisted I choose. Mom didn't. While Pop starved me, she fed me, trying to soften the sting of his rejection. College was foreign to her, and living as an unmarried girl anywhere other than under one's parents' roof was unheard of in Mashhad. I had gone way beyond morally acceptable bounds, yet, each Tuesday, Mom came to Morningside Heights, rosy-cheeked, impeccably dressed, arms wrapped around warm tins, enduring three trains and steep subway steps, all in high-heeled shoes.

She was a brain-boggler, a bundle of contradictions. Outspoken, outrageous, fearless, defiant, and yet disinterested in my schooling. Repeatedly running away, not wanting to be touched, and yet when I left home, she touched me deeply with her weekly visits, keeping us linked. Mom sat at the very center of our family maze and in her jagged-edged way kept us all together.

Checking my pride at the door, I continued to visit my parents on weekends, hoping Pop would eventually come around. Our worlds did not mesh. He didn't believe in multiple perspectives, alternative views. It was as if he had locked himself in an echo chamber inside a windowless dungeon, where self-validating proclamations were constantly reconfirmed.

It was six months, six agonizingly long and suspenseful months, before my father made eye contact. A lackluster look, at that, but nevertheless a look, which led me to invent more subtitles for his silent signals. *Rupture and repair,* I captioned this one, translating Pop's grizzly gaze as saying: *Keep visiting and, who knows, I may one day speak.*

1. *Va-veylah!* (Persian/Farsi)—Oh, my goodness! Oh, my gosh!

So I did. And, sure enough, one evening, speech came to the fore. "Pass sugar" slipped through his tobacco-stained teeth as he reached for his chai. Later, as I was telling Mom about a free concert that had been held on campus, Pop shouted at me, "Change subject!"

He had thawed. We were back on track. Never to speak of naked Carmen or these difficult days again. ▨

CHAPTER 30

Barnard

As a campus resident I was now experiencing college from within. Many of my Barnard classmates came from finishing schools, were multilingual, had laser-sharp minds, photographic memories, and were sexually on fire. At night, practically every student had a male or female companion in her bed. Even Orthodox Jews had their secret lovers. One sophomore from down the hall told me her boyfriend, a Columbia Law School student, wore his velvet *yarmulke*[1] while having intercourse. I didn't understand that. Other classmates, I knew personally, were sleeping with their married professors in nearby hotels. Anorexics, bulimics, girls experimenting with LSD and heroin lived on almost every floor. I found each of them fascinating but was especially drawn to those with hidden lives and harrowing histories.

There was Georgette, who had lost her mother, brother, and grandfather to suicide and had been raised in the Texas boonies by her maternal grandmother. By day she was a sophomore majoring in philosophy, and at night she worked for Gil, a Harlem pimp. When I told her about my mother's water cures—her Sunday night administration of enemas as a treatment for my childhood ailments—she told me about Gil, who hooked her up with johns and took half her pay. All quickly said, without looking up from her soup.

Georgie was ethereal, skinless, in need of protection. One evening she and I were eating pizza around the breakfast table in her suite when six-foot-six Gil walked in, wearing a high-crowned,

1. *yarmulke* (Hebrew)—skullcap worn during prayer by all Jewish men and all day by Orthodox Jewish men

wide-brimmed felt hat and boots with spurs. Like some cowboy gunslinger, he spread his legs, unzipped his pants, and whisked her into her bedroom. I left, stupefied. Later she told me that Gil was not only the love of her life but also a magnanimous drug dealer who supplied her with free heroin. I knew how to ask questions and I knew how to listen, but for the life of me I couldn't get through to her, I couldn't help her see Gil for who he was. A year later Georgette stopped attending classes, left the dorm, and disappeared.

There was lily-white Mary from Ireland, who at age 14 had started sleeping with Luke, the 40-year-old black janitor of her apartment building back home. After getting pregnant and giving birth, she handed her infant over to Luke's mother to raise so she could finish high school. She and Luke parted after the baby was born. Due to outstanding grades, Mary was granted early admission to Barnard. "If it wasn't for his mom, I wouldn't be here in New York City studying physics," she said.

"Do you miss your son?" I asked hesitantly.

Mary shrugged. "I barely know him. As far as I'm concerned, Luke's mom is his mom."

I was gobsmacked. Could I give away my newborn and move across the Atlantic to study physics? Could I leave a child to pursue my own core mission? I had trouble leaving Mom and Pop.

Escaping through hinges, from behind closed doors, potent scents wafted through dormitory hallways. Pot was identifiable; other pungent smells weren't. But drugs didn't intrigue or entice me. Instead I found them frightening. The slightest whiff of marijuana made me think of the story Mom had told me about Layla, Albert and David's Muslim nanny—a cautionary tale.

The possibility of becoming an addict like Layla terrified me, especially once I discovered how accessible opium was, not only on the streets of Manhattan but within Barnard's own corridors.

Seated in the dorm's lobby lounge with Mary, I was sharing swatches of my life when Christine dropped by.

She gave me a big thumbs-up. "I told you so. Didn't I say your father wouldn't kill himself?"

We wrapped our arms around each other and hugged. Squeezing her tight, I mumbled, "You know, I could never have done it without you. It was *you* who got me through this whole ordeal."

Stroking my thick hair like a doting mother, she said, "You did it. Not me. But now that you've left home, and not in a bloody body bag, we have to celebrate your newfound freedom. Have you ever had a drink?"

I smiled. "Does a sip of Extra Heavy Malaga wine on Friday nights count?"

"No Es," she chuckled. "That's your weekly Sabbath ritual. I mean a mixed drink from a bar."

I looked into her Greenwich-Connecticut-blue eyes. Chris had told me that by age 12 she had already been introduced to hard liquor.

"I haven't had a mixed drink, but I'm game."

She winked. "This is your next *first*."

That night Chris took me to The West End bar, an ever-popular Columbia-Barnard hangout. Wearing bell-bottoms, tank tops, and stilettos, our hair loose and long, we linked arms as we strutted over to Broadway and 114th Street. I followed her into the dark bar. It smelled of sweat and billowing clouds of pot. Agile and bold, Chris grabbed two chairs from another table and swung them around to an empty table in the center of the crowded room. On a small stage a few feet away, a performer was strumming his guitar and singing the Beatles song "I Want To Hold Your Hand."

Cradling my head between her hands as if to read my mind, she said, "In celebration of freedom, choose your first drink."

"I have no idea. You tell me."

"Let's each start with a Bloody Mary." Chris squeezed my shoulders. "It'll be so much fun watching you loosen up."

"You just want to see what comes out—against my will. Right?"

She pinched my cheeks and looked me straight in the eyes.

"Even if I meet the hottest guy, I'm staying by your side all night. And I'll make sure to get you home safe and sound."

I trusted Chris.

Out came our drinks, each with a red plastic straw topped by a tiny paper umbrella.

"I feel like a lab experiment," I said to Chris. "Just because I never drank doesn't mean I don't know how." I reached for my glass, swirled the straw, and took a large gulp.

She crossed her long colt-like legs and laughed loudly. All the Columbia guys at neighboring tables looked up and, like metal chips, were magnetically drawn to Chris. Tossing her blond hair to one side, she raised her glass.

"Here's to Esther and upending the balance of power. Here's to internal and external combustion. Here's to counterintuitive living."

We clinked glasses.

I tacked on, "Here's to knowing ourselves to the extent humans can."

"I'll drink to that," Chris seconded. All male eyes were on her, and she knew it. She was used to it. She turned and smiled at each of her admirers.

I felt a band of warmth rise from my chest and turn my cheeks hot. My mind melted like butter.

"Chris, I like tomato juice and vodka."

"Take it slow, Es. Sip, don't gulp. Eat some peanuts so it doesn't go straight to your head."

After the second drink my words began to slur, while Chris, after her fourth, was clear as a bell.

"How do you feel?" she asked.

"Pop's not here. Or is he?" I tittered.

She inspected the room. "Nope, he's not here. It's better to be whole than to be good. Keep that in mind."

I had no idea what she meant. "Am I being whole now?"

"You're strangely blended—American and Mashhadi—but you're getting there." Chris and I giggled.

While we prattled on, juggling words, two Columbia men veered toward us. Through glazed eyes I saw a fellow with a kangaroo-shaped head and a face full of acne pull up a chair and place his nose an inch away from mine.

"Hi, I'm Cal, short for Caligula—the imperious Roman Emperor. Are you getting a bit liquored up?" He licked his teeth.

I gripped my purse straps, wrinkled my forehead and thought, *Chris, save me.*

But her hands were full. The other fellow, who looked like a self-infatuated literary type, sat down next to her, sipping from a flask.

"I'm Dan," he said, giving her the once over with huge bonfire eyes. "Columbia undergrad, English lit."

Oh shit, I was right. English lit.

Cal grabbed my hand as if he wanted to crush it. "Ya wanna dance?"

I noticed dirty fingernails, complicated shoulder-length hair, and sweat drizzling down the sides of his face.

"No, thanks," I stuttered.

I had nothing else to say, nothing to work with. In an instant I was back to being my scared and silent younger self. I became child-small, pushing age seven at best.

Mr. English Lit shoved his thumbs into his armpits. "What have you two been intently discussing?"

The image of my father picking at his whiskers jumped into my head. He *was* here—blowing a gasket, seeing me at this bar, tipsy on Bloody Marys, squeezed between two men and their unchaste fantasies. I felt his presence. With Godlike powers, he reined me in. Pop and I united. Of one mind. *This is not for me. This is not my world.* Not that I knew what mine was. But it wasn't this. I could never bring Emperor Caligula home. Whenever I met a guy from Columbia, that was my first thought: Could I bring him home to Mom and Pop? Was it even conceivable?

Chris politely answered Dan. "I was saying to Esther, instead of pyramids there are circles."

Glancing at me with bright blue eyes, she was telegraphing messages: *Stop thinking about your father. You're here to disengage. As for these guys, empower yourself, hold your ground.* If there was more she was saying, I was too sloshed to hear it.

Dan looked smugly at Chris. "I can tell, you're a woman of almost masculine intellect."

Vodka-steeped or not, I almost threw my glass at him. How much of this crap had I heard growing up? Masculine intellect. As if intellect had a gender. A vein in my neck throbbed.

Chris, a sure-footed tightrope walker, second in courage only to Mom, stood up and told them to leave.

Left to ourselves, we ordered refills.

"Es, tell me how you're feeling."

"I can't see straight. My mind is a trampoline. No control. Hard to talk." Struggling to form words, I muttered, "Hearing myself think feels intrusive."

She slapped her knee and giggled as if on laughing gas.

Chris helped me to my feet and took my arm. Teetering on stilettos, I hobbled out of the bar holding onto her.

"You're amazing, Chris, amazing, just amazing," I babbled as we made our way back to my dorm. She was light-years ahead of me. She knew how to speak her mind, stand up to Cal and Dan, and protect us.

I wished I could be that strong and smart. But I knew I never would. 🔲

CHAPTER 31

Confession

The Columbia-Barnard campus was a hotbed of political activity. Barnard girls from South Dakota, Istanbul, and Tokyo
huddled around bullhorns, shouting slogans promoting feminism,
lesbianism, and Black Power.

One Sunday afternoon as I walked through Columbia's gates, a
Barnard student with a shaved head came marching down Broad-
way banging a drum. She approached me wearing an OVERTHROW
THE ESTABLISHMENT banner slung across her chest.

"Hey, girl! You there. What are you majoring in?"

"Art History," I answered.

"Shit," she snarled. "You're not serving the movement. Art is
capitalistic, worthless, antithetical to our cause. These are revolu-
tionary days. We're changing the world. Get on board."

Giving me the middle finger, she huffed off.

That evening, needing a break from campus fire and fury, I sub-
wayed back home to Forest Hills. Coming in through the back door,
crossing the kitchen, I heard my father in our living room say, "I'm
in deep trouble."

I halted. Peeking through louvered doors, I saw Pop in the living
room, wearing a tux and sitting hunched in his arm chair. Albert
and David sat across from him on the sofa, looking grave. Mom
stood next to her sons dressed in a crisp powder-pink taffeta gown
and pink open-toed shoes, her chest bedecked with jewels. *That's
right*, I remembered. *They're going to a wedding.* Staying as quiet as I
could, I listened.

"For the past twelve years, I've been buried in debt," Pop said, pressing the palms of his square hands over his eyes. Sweat oiled his face. "There is no way out."

I stifled a gasp. I had always thought Pop to be excessively cautious and risk-averse. Now, listening, I discovered that he had been reckless, borrowing from loan sharks at mind-boggling interest rates to keep us afloat. Concealing the truth from his wife and children, he had believed he would find his way out. But his strategy had backfired, leaving him even more distraught. For 12 years Pop had been hiding more truths than he could ultimately bear: not only the fact that he hadn't been earning enough to financially support us, but also the truth of who he was, what he had done, and, throughout these years, how he had felt. Were these well-kept secrets another form of hiding, of duplicity—Fatulla aboveground and Nissan underground?

Pop lowered his hands, his eyes two pits of terror.

Hearing his words, Mom's face turned yolk-yellow. She sank into a chair as Pop confessed that loan sharks had been paying their mortgage, their real-estate taxes, buying her Oscar de la Rentas, her jewels. When she could take no more, she sprang from her seat and cursed. "*Khar.*"

Pauperized by America, Pop's hopes of financial success had been dashed, his aberu destroyed. Yearning now for ancestral soil, he recast the anti-Semitic homeland from which he had fled as The Promised Land. "This would never have happened if we had stayed in Iran," he heaved.

Mom, looking catlike, unsheathed her claws. "By leaving, I thought I was leaving behind the scum of Iran," she fumed in Farsi. "But you are the scum that has followed us to New York. Once again, because you are weak, you've put our lives at risk!" She made a spitting noise with teeth, tongue and lips, as if spitting him out like a wad of bitter tobacco.

Envisioning Iran from his Forest Hills armchair, Pop said nothing. A stench of failure seeped from his dry mouth.

I stood in the kitchen, thunderstruck. *A counterfeit...a liar.* A biting chill sped through my limbs. *Our lives are a lie.* Fancy clothes, sumptuous dinner parties, my college tuition, were all borrowed and owed. All I believed to be true wasn't.

Out of the corner of his eye Pop noticed my presence.

"Go to your room!" He thundered, thrusting an index finger and shakily pointing at the staircase.

I was almost 20 years old, living on my own. And still Pop saw me as a little girl who had to be kept from sad, cold truths—as a daughter whose destined path was from cradle to wedding canopy. His message: *You're merely a sweet confection, to be viewed and eventually eaten. That's all.*

I stomped out.

In my room, my imagination ran wild. Loan sharks. Attempts on Pop's life. Prison. Through my slammed-shut door I heard Mom twist the knife. "You're worthless! Stupid! A failure! Always failing!" she shouted in Farsi. She then called him what I knew she deemed most despicable: simple-minded. My heart jumped into my throat as I ricocheted between wishing to shield him and wanting to shoot him.

I thought we'd plunge into poverty, lose our home, I'd have to quit college. But none of that happened. Maybe Pop sold his share of family lands back in Mashhad. Maybe he asked other family members to help bail him out. If Albert and David knew how we survived until they ultimately rescued my parents, they kept that information to themselves. No one outside the family ever knew about Pop's confession. And no one in the family ever brought it up again.

My father, for the next few weeks, trapped inside a cage of dread, shuffled about the house with a hangdog face, scorned—like a squatter, an illegal lodger in his own Queens home.

Pop went to work, came home, watched the news, read his bible in bed, went to work, came home, watched the news, read his bible in bed. He and Mom seldom spoke. Gradually, gardening became Pop's main pastime, as he gave all his attention to his flowers and vegetables. In morning sunlight, making a visor of his hand, he'd inspect his efforts, looking for new growth, checking to see what had made it through the night. On Sundays he spaded, tended to patches of mint, cucumbers, and tomatoes as I lay on my back, swinging in a hammock, watching. Two-fisted, ripping out weeds, he cultivated his garden. Pop and his plants bonded, sharing sacred interspecies time as he tilled, fed, and watered the soil.

With praying mantises swiveling their heads, dragonflies and bees hovering, he said to me one day: "Estaire, respect the earth under your feet. There is life here." I assumed he meant ants, worms, slugs, seeds—all that he uncovered. Lying in the hammock, watching him fertilize flower beds and vegetable patches, I wondered if, bent over, he was also planting hope.

Outside our house was an intersection with four sewage drains, one at each corner. Bare-armed, Pop allotted himself the weekly task of reaching down into these drains and removing wet, clogged-up leaves. While this was an activity Mom found offensive and repeatedly forbade, he wouldn't give it up. If he wasn't indoors and wasn't in the backyard gardening, then he was on his knees in the street, reaching into sewers with rolled-up sleeves. While neighboring fathers jogged, golfed, and played tennis, mine dug elbow-deep into slimy city sewers, fishing for obstructions. With one arm sloshing about in the muck, he persisted, not knowing what his naked hand would find—be it snakes, rats, dead birds. His arm would emerge covered with insect bites. After each rainstorm, he'd be back at it, going where no one else dared to go.

When I asked him why he did this, he answered, "I clean out corner drains so rainwater doesn't back up into our basements." But given when he took up this new pastime, I was certain there was more he wasn't saying. Perhaps, like working in his garden, this was his Africa, a jungle-like retreat and escape from human engagement. Left alone, he'd grapple with nature, which he much preferred to do.

As he entered his retirement years, my father grew even quieter with less and less to say and nothing he felt a need to ask. He ate sparingly, read the weekly Torah portion, slept as much as my mother would permit, and developed a kinship with pigeons.

Stale bread was saved in plastic bags for park benches, where he sat in suit and tie sprinkling dry crusts. Flared wings settled by his laced shoes as pigeons rammed into one another, pecking, cooing, fighting over bread. Transported to some mystical world, Pop's narrow lips would lift into a faint smile as he scattered more crumbs, making one full circle for all to have—even the late arrivals. I'd sit by his side, watching birds descend, not speaking, not asking, not pushing any further. 🔲

Esther Amini, age three, a timid, nonverbal child.

Esther with her father, both reading in silence.

Esther at age six (second from left), dressed as a Boukharian shepherd for a Purim costume competition.

Esther at age eight (center) at Rockefeller Center, where her mother took her for ice-skating lessons.

Esther at age ten, approaching marrying age in her parents' eyes.

Esther's mother, Hana (right), shaking hands with Shah Pahlavi of Iran at a reception for the Shah and Empress Farah Diba at the Waldorf Astoria in 1962.

Esther and her mother in 1982, when Esther was pregnant with her son, Aaron.

Esther's father at age 80, ten years before his death.

PART FIVE

Lost and Found

CHAPTER 32

Homecoming

Pop did have sons, and Persian sons are a hedge against sunken states. Since my brothers had grown up with a strong sense of filial responsibility, fathering our father, they put their heads together, brainstormed, and hatched plans.

On the brink of rewarding careers, Albert and David left their respective professions and teamed up. With the help of family connections, they recast themselves as merchants and became importers and distributers of Oriental rugs, just as my father had once wished. After a few years, they attained success, nudged Pop out of paralysis, put his stymied world in order, and restored him to his rightful place, his sovereign seat, as family patriarch.

In the meantime, I spent the remainder of my undergraduate years crouched on museum floors in faded jeans, pad in hand, eyeing, then sketching paintings, sculptures, artifacts: all that couldn't speak. Studiously I stared, scrutinizing details, recording thoughts, translating the visual, the nonverbal into words. Living with Pop and deciphering his silences had been my training ground.

In the 1960s and '70s, Barbara Novak was the revered professor of art history at Barnard. I took all of her courses, and, just like her, wore prairie skirts, turquoise earrings, and went makeup-less. Her field of specialization, Nineteenth- and Twentieth-Century American Art, became mine.

Edward Hopper's paintings portraying isolation and alienation spoke to me, so I sub-specialized, studying his entire body of work. After Professor Novak read my senior thesis on Hopper, she called me into her office. Her wire-rim glasses sat slightly askew on her nose as she braced my shoulders and in her gentle way of speaking—slow and fond—urged me to apply to graduate school, pursue a Masters, a PhD, write, and someday teach.

My eyes moistened. She must have assumed I was tearing up from joy. I wasn't. She had no idea she was weighing me down with ambitions my center couldn't hold. Hearing her say I had the chops and should shoot for the stars turned my gut into a roiling pot of terror, shame, and guilt—a stomach-wrenching landscape. I couldn't push for more and I couldn't tell her why. Fear seized me by the throat.

I had made a deal with Pop. All I wanted was four years of college. I had promised him that after receiving a B.A. I'd return home and be the Iranian daughter he wanted, remaining under his roof until I married. It was a trade-off I had made for the sake of an education, and I had to keep my end of the bargain. After Pop's hunger strike, confession of his loan shark debts, his sunken financial and emotional states, how could I add to his burdens and have the audacity to even think of wanting more? I had stretched our bond almost to the breaking point. How much more could I test it before it snapped? If for no other reason, I couldn't add to my own guilt-ridden feelings of no-goodness by asking for more.

Pop had fought hard against his major adversary—my education. And yet, in spite of temper tantrums and hunger strikes, he had paid my school expenses and survived my Barnard years. I was wholeheartedly grateful. Now, as a senior, with college coming to an end, I needed to show gratitude and prove to him that he hadn't lost me, that I remained loyal to Mom, Pop, and our Persian-Judeo roots. Even if costs had not been a consideration, the prospect of distancing myself even farther from family and upbringing by pursuing an advanced degree frankly terrified me. No, graduate school was out of the question. I imagined Professor Novak sitting on one side of an imaginary scale while Pop, with arms tightly crossed, sat on the other. Even though he was shorter and much lighter, he outweighed her.

But, for now, I was still in college. Gingerly pushing limits, I remained on campus and now commuted home every *other* weekend. On Saturday nights my dorm exploded like fireworks, and I stayed put to see the sparks fly. With hoopla and hullabaloo, girls rushed in and out of showers, shaving armpits and legs, brushing teeth and gargling, popping in contact lenses and diaphragms, borrowing each other's spermicidal gel, all to the background heat of handheld hairdryers. Surrounded by crackling force fields, they reeled about, leaping from mirror to mirror, applying mascara, eye shadow, and lip gloss.

I sat on my bed in pajamas and told my suitemates which bra, which pair of jeans, shoes, and earrings to wear. We mulled over the pros and cons of parting hair on the right, the left, or simply leaving manes wild and unruly. Carmen's Jason would show up extra early, practically drooling at the sight of her. Francesca's beau would be downstairs, double-parked in his Ford Mustang, honking his horn, all set to dance. Bridgette, Chloe, and Suzanne would dress up in tie-dyes, love beads, and with daisies in their hair sprint to the Columbia dorms to snuggle with their fiancés. I listened to their stories of love and heartbreak, lived their romantic lives, and sent each one off for the evening, reassuring them I was fine.

I wasn't.

I, too, needed a boyfriend—urgently. Left with my lonely self, I'd raid the freezer and consume a tub of mint chocolate chip ice cream, thinking it would keep me company and sub as a date. It never did. It left me numb and cold. For three years Barnard had fed my intellect while the rest of me went hungry. I was educated but inconsolably sad. Unpaired, I felt a stinging void—a biting crick and kink, as if I were a partial person with huge missing pieces. Drafting a letter to myself, I asked: *Are you grown up enough to face the truth? Stop lying to yourself. You want a love life… You want to feel what your suitemates feel—all giddy inside. You want to adore, feel adored, and someday marry a man you're wild about.*

But it wasn't happening. Why? Was I ugly? *Ugly* gnawed at my stomach. I cascaded back to early memories of Pop shaving my head. Tufts of hair tumbling onto cold bathroom tiles. I remembered looking in the mirror, seeing my unsightly scalp, and feeling so ugly. A lingering, paralyzing sensation, coupled with silence.

I wanted what my friends had—a guy who would love me, who couldn't live without me. *But what do I look for and how do I find him?* I asked myself. I didn't know.

Meanwhile, Mom and Pop maximized the weekends I did spend with them. Twice a month, on Friday nights, Mashhadi bachelors strode in for Shabbat dinner. Pop made sure to invite suitors ten to 20 years my senior. Some didn't speak a word of English but showed approval by slowly scanning me up and down, lecherously ogling every inch, putting to rest for just a moment my fears of being ugly. And then there were those who were fluent in English but chose not to speak to me or even look in my direction. I helped Mom serve, clear the table, and finally slipped away to help wash dishes as the men sat and talked. I hid in the kitchen, humiliated, feeling like a rack of raw meat being auctioned off to the highest bidder.

A sharp contrast to weekends at Barnard.

But my college world, even though different, was still an all-girls one. I hadn't learned how to socialize with the opposite sex. At Barnard-Columbia mixers, I leaned against a stone wall, gazed at the concrete floor, hoping I would and wouldn't be seen. If someone approached me, it could mean I was appealing. But it would also mean having to engage, self-reveal, ask questions, find ways to get to know this person, participate in co-ed, college-age conversation. Language I didn't have.

Then, one evening, a buff, broad-shouldered Columbia student with light blue eyes and a corn-yellow crew cut shambled across the room and asked me to dance.

His name was Kevin. He was a Columbia College football player and a good foot taller than me. After our dance, he asked me out on a date.

My thumping Persian sense of aberu and protocol told me not to accept.

"Sure," I answered. I'd never been on a date. This was my chance.

Kevin suggested we meet the following afternoon at a near-by Hungarian café. Seated opposite each other on plastic webbed chairs, we each ordered coffee. Dressed in a motorcycle jacket and denim shorts, he sat in silence.

"Where did you grow up?" I asked, giving him a cordial smile while digging my nails into my palms under the table.

His yellow crew cut, like porcupine quills, stood on end. "Cattle farm in Nebraska."

"Oh, really." I tried to look enthused. "What kind of cattle?"

"Black Angus." Kevin's hooded eyes avoided mine. He was worse at this than I was.

"I've never been on a cattle farm. Where in Nebraska?" Trying my best to show interest.

"In the Sandhills." He crossed his callused knees, lazily stirred his coffee, and kept his eyes on the spoon.

"So you grew up in the Sandhills of Nebraska. What did you do out there for fun?"

Kevin ran his forefinger inside the cup and licked it.

"Hunt. Fish."

Why wasn't he asking *me* any questions? Didn't he want to know *me*? When I came into his line of vision, he hummed tunelessly to himself and looked away.

Suddenly, Pop invaded my thoughts. *Enough talk!* he chided. *You shouldn't be with Black Angus! Estaire, you're a disgrace!*

Yes, it seemed I was. Kevin said little, but I did learn he was a devout Catholic, attended church every Sunday, and had never before met a Jew. "Folks from Nebraska say Jews have horns," he dryly remarked. "That's what we say back at home."

His words, jolting like a shock collar, shot down my spine. I froze. How could he say this to my face?

If I had been Chris, I would have asked him to leave, or left myself. But I wasn't. So I finished my coffee. After the longest half hour of my life, I finally stood and shook his hand. "So nice meeting you, but I think we have nothing in common."

He nodded, politely.

Undone, I cried all the way back to my dorm. My deepest self knew Kevin and I could never be, but still, I was in dire need of a second date. I didn't want Kevin—but I needed him to want me. I wanted to feel I had the power to attract, steal hearts, exude inescapable appeal, just like Chris. Was I that unlikeable? Kevin had said something abhorrent to me, and yet I hammered myself hardest. Unable to captivate Kevin, I blamed me.

The more I compared the college men I was meeting to the men my parents wanted me to meet, the more I felt lost. My American hippie generation seemed confused and rootless. TV programs, newspapers, and magazines were filled with stories of young males running off to Canada, dodging the draft; graduate students dropping out of school, settling on communes, smoking pot, tripping on LSD. Getting high and staying high seemed to be a new national norm.

I didn't belong, didn't fit in. *I was born in America*, I told myself, *but I'm not American. It's not my core.* Pop didn't have to worry, I realized. He'd done his job well. I'd never be one of the girls shaving her legs and popping in a diaphragm before running off to have sex with a boyfriend at a Columbia dorm. I would never even be one of the girls I saw sitting on park benches with their boyfriends, nuzzling and kissing. I passed as an American, but that was just an outer garment. A chador. In truth, I was a traditional Mashhadi Jewish girl, like it or not. And maybe that wasn't so bad. Maybe being American wasn't all it was cracked up to be, anyhow.

Months after my coffee date with Kevin, my parents insisted I attend a distant cousin's Iranian wedding at the Hilton Hotel in Manhattan. Reluctantly, I complied. After the ceremony, as I entered the ballroom in magenta strapless silk with my hair braided in a bun, I was aware of a slew of male heads swiveling in my direction. A place card seated me at a table of single Mashhadis, most of whom I did not know. A ten-member band of drums, trumpets, saxophones, trombones, and keyboards electrified the room as the female vocalist alternated between traditional Iranian and contemporary American tunes. When she burst into "Build Me Up Buttercup," a tall, dark-haired, good-looking fellow slid through the crowd and asked me to dance. With a firm grip and grin, he swept me into the center of the ballroom and, within seconds, we were bouncing to the beat. We exchanged first names with no need to know more. Jack's long, lean legs fluidly moved in ways I didn't know were anatomically possible—as if he were jointless and made of rubber. He was a natural, like an *American Bandstand* winner.

To my surprise, I was in high demand, bopping from partner to partner, kicking my heels, rock 'n' rolling—with no questions asked and no strings attached. Pure fun. That night, not given a moment's rest, I never even tasted the salad, soup, or main course. It seemed as if every unmarried Iranian male asked for a dance. A deliriously dizzying, empowering high. The evening came to a close with me nipping a Bloody Mary while rollicking to Diana Ross's "Love Child."

I woke up at home the next morning peppered with goosebumps. *Bewitching, ravishing, captivating—is that who I am?* For one night, I had been irresistible, desired by every Persian bachelor at the Hilton Hotel. Feeling physically alluring was a brand-new sensation. Over-the-top intoxicating. All through college I had wanted to lose my heart, like other Barnard girls, to a magnificent man who was smitten and enthralled by me. I, too, had wanted to become someone's *beloved*. The night before, at the Hilton, among English-speaking Iranians, I had had a taste of what that felt like. For the first time, it seemed attainable. I had spent most of my life bucking cultural barriers, fighting family expectations and traditions. Now, at age

21, I decided to embrace them. Damming up one set of dreams in pursuit of another, I returned to hearth and home, feeling an overpowering gravitational pull back to family.

During the rest of my senior year, my Sundays at home were now spent in the kitchen at Mom's side, learning to cook. She masterfully rushed through countless steps, making *Polo Safi*,[1] as I slowed her down, meticulously measuring her palmful of this and pinch of that, penning her every move on index cards. I recorded each step as she made her khoreshes, her samboosehs, her cakes, puddings, and Persian candies, neatly filing her talents in a tin box. I learned to crochet leefs, embroider tablecloths, hem skirts, and even mastered the art of ironing Pop's white shirts.

One Sunday morning, frying halibut, with fish scales under her nails, she muttered to me, "Estaire, I no vhant you burn, like me. I vhant you happy."

That, too, was indexed and filed away. I was on a path to marriage. Mom knew it. I had decided it was, after all, what I wanted, and I had expected she would be pleased. Now, though, when I stood beside her, eager to learn housewifery, she somehow seemed subdued.

But I'd made up my mind. I had no post-college plans and was terrified of the future. My fear was physical, pulsing from my chest and digging into my ribs. No way could I leave my parents' home and live on my own. Undoable. Nor could I go to graduate school or get a job. It would kill Pop for sure. Marriage was my only option. And I wanted romance. I wanted to feel the way I had felt at the Hilton—bewitching, irresistible. And the only men who saw me that way were Iranian. Approaching graduation, my fears and desires shifted. It was time to come home, where I belonged.

David was now happily married to a Jewish-Mashhadi girl, and Albert would soon follow in his brother's footsteps. Love-starved and directionless, I came full circle and agreed to marry a college-educated Mashhadi selected and vetted by my father. *Pop knows best, I told myself. He knows men far better than I. Didn't he rescue me from Bill, the postal clerk, when I was 16? Pop loves me and looks out for me. What's the alternative? Traipsing through a world booby-trapped with hazardous men?* Rushing into marriage, I chose Persian—believing it was my blood, the blood of generations, my authentic self that

1. *Polo Safi* (Persian/Farsi)—Persian rice that has been soaked overnight in saltwater, then drained, boiled, and steamed so each grain is separate and firm

needed raising as I razed all else.

When I told Pop of my decision, he let out a sigh that could be heard throughout the house. His jowls unclenched, his forehead smoothened. His face settled into a peaceful smile. He got up out of his armchair and held me in his arms, weeping his thanks to God.

"You returned my one and only daughter. You brought Estaire back home. For twenty-two years I worried and suffered. *Am-ree-kah* is dangerous. You didn't allow her to ruin her life, to go astray, and for that I am eternally grateful."

I had never seen my father happier. His life was complete, and I knew mine would be too. 🔲

CHAPTER 33

Matrimony

Pop invited a young man by the name of Saul to come over one Saturday afternoon and join us for tea in our backyard. Mom handed me a platter of cakes and cookies to serve. Before I could swing open the screen door, she quickly filled me in. Saul had been born in Mashhad and had come to the U.S. on his own to further his education. Mom made sure I knew that this Mashhadi bachelor, who had been carefully appraised by Pop, was now a graduate from an American university with a degree in architecture. She nodded with approval.

Saul was sitting next to Pop. He was tall, slim, serious-looking in his tortoiseshell glasses. He was wearing a Prince of Wales check sport coat. Given Pop's soft spot for the British and their articles of clothing, I knew Saul's jacket would win him points. When I sat beside Mom after serving the sweets, she suggested I tell our guest what courses I was taking at Barnard, perhaps thinking he would see some overlap, some kinship, in our respective fields of study. Saul listened politely as I listed the senior seminars I was taking and he even asked me a few questions in fluent English. I was relieved to see my education didn't frighten him.

The following week, while I was in my dorm room writing a paper on Northern Renaissance Art, Saul called and asked me out to dinner. No unnecessary chit-chat, no awkward adolescent hemming and hawing, just directly asked for what he wanted—a date. I liked that.

"Sure," I said.

As far as I was concerned, all boxes had now been checked. He spoke fluent English, was college-educated, decisive, and mature. After hearing me talk enthusiastically about my art history classes, he had still called to ask me out. Most important, he had been vetted. My parents and my brothers all knew him and liked him.

By now, some of my girlfriends were applying to law, business, and medical schools, preparing for meaningful and well-paying careers. Some were looking for museum internships or jobs in upscale art galleries, while others had decided to take a year off and travel. Pop would never allow me to work, become a wage-earner, or enter graduate school, let alone traipse off to see the world. Once I completed college, my only option was to move back home and live with my parents until I wed.

After our third dinner date, Saul asked me to marry him, and I accepted.

The wedding took place at the end of May, shortly after my graduation. It was a typical Persian-Jewish affair in a Long Island banquet hall that comfortably held all 1,000 of our guests. For Mashhadi Jews, this was the customary size. Relatives, friends, business associates from all sides of both families were invited. I wore a wedding dress, but I don't remember it. I can't recall the ceremony, the flowers, the reception, the wedding night. It's all a blur, lost to me and forgotten—and better left that way.

In June, 1971, one week after the wedding, Saul and I moved to Israel and settled in Jerusalem, a lifelong dream of his. Mine were Cinderella-like dreams, 3-D fantasies in technicolor: Saul was my knight in shining armor, carrying me off to wherever he chose. At 22, it was totally irrelevant where we lived. I would have moved with him to Timbuktu, anywhere. All I wanted was to feel deeply loved. I imagined the two of us living in a state of eternal bliss, in a marriage dramatically different from my parents'.

On the day of our departure, Pop kissed the crown of my head and blessed me in Hebrew while Mom bit her lower lip, wept and said nothing, not one word. I knew she wanted the best for me and expected her to be happy. I decided she just couldn't bear to see me go. 🔲

CHAPTER 34

Jerusalem

In Jerusalem, Saul worked as an architect for a firm near our apartment while I attended Ulpan[1] five days a week to improve my Hebrew. Many months later, I was accepted to Hebrew University's Master's Program in Art History. Saul didn't mind if I once again became a student, as long as I tended to the home, kept it spotlessly clean, and kept the refrigerator stocked with homemade Persian dishes. While he worked long hours, laundry, food-shopping, cooking, cleaning, and classes filled my days. Tuti was still living in Jerusalem and was almost 100 years old. I visited her a few times, but her sight and hearing had dimmed, and she didn't seem to know who I was.

Every month a heavily stamped manila envelope, addressed to me, arrived from Queens. Each package contained Mom's freshly crocheted leefs. No letter enclosed, just leefs. I stacked them in drawers and privately bawled, knowing these leefs had nothing to do with bathing. She was reaching out, sending smoke signals, saying: *I am with you. You're not alone, not even in the distant, dusty hills of Jerusalem. Are you happy? Tell me, Estaire, are you happy?* I didn't answer. I had learned long ago to keep things to myself.

It was my decision to get married, I reminded myself. No one twisted my arm. Okay, so I didn't know Saul was domineering, critical, explosive, and prone to mood swings. So I never explored our differences. *Big deal,* I told myself. *Maybe I didn't know how. I can learn to live with them. I can. I can be like Tuti. I can be deferential. I*

1. Ulpan (Hebrew)—Hebrew language school

can agree when I disagree. I can perfect my cooking and cleaning. I can pretend I'm content. I can perfect submission. My ancestors did, and so can I.

I'd learn to steam Persian rice just like my mother, I told myself—each grain firm, separate, and whole. I'd darn his socks and master an inconspicuous cross-stitch, just as he wanted. I'd prove my worth.

One evening, Saul shot out of our bathroom, livid. "Didn't your parents teach you anything?"

It seemed they hadn't.

"You don't even know how to insert toilet paper! Toilet paper must always roll off the top. The sheets should never unwind from under. When pulling the paper, it must never touch the wall tiles. You understand?"

I didn't know. I couldn't remember how Mom inserted rolls at home. I hadn't paid attention. Here I was, 22 and doing it wrong. I was sure my ignorance was rooted in some failure in character. From then on, whenever unfurling toilet paper, I was highly aware of right versus wrong and couldn't help think there must be so much, so much more I didn't know.

There was the day I hadn't sewn a missing button on his shirt.

"Just be damn grateful I married you!" he hollered. "No one else ever would have!" Slamming every door in our apartment, he left. His words sent me reeling back to Mom standing in my bedroom, shaking a stalk of rhubarb: "If you don't learn to cook, run a home, no man will ever want you."

One morning Saul opened the refrigerator and spotted a beefsteak tomato so ripe its cap had split in two. He rolled the leaky vegetable in the palm of his hand, then looked at me, looked at the tomato, and back at me. Suddenly, with tremendous force, he pitched it across the breakfast table at the kitchen wall. Blood-red pulp with wrinkled skin, translucent seeds, dripped down white plaster, pooling onto the floor.

The room spun. I stared at the mess feeling waves of involuntary tremors. The tomato was me, my skin, my torn flesh puddling at my feet—despicable me staining the kitchen.

"Are you a child? From now on, check every bin!"

His rage hunched my back. While he stood ramrod straight, I stood bent over with downcast eyes, just as I had years ago when my father, gritting his teeth, demanded obedience. "You're only a child," he'd thunder. "What do you know? When you're matched with a man I know and approve of, there's permanence."

I wanted permanence. So I scrubbed tomato off the wall and floor, repeatedly scouring the same spots, seeing red everywhere, even when there wasn't any. I had botched up big time. It was all my fault. *Dimwitted—I'm dimwitted,* I told myself. *If I had checked the refrigerator, thrown out the rotten tomato, I wouldn't have driven him to this point.*

I now understood why no man would want me. It was clear: I knew nothing. I searched Saul's angry eyes as if to say, *Tell me more. Tell me who I am and who I should be so I can know.* For two years, that's where I lived: on a hill in Jerusalem, learning all that I was not. That I was worthless.

Chris had once said, "Every deficit creates an equal and opposite strength." I hadn't understood what she meant at the time and still didn't. But it certainly didn't apply to me. My deficits were obvious and many, but my strengths were nowhere to be found.

There was no *me* within me to consult. *Should there be?* I asked myself. *Or to be a cherished wife must I make sure an inner me never sprouts?* I dared not keep a journal for fear it would be found and read. If I had had the courage to write, I probably would have inked in secret script: *HELP! I made a mistake! Mashhad and New York should never have married.*

Eventually, like clockwork, every Saturday and only on Saturdays, I began experiencing sledgehammering migraines. They were so sharp-shooting that all I could do was tighten a kerchief around my head, swallow aspirin, darken the room, and lay motionless until forced to lunge out of bed and into the bathroom to retch into the toilet. Never before had I been a once-a-week Sabbath invalid besieged by migraines. I didn't get it. *Why is this happening? Do I have some sort of brain disorder? Hasn't Saul been saying so?* As I lay in bed, I thought of Pop. I wanted him with me, holding me up, bracing my forehead as I vomited. I wanted to hear him whisper, "Estaire, you're not bad. It's not your fault. Soon you'll be well."

I didn't tell a soul about my marriage—not fellow students in school, not neighbors in our building, not the few distant cousins who lived in outlying parts of Israel. I made sure to wear a happy mask. That, I was good at. However, my eyes never matched my smile.

Even though I felt terribly alone and scared of Saul, I didn't want Mom to know. If she found out I was crying myself to sleep, she'd be screaming bloody murder from Forest Hills rooftops and flying direct to Israel to bring me back home. Matrimonial misery is what she had and never wanted for me. I could hear her words: *I burn...I no vhant you burn.* I could never let her know I had failed at marriage. And it would destroy Pop. This problem was mine and mine alone to fix. Gone were the days of visiting Albert at Cornell, moseying through MoMA with David, battling with Pop to attend Barnard and live in a dorm, hearing an esteemed professor tell me I had promise. This was my life now, and I reminded myself again that I had chosen it. The only way to see it through was to seal memories and send them underground.

Jerusalem, dating back to the fourth millennium BCE, sits on a plateau between the Mediterranean and Dead Sea, elevated like a crown, surrounded by valleys. Every other day, I dragged my cloth cart down a rock-ribbed hill towards the nearby *shuk*.[2] On the way, I passed a blaze of ruby-red anemones, inhaled patches of eucalyptus, and walked beneath a canopy of pomegranate trees. Wandering the shuk's narrow lanes, stopping at favorite stands, I rummaged, carefully selecting, squeezing, smelling cantaloupes and eggplants, just as my mother would do. Fruits and vegetables displayed in rows of primary colors, a blistering sun, noisy hagglers, the overhanging stench of raw fish split wide open, Arab women heavily cloaked, faces concealed, doing their marketing.... It all brought Mom to mind—front and center. I went back in time to when she and Yocheved, hand-in-hand, hidden behind black chadors, ambled through open markets in Mashhad. I saw her as a girl, a child bride, living in a city where she never felt she belonged. And now, here I was. Place and time differed, but the feeling was the same. Choked by parallels, a few too many, I blunted my mind and stopped myself from thinking.

On a raw December day my husband told me to pay a call on Isaac, the carpenter we had hired to build us living room cabinets. I was instructed to first check on his progress, then hand him his monthly pay.

It was beginning to rain as I left. Wearing a thin winter coat, jeans, and sneakers, I briskly walked through Jerusalem's cobble-

2. *shuk* (Hebrew)—outdoor market

stone streets, steadying a black umbrella over my head. I had visited Isaac many times and was familiar with the labyrinthine path to his workshop. Holding a scrap of paper with his address on it, I made a left, then a right, walked 15 blocks, made another right and another right, certain I could find the way blindfolded. The sky darkened. Suddenly a cluster of clouds burst, releasing buckets of water. A fierce wind grabbed my umbrella, turning it inside out. I fought to flip it back and stay dry, but I couldn't. Torrential wind and rain whipped the spokes, cracking them one by one. My canvas sneakers filled with icy water as my dripping-wet hair flew around my head and clung to my face. I couldn't fight the winds and I couldn't find my way. Suddenly, I was lost. Every winding alley was identical to the last. Which one was Isaac's? The open garage, the bay he worked from, where was it? There were no street signs. No numbers. And all at once, the wrinkled slip of paper, pelted by rain, blew out of my hand.

"Isaac! Isaac!" I shouted. "Where are you?" No response. Just the sound of my own voice calling, echoing, bouncing off locked metal doors, and the howling rain and wind. Another black cloud cracked open and dumped its load on my head. My shoulders ached from trying to hold onto my umbrella. Pushed along by the wind, I sped through alleyways, not knowing where I was going. "Isaac!" Soaked, freezing, my mind a swampland, I ran, not running toward but fleeing, running away. Away. I wanted it all to end. I wanted *me* to end. I dropped the umbrella, my ankles caved, my knees collapsed, and I went down, my face smacking hard against wet cobblestones.

Coming out of a deep, dark slumber, I opened my eyes slowly. I could barely see. My mouth was parched. I was in bed with my wrists tightly strapped to the bedrails. Ever so slowly, as my eyes struggled to focus, I regained sight.

A tall, angular man in a white coat stood in front of me.

"Wake-up!" he commanded.

Behind him stood another man. I squinted at him. He stared back coldly.

"I'm Doctor Crone," the man in the white coat said. "I'm here with your husband." He consulted a chart he was holding. "Tell me your name and date of birth."

I locked my lips.

"Answer me," Dr. Crone demanded. "I need to know if you know who you are."

I remained silent.

"What's your name? Answer!"

Simmering blood heated my face.

"Answer me!"

I refused.

"I said, answer me!"

"Fuck you!" shot out from my mouth.

Dr. Crone was jolted backwards. My husband's eyes widened. I was as stunned as they were.

A dam had just broken. Someone had hijacked my vocal chords. Someone deep inside who didn't give a shit had taken control.

With clenched jaw, as if what he was about to do was medically indicated, Dr. Crone slapped me hard across the face.

"Give her morphine," he ordered, and walked out.

Later that day, I was discharged and sent home—back to the home I had been fleeing. ▨

CHAPTER 35

Scandal

I returned home, disappeared deeper into myself, saying nothing. I quit graduate school, attended to my domestic duties, remained at my husband's beck and call, feeling trapped. History had come full circle.

The success and recognition Saul was receiving as a rapidly rising architect didn't satisfy him. He felt confined and limited in Israel. After two years in Jerusalem, Saul decided we should return to the States. Wholeheartedly, I agreed. I wanted to end our marriage and knew it could be done more easily in America, but I kept these mutinous thoughts to myself.

In 1973 we were back in New York. I filed for divorce and, the next thing I knew, my migraines departed.

But my decision to divorce drove a knife through Pop's heart.

"Scandalous! Divorce is scandalous!" he said repeatedly, when I called my parents into the living room to tell them of my decision. "Estaire, don't! Americans divorce, Iranians don't. It will be a disgrace to our family. We will lose all *aberu*."

The rant was vintage Pop. Since every Iranian man wanted a virgin, my father was certain I would never again marry. Persian men believed inexperience made young girls deferential and much happier with their lot. The less a girl saw and knew, the more she was desired.

"Listen to me," Pop advised. "Men, even the most difficult, can be softened and changed. Your husband can be molded to your liking." Then he lowered his sagging eyes and said uneasily behind one hand, "It can all be done through sex."

I was aghast. He was suggesting sex for favors. Sex as a bargaining chip.

Like a smoldering brushfire, Mom burst into flames. "Stu-peed! Stu-peed talk!" she shouted. She jumped up, grabbed a Chivas Regal bottle from the liquor cabinet, and ran around the living room counterclockwise. "Estaire, don't leezen! Sex change no man!" She stopped, poured herself a tall drink, gripped the glass as if wanting to strangle it, and took a huge swig. "Estaire, I burn," she said, glowering at Pop. "I no vhant you burn!"

My father took to his bed, and once again, unshaven, in pajamas and robe, drowned in sorrow, mourning my demise.

Chafing against authority, braving all obstacles, Mom paid my legal fees with money she must have withdrawn from their joint account. Pop knew but said nothing; at the end of the day Mom always got her way. Now that I was tarnished goods, I had more freedom. I moved into a one-bedroom rental a few blocks away from my parents and worked for my brothers as a secretary and receptionist in their rug business. Mom frequently came by to fill my freezer with rich stews and slip me $20 bills, whispering, "Een-Joy"—reminding me of her Barnard visits. Defying husband, community, convention, she supported me, wanted me to have what she hadn't had—one more shot at happiness.

Different people at different times had mothered me in various ways: Albert, David, Mrs. Storch, Christine, Professor Novak. But now it was hard-nosed Mom. My fierce defender. She was the real deal, and I loved her for it.

There was a wide gap between her two front teeth—a portal allowing air to flow and spit to spray. As a young child I'd stare, imagining myself cradled in that space, claiming it as mine, harnessing its power and calling it home. With shut eyes, I'd pretend I was curled into a lap that lived in her mouth, somehow knowing, even then, that this mouth I feared would also fight to protect and defend me. Now it did.

Esther wasn't just my maternal grandmother's name but a name passed on in the Mashhadi community for thousands of years, dating back to Queen Esther. In my family, a long ancestral line of illiterate child brides married to first cousins, tending to home and hearth, food and family, stuttered to a stop with Mom and came to a full stop with me. Why? How did I escape the chador, bypass illiteracy, duck a latency-age marriage? Why was I the first Esther in our family to enter a classroom, much less college?

Ancient wheels turned and would have continued turning, if not for Mom. Staunchly, she stood behind me, backing my decision to divorce, turning a page in history, and bringing two millennia of female bondage to an end.

The Mashhadi communities in Kew Gardens and Forest Hills were appalled by the news. Nobody had ever heard of a Jewish-Mashhadi girl electing divorce. Gossip buzzed:

"It's because Estaire has an unfiltered mother—a mother with a latchless mouth!"

"Estaire never learned to bend and buckle in marriage. She discarded her husband because she's a college graduate. Over-educated. That's the problem."

The gossips were sure there would be crippling consequences. Rumors spread that, as a divorcée, I would be just a step away from becoming a girl gone wild, leading a reckless jezebel life.

Privately, I wondered if all this would come true. It was a changing of the guard, and in many ways I didn't know who I was or what the future held. I was new to myself.

I once again began writing in a journal: *What does it mean to claim me...to make me mine?* My self-description stirred confusion. I was a mix that didn't add up, a poly-hyphenated self: an Iranian-Mashhadi-American-Jewish-educated-divorced female. There were too many selves, in sync and at odds with one another, clashing cultures spliced together, causing commotion.

As a child, more than anything, I had wanted to be seen and known as American, with no trace of henna, rose water, or Farsi. Yet, within me lived two sparring spirits. When I stood among Iranians, I felt like a fraud. Yet in the company of non-Persian Americans, couplets from Ferdowsi's epic *Shahnameh* and Rumi's mystical verses thrummed through me. Ground beneath my feet kept shifting, throwing me off balance.

Being a Mashhadi Jew was also problematic. In the 1950s and '60s, Jews from the Middle East were regarded as inauthentic by European Jews. Even our celebration of *Sukkot*[1] was suspect.

When I was seven, my father, with the help of my brothers, assembled a beautiful *sukkah*[2] in our backyard in remembrance of the temporary dwellings Israelites had built for shelter during their 40 years

---

1. *Sukkot* (Hebrew)—Festival of Tabernacles
2. *sukkah* (Hebrew)—temporary hut, booth

crossing the desert. Ours was free-standing, built of wood, and roofed with cut tree branches. Albert had asked an artist-friend to decorate the four inner walls with hand-painted scenes from the Book of Exodus, including one of Moses receiving the Torah on Mount Sinai. Mom placed a table in the center with five folding chairs and adorned the interior with hanging pomegranates, green peppers, corn on the cob, and red apples. I was sure no one had a sukkah as stunning as ours.

That week, my Hebrew School teacher, in preparation for the holiday, asked our class, "Which of you have a sukkah in your backyard?" My hand proudly shot up. Ignoring the other students who had raised their hands, the teacher came over to me. "Is your sukkah kosher?" Before I could ask what he meant, he continued, "Can you see the stars through the branches of the roof? Is there an overhanging tree obstructing the sky? Of what are the walls made?"

Unable to answer his questions and certain I shouldn't have raised my hand, I gave him our home phone number so he could ask my parents directly.

Later that night, my teacher and a band of rabbis came to our home with flashlights. They had come to inspect our sukkah and make sure it was kosher.

We passed inspection, but after this self-appointed group of judges walked through and examined our sukkah, it somehow felt sullied. I broke down and cried. "Mom, I'm so sorry I raised my hand. I shouldn't have told them we have one. I'm so sorry."

"It's because we come from Iran," my mother seethed in Farsi. Mom called it Ashkenazi Supremacy. "They believe they're the only true Jews and we are false."

I didn't believe her at first, but by the time Sukkot ended, I did. My teacher didn't grill any of my classmates about their sukkahs, and he and the rabbis didn't visit any other homes.

And then there was that last dangling, gender-sensitive component of my multi-hyphenated self: female. Inside me lived two women: a near-mute, submissive, ornamental Persian female, honoring the past, adhering to the old ways, preserving aberu, deeply beholden to her Aminoff and Levi lineages; and her American twin, a whistleblower unconcerned with losing face, passionately disagreeing, unapologetic, saying it all, choosing her own path.

I was a hybrid through and through: a Yankee—with a Boukharian shepherd costume tucked in my closet.

At age 25, I ended my marriage and began afresh. ▨

CHAPTER 36

Second Chance

Mom had mixed feelings about divorce. She exhorted members of her Mashhadi baking crew to "Divorce the swine!" but was too bound by tradition and lacking in earning power to consider it for herself. Sorely mismatched and stuck in place, she nevertheless found the concept intriguing. She wasn't happy that I was divorcing, but she also didn't want me to "burn" as she had. And was ready to take on anyone who tried to make her, or me, feel bad about it.

Her chance came six months after my divorce, when Mom and Pop attended their next 950-guest Iranian wedding, fully aware that other Mashhadis would be spreading stories about the destruction of my marriage and calling Mom the instigator. She was prepared. With hair bound in a tight French twist, her torso wrapped in jade-green Oscar de la Renta, her ears, neck, wrists adorned with emeralds, she entered the hotel ballroom with Pop looking like a high-society swan. Sequined wives sidled up, crowded around her, eager to witness her shame. After exchanging pleasantries, Mom swerved from chitchat, threw out her chest, and with over-arching confidence said in Farsi, "I have my second life all planned out. After I die, I'm going to return to this world as an American. I'll go to school, become a successful lawyer, and marry a modern American man. They make the best husbands. They're open-minded, smart, happy, and devoted to their wives. Iranian men are mules. They're meant only for fools."

Faces coated with thick foundation creased as women nervously giggled.

Pop, standing nearby in a tux and curling twisted collar, grabbed her elbow and blasted in Farsi, "Be ashamed of yourself. You just insulted every woman here!"

She pulled away. Tidying a stray hair, she enunciated clearly: "*Mikhastam.*[1]" Then, with a sassy shrug and surplus energy, she sashayed away, leaving her fragrance behind.

Mom thoroughly understood the benefits of divorce.

"Estaire, your life story is about a second chance," she often said in Farsi. "You've been given a second chance—a chance I never had."

But when I told Mom I had decided to go to graduate school, live off student loans, and eventually have a career of my own, she grew prickly. This wasn't what she had in mind. The more self-sufficient I became, the more she felt betrayed. The fact that she had been supportive through college and my divorce didn't mean she wanted a truly independent daughter; and the fact that she fought furiously to live her life as freely as possible didn't mean she wanted me to do the same. One had nothing to do with the other.

Mom gave herself license to wander without me through Manhattan's boutiques and museums, attend Broadway matinees, swim weekly laps, and meet up with her Iranian cohorts at The Plaza's Palm Court to sip flutes of champagne. But if she heard I had done any of the above without her, I was in serious trouble. "You are mean, meez-ra-bull," she'd lambaste me. "Enemy. You are my beegest enemy." Her tongue-lashings were followed by weeks of silent treatment, my punishment for having broken a cardinal contract. I was expected to make up for the mother who died and left her behind by always being present, available, and never going anywhere without her. Despite her need for independence, I was to stay put, orbiting her the way a mommy revolves around her newborn, constantly there.

She wanted me always to be on call, ready to nurse, ready to soothe, never separate or apart. She would remind me that her mother's name was Esther. Sitting cross-legged on the floor, tailoring her newly bought outfits, she'd say with a mouth full of straight pins, "Estaire, whenever you buy clothing, you must buy for me, too—remember, you are my mother." She would remind me that her mother had named her Hana after her mother's older sister, Hana, her father's first wife, who had died in childbirth. With historical certainty, Mom would add, "Hana and Esther were sisters, so

1. *Mikhastam.* (Persian/Farsi)—I wanted to; I meant to; I did it on purpose.

you're not only my mother but also my sister. You have two responsibilities. Never forget!"

When I was a child, she'd rail in Farsi, "If you finish food on your plate, you're loyal." Feeling forced to eat, I ate less. Later, when I was old enough to attend social events, she warned, "When you talk to women I hate, you're my enemy." Already uncomfortable speaking, I spoke less. I was loyal when sitting beside her in synagogue and disloyal if I allowed anyone to sit between us. The loyals and disloyals mounted, and by the end of each day, disloyal won out. If I went away for a weekend, she'd scold, "How could you leave me behind, all alone with your boring father? You should take me with you wherever you go." Now it became, "Why do you want to go to school? Why do you need to work? You're poor? You need money? I'll give you money. If you truly loved me you'd stay home and be with me."

I was stuck on the horns of a dilemma. I couldn't win. Handing over my reclaimed life felt deadly, while insisting on having one meant I was heartless and cruel.

If Mom called and was greeted by my answering machine, the message she left would be: "Estaire, vhair you now? A-LAZ-KAH? You nevair home."

Alaska was code for traitor. You're not where I want you to be.

One evening, I returned her call. "Mom, I just came home. What's up?"

In a steely voice she replied, "Too late," and slammed the phone.

Thinking something might really be wrong, I ran over and found her in the kitchen, sorting rice. She coldly stared and said, "Vhair name tag. I no know you."

Eyeball to eyeball, I confronted her. "I live only a few blocks away. I call, I visit, and we go out together. But, Mom, I can't give up my life and spend the rest of my days sitting by the phone, waiting for your calls."

With a jutting jaw, she cut to the core. "Vie not?"

I tried to remind myself that Mom's feelings of abandonment and betrayal predated my birth and had nothing to do with me. Whenever she widened her milky eyes, peered into mine, scanned my cheeks, nose, lips, and hair, I felt her searching for her phantom birth mother. As a child, I longed to rid myself of the *me* that stood in her way. What was I supposed to do with the *me* she didn't need or want? Sometimes I stood silently and withdrew into myself, saying nothing, trying to make myself invisible and let the Esther she was searching for, the one who had birthed her, take my place. At other times I'd hole up in my bedroom, trying to avoid her altogether. During my hormonal teens, I reacted savagely. "Get out of my face! I'm not who you want!" I'd blurt as I ran out of the house. Outbursts that left me more guilt-ridden than giddy. Now, I was more understanding, but also more aware of how dangerous she could be when she felt her needs weren't being met. I swung back and forth, lionizing and demonizing her. She was a giant, multilimbed octopus—a gnarled, mythic creature, twisting and grabbing, horrifying and mesmerizing.

During the two years I worked for my brothers, I also attended therapy sessions with Mr. Hanse, a psychoanalyst who had been recommended by a trusted friend. Therapy, like divorce, was unheard of in our community, so I kept it a secret and didn't tell my family. Initially, I went to better understand why I had mindlessly married, and why I hadn't known my own needs. I was terrified that if I didn't examine my behavior I might repeat it and make the same mistakes again. Over time, the work deepened and turned to my attachment to family and fear of doing anything that would threaten these bonds.

Mr. Hanse was an extraordinary listener—supportive, noncritical, adept at knowing when to remain silent and when to probe. Step by step, with his help, I began to hear myself more clearly, and trust the person I was becoming. Was I unconsciously attracted to men like my father? If so, why? Were there parts of him I admired and valued more than I realized? Were there parts of me that were drawn to traits I abhorred? Mr. Hanse helped me find words to clarify fuzzy feelings and enable me to begin speaking with confidence and conviction.

Part of the work focused on helping me figure out my next step. I didn't want to continue being a secretary, nor did I want to remarry. I had loved studying art history, both at Barnard and at Hebrew University, but I was disinterested in academia and no longer wanted a career in that field. The work Mr. Hanse was doing spoke to me. I found it life-altering and began wondering if I could give others the gift he was giving to me—the insights, self-awareness, and self-confidence to live a more authentic, satisfying life. In some ways, I thought, analyzing patients wasn't so different from analyzing paintings. Both involve studying surfaces while exploring what lies beneath, hidden in the subconscious.

My therapist felt I had what it takes and encouraged me to look into MSW programs. I could begin my training there, he said, and later pursue postgraduate psychoanalytic training.

So I did.

I was accepted into NYU's Graduate School of Social Work. After earning my master's, I did post-graduate training at The New York School for Psychoanalytic Psychotherapy and Psychoanalysis, better known as NYSPP, in Manhattan. I supported myself through five years of study with savings and student loans. It wasn't easy, but I made ends meet.

My parents couldn't understand this newfound passion of mine, but they didn't interfere. And for that I was grateful. Occasionally, Mom would ask me what I was learning and then rapidly change the subject, not really wanting to know. Talking about subconscious fears and drives spooked her. Pop, on the other hand, shocked me by suddenly exhibiting pride. He boasted and bragged to his Persian friends and business associates, introducing me with great pleasure at gatherings and events as "Doctor Amini." It wasn't true; I wasn't a doctor. But he reveled in saying I was. Maybe, in order to make peace with the direction my life was taking, he had to turn me into some sort of Albert Schweitzer, the doctor *he* had always wanted to become.

It was during my last round of post-graduate training and the beginning of my clinical career that I experienced a stepping into myself—a second incarnation. As a psychoanalytic psychotherapist in training, I learned to listen for the subconscious—its concealed voice—and shine a light, illuminating the disguised and buried. I learned to help patients know themselves, dive into submerged realms, and examine fears, truths, and memories.

Exposure to Pop's strain of silence had had its effect on me. I had seen it feed on itself, watched it grow, felt it trying to infect me, turn me into a "carrier." Siding with speech, I worked on myself first, then applied what I learned to helping others articulate the unarticulated, create order out of confusion, explore the foreign recesses of their minds, and not be afraid of what they discovered. I worked on separating fantasy from reality, examining assumptions, preconceptions, conjectures, distortions, self-sabotaging impulses, and self-limiting beliefs. I discovered the power and possibility of words and learned that more language means more life.

Helping patients free themselves and grow became my calling. And as they grew, I grew as well, discovering the power of one—me within me—forging my own voice. ▨

CHAPTER 37

Ira

While attending graduate school, I socialized, met men, and dated in a wary and extremely discerning manner. I no longer trusted what I saw, and suspected there was a Mr. Hyde inside every Dr. Jeckyll. In the midst of my final year of classes, field placements, papers and exams, my dearest and closest friend, Lin, insisted on introducing me to a special friend of hers named Ira. "I just feel you two will hit it off," she said.

I was reluctant, but she was persistent. Eager for me to meet him, Lin decided to throw a Saturday night party in her Rego Park apartment so I could casually check him out without feeling pressured. "He's on the shy side," she told me, "so it'll be up to you to go over and introduce yourself. But I'm sure you're going to like him. He's really smart and has a terrific sense of humor. And he has a big heart."

About a half an hour into the evening Ira arrived. Lin signaled me from afar. *That's him! Go get him!*

He was thin, of average height, with dark, thick, chin-length hair—a popular style then—and wire-rim glasses. His hazel eyes looked gentle. I introduced myself and, immediately, the conversation took off. Ira was easy to engage. As we talked and laughed, I learned he was Jewish, had grown up in Brooklyn, was the middle of three brothers, was one year older than I, studied psychology at Brooklyn College, was now working in advertising and marketing for a large lighting company, and had never been married. A good listener who asked many questions, Ira learned as much about me that night as I did about him. Lin was right. I felt a visceral connection from the get-go. Ira did, too. A few days later he called and asked me out. After that first date we were inseparable.

This Ashkenazi American with no hint of Persian fumes was unlike any man I knew. He was smart, calm, even-keeled, with a wicked sense of humor. Six months into our relationship, Ira told his parents about me and took me home to meet them. The moment I stepped into their Sheepshead Bay living room, his short, thin, gray-haired mother ran to me, wrapped her arms around my waist, and squeezed hard. Teary-eyed, she kissed my cheeks, took both my hands, led me to her couch, and sat down beside me. "Ira has told us so much about you," she whispered, her hazel eyes, the same shade as her son's, shining. "We already adore you." It didn't matter to her or to Ira's dad that I was a divorcée of Iranian descent. All that mattered was that their son loved me and I made him happy. Ira had told me his mother's first name was also Hannah, the same as my mother's though spelled differently. But this Hannah was affectionate, uncomplicated, with no hidden agendas—nothing like Mom. Ira's dad was more reserved but also nothing like Pop. He had the same warm manner as his son. I could see Ira's parents enjoyed one another and were a compatible couple who didn't engage in angry explosions or ugly fights. Visiting them was a pleasure, and whenever Ira suggested it I was game.

Introducing Ira to my folks was a different story. The first time I brought him home, he respectfully sat by Pop's side in silence, intuiting that Pop should be the one to decide whether they spoke or not, what they talked about, and even what they should think about a chosen topic of conversation. Ira abided by my father's unspoken rules. He knew not to refute, not to challenge, even when my brothers disagreed with Pop and even when Pop was glaringly wrong. He understood my father's need for honor and gave it bountifully, never feeling diminished or short-changed. As for Mom, he found her endearing and fondly offered her all the space she needed, to be and say whatever she chose. He gently sidestepped their brawls and chase scenes, remained serene in the midst of the chaos and clamor, while I, struggling to contain myself, turned from pink to purple. Seamlessly, he stepped into their world, savored Mom's Ghormeh Sabzi, danced to their tambourines, picked up Farsi, and decided that he preferred our traditional Persian *Seders*[1] to his own Ashkenazi ones.

---

1. *Seder* (Hebrew)—ceremonial meal held on the first night or first two nights of Passover, commemorating the exodus of the Jews from Egypt

Swiftly embraced by my parents and brothers, Ira passed tests he wasn't even aware of taking. Baffled by his ease, I asked how he was able to so graciously glide in and so tenderly handle Mom and Pop. He smiled. "They're not my parents. It's that simple."

It wasn't that simple. It had more to do with his sensibility. He was a natural—strong and centered, able to put his needs aside and accommodate others.

We fell in love. A few months after we met, Ira proposed, but I wasn't ready. For the next two years we shuttled between apartments, before finally deciding to rent one together in Manhattan. I didn't tell my parents and kept my Queens apartment for propriety's sake. But I knew I needed to see him under all kinds of circumstances, find out if he had a violent, vicious, tomato-throwing side before I could consider marriage. Because he knew all about my past, Ira understood and agreed. After a year of living together, I was certain he truly was the person he seemed to be. There were no hidden monsters.

In October 1980, we took the plunge. A simple, low-key ceremony at a nearby Manhattan synagogue was all we needed. After our wedding, relatives and friends, 30 in total, accompanied us back to our apartment for wine and French pastries. How right it felt.

Now, at the end of each Shabbat visit, my father placed his hands on his son-in-law's head, and with shut eyes, blessed. He then steepled his fingers and whispered in my ear, "Estaire, he's a very good man. *Najib*. No man is like Ira. God bless him." On one occasion, he gave Ira a bear hug and said with a chuckle, "With one more letter, your name becomes Iran. Maybe that's why I like you so much."

My father was right. No man was like Ira. Mom and Pop's war-torn marriage would not become ours. From the start, Ira offered a serenity I had never known. As I grew and advanced professionally, treating patients, supervising therapists, and teaching at an analytic institute, it was Ira who beamed, gently coaxing me on. I was no longer in hiding, no longer reading and writing under the sheets with a flashlight in hand. Our lives were well lit, lived happily out in the open.

And yet, inside me was a whirlpool of fear having less to do with matrimony and more to do with motherhood. By now, Albert and David were both dads: David had two little girls, and Albert had a daughter and son. I loved their wives and adored my nieces and nephew. But that didn't mean I felt ready to have children of my own.

Feeling unmoored, I doubted I could mother in ways I had never been mothered. My married female friends who were having children were able to reach back and draw on how their moms had raised them, making minor tweaks here and there, while I was stuck without map or manual. How I envied women with blueprints in their hands. Mothers who had had mothers. Women whose own mothers had felt whole, who could care for infants and didn't themselves need daily infant care. Who didn't expect their daughters to sit by the phone, waiting to be called. Mothers who watched their words, fretted over consequences, and could say: "I'm sorry. I was wrong." Moms who coped with conflict, were steadfast, and didn't disappear for days, like a 14-year-old runaway bride.

The more I reviewed my past, the more I felt there should be no drawing from or tweaking of my upbringing. But so much filters down from generation to generation intentionally and unintentionally. Could I vigilantly listen for echoes from the past? If I became a mom, would my tongue morph into Mom's? Would I mimic her and trade in self-restraint for full release? Would I slam phones, call my child a traitor for having independent wants? Would I use Mom's silent treatment as a ploy to bend a child to my will? And what about Pop's dread of the outside world? Would his thick fog of fear pass to my children through me? I came from a culture, a tradition of duplicity, descended from ancestors who juggled aboveground and underground lives, posing as one thing while being another, be it Jews passing as Muslims, women concealed behind chadors, or, as in my case, daughters secretly reading beneath the sheets. Could I be the good ancestor who brought duplicity to an end?

My brothers were fathers now. I watched them with their children and didn't see any fog of fear, silence, and dread hovering over them. Was I wrong to think I needed to reject all aspects of my childhood? Were parts of it worth embracing? Might some of it be valuable? Perhaps precious and priceless? Worth preserving and not discarding in haste?

I wrestled with my fears, shared them with trusted friends, and, of course, confessed them to Ira. Over time, I began to see that, although my parents had huge flaws, they also had remarkable strengths: Pop's fierce protectiveness, his Schweitzer-esque need to heal, and his deep love of nature. Mom's fearlessness and outspokenness, her determination to stay connected to me during my college years, and the way she had supported me through my divorce.

And I deeply admired their bold and daring decision to leave Iran and begin anew. My parents were far from perfect, but they had done their best to give their children a better life. The more I grew and the stronger I became in my own sense of self, the more I was able to forgive and value them.

I also drew on all I learned during my professional training. Many of my courses delved into early psychic development and what infants and children need to grow up healthy and well-adjusted. I drank it all in and began to think the lessons I had learned from my own upbringing could actually work in my favor, making me more finely attuned to my own children and to what I, as a mother, needed to give. These fortifying thoughts helped me feel better prepared for the challenges ahead.

I had no doubt Ira would be a great dad and would be ready when I was ready. One year after our marriage I became pregnant, and the following year, in July 1982, I gave birth to our son. We named him Aaron, a biblical name we both loved that was also the name of my mother's brother, who had died when I was seven—my childless Uncle Aaron, who had encouraged Mom to come to America and had deeply loved me and my brothers.

As a first-time mom, I relied on vigilance, self-scrutiny, and self-invention. Catching impulses as they arose, I'd examine and label them as Mom's, Pop's, or belonging to my newly renovated self. My mantra became: *I self-monitor, self-edit, choose restraint over verbal spillage.*

I studied subway moms, supermarket moms, Central Park moms; no one escaped my scrutiny as I hunted noteworthy skills. Other women were emulating what had come before while I was scrambling to concoct a present tense.

Day by day, as Aaron grew into a healthy and happy child, I became more relaxed and confident. Five years after his birth, in November of 1987, Ira and I had our second child, a girl. We named her Miriam, another biblical name we adored. We knew that, in the Torah, Miriam was the sister of Aaron and Moses. We hoped our Aaron and Miriam would always have the same tight bond the biblical brother and sister shared.

Snuggling my children in the crook of my arms, I searched their luminous eyes and pursed lips. Peering into the center of their pupils, I wanted to find them and no one else. A switch I couldn't turn off. Could they feel it? Did they know why?

Could I be the mother I had wanted? Making calculated shifts with legacy in mind, I felt an evolutionary responsibility to think carefully about what to pass on, what to chop off, and what to bury. I worked hard at erecting boundaries, encouraging noise, fanning speech, embracing dispute, fostering locomotion, and offering my children a lap with staying power.

In the process, I discovered that one of Mom's many hand-me-downs was a shared quest: We each were a mother in search of a mother. All along I had been convinced that we had nothing in common, that we were diametric opposites, only to realize that, at core, we both came from a place of hunger. It was a humbling insight that brought me closer to Mom. And more than anything, it made me determined not to pass this inheritance down to my children—this legacy of hollowed-out loss. ◆

PART SIX

BIBI

CHAPTER 38

Persian Paranoia

Pop, obsessed with pedophiles, had begun protecting me from child molesters, kidnappers, and rapists long before he ever had to chase off Bill, the postal clerk. When I was a child, he instructed me never to trust good-looking men because they had been molested during their childhood and would want to do to children what had been done to them. He told me not to trust ugly men because they had undoubtedly been repeatedly rejected by women and consequently would turn to children for sexual gratification. Dwarfs couldn't be trusted because they were the same size as children, which automatically turned them into pedophiles.

The arrival of grandchildren only heightened his fears. When I became a mom, I was further warned not to trust men who enjoy being with children or men who pretend not to be interested in children because they are, in fact, the most interested.

My father's teeth-grinding paranoia made all men suspect, with no one but him left to trust.

"Pop," I asked, "how can every man be a sexual pervert?"

With short square thumbs he slowly rubbed his temples. "In Iran I saw *plenty.*"

Ira and I had moved to a larger apartment in Manhattan after we had our second child. Mom, determined to live near me, twisted Pop's arm and forced him to give up Queens and buy a two-bedroom apartment a few blocks away from us. Now that they lived in our neighborhood and were able to spend more time with our son and daughter, the frequency and intensity of Pop's pedophilia alerts dramatically increased.

One Sunday afternoon, Ira, the children, and I paid them a visit. As we entered their apartment, Mom proudly handed me a large shopping bag filled with leefs. She had just finished crocheting batches of washcloths in a range of sizes to fit each growing grandchild's hand and wanted me to store them in my linen closet and be fully stocked with enough backup leefs, in every dimension and color, to last us a lifetime. Pop, seated in his winged armchair, ran through his list of predators, warning me of pedophiles disguised as: mailmen, window washers, policemen, doormen, bus drivers, pediatricians, plumbers, electricians, and any other male worker or professional I might happen to encounter during the week. He then tightly clasped his hands in his lap and fell silent, impatient for us to leave. While my mother had an insatiable hunger for company, Pop, as always, craved solitude—his aphrodisiac. It wasn't personal. It had nothing to do with who came by or what was being discussed. My father silently suffered in anyone's company. He found his grandchildren sweet, but one quick glance was more than enough. Every five minutes during our stay, he lifted his cuff and studied his watch, letting us know he thought we should be in our own home and not in his. I was only too familiar with Pop's nonverbal messages, but on this day I chose to ignore them.

My mother, tingling with excitement, spilled the same carton of toys I used to play with onto their Persian Sarouk carpet and got down on all fours with six-year-old Aaron and one-year-old Miriam to stack blocks. Pop instantly sprung from his chair and walked off toward the bathroom with a can of insecticide.

"*Babai Albairt!*" Mom called after him. "Seet down! Een-joy A-ha-rone and Meer-yum."

Pop shut his ears, spraying bathrooms with a vengeance.

After we'd finished eating, Ira took the children home, and I stayed behind to talk to Pop. I wanted to get to the root of his pedophile fixation. He had said more than once, "In Iran I saw *plenty*." What had he seen?

I waited until he had settled back into his armchair and asked. He stiffened, but slowly, with a bit of pressure, history leaked.

In the 1930s and '40s, he said, homes in Mashhad did not have bathtubs or showers. Men gathered in hammams for their weekly wash.

Mom served tea and sat down beside me on the sofa.

"I saw *plenty* there." Pop's pitch had heightened.

I needed hard facts. "And what did you see?"

His eyes snapped shut.

"Enough!" he belted, crashing his hands on his thighs. "Change subject!"

Mom, on the other hand, had only warm memories of her visits to Persian hammams. Whenever she talked about them, her eyes glowed. On days designated for women, she said, they came in droves with baskets of chicken, bread, pickles, pistachios, sunflower seeds, dayerehs, and overripe gossip. Unleashing their tongues, women sang, danced, ate, drank, exchanged rumors, created new ones, and even decided on prearranged marriages. She closed her eyes and leaned back on the sofa, dreamily recalling the ancient stone walls and vaulted, womblike domed ceilings, all softly lit by oil lamps and skylights.

This was much too much talk for Pop. With hands covering his ears, he marched into his bedroom.

Mom kept reminiscing. She spoke of the women who threw water on hot tiles to create steam, and the *dallaks*[1] who powerfully scrubbed their backs with *kisehs*.[2] After scalps were soothingly massaged and shampooed, mounds of henna were heaped on top of each woman's head. With piled hair turning red and henna running down their faces, they jabbered for hours. Comfortably naked, bearing breasts and vaginas, they spoke of demanding husbands and bedroom dramas. My mother said she often held court because her stories about Pop trumped all others. The dallaks would quietly eavesdrop as they attended to palms of hands, soles of feet, softening and smoothing them with *sang e pa*[3] just like the worn pumice stones I had seen dangling from the shower faucet in our American bathroom as I was growing up. Mom sighed longingly, remembering. She could still feel the hard scrubs.

Hammam parties were brought to a close with the women seated in a circle on the floor, around the ghelyoon. Each sucked in a deep puff of tobacco, then lazily passed it along. It was their Women's Day: cracking pistachios, slapping dayerehs, and telling dirty jokes—leaving husbands, etiquette, and domestic chores behind.

Mom lowered her voice as she continued.

1. *dallak* (Persian/Farsi)—hired washerwoman
2. *kiseh* (Persian/Farsi)—rough-surfaced, rectangular washing mitt
3. *sang e pa* (Persian/Farsi)—pumice stone

"Hammam dee-fair-rent for heem," she said, nodding toward Pop's closed bedroom door. "He no par-ty in hammam. He rush in, rush out."

"Why?" I asked.

Mom switched to Farsi. Two dirty old loincloths hung in front of the hammam's entrance on Men's Days, she said. "Disgraceful! Muslims should be ashamed of themselves."

"Why?"

"Estaire, imagine hanging old bras to announce Women's Day. They were advertising sex."

On Men's Days, Mom said, my father would zip through steam rooms, be quickly scrubbed by a male dallak, and then race home. On days assigned to men, the hammam became a clandestine meeting place for males of all persuasions. A place where young boys, teenagers, and grown men lounged, steamed, were massaged, and bathed: an erotic haven for men seeking men or young boys. Male same-sex relations had a complicated history in Persian culture. In 1925, the year my mother was born, homosexuality was declared a crime punishable by death, and men began restricting these activities to places like hammams.

According to my mother, men met in the bathhouse, sexually engaged, and after "spilling their seed," went home to their wives and children.

She paused, as if unsure whether to continue. She cupped her hands over her mouth and spoke through her fingers. On Men's Days, pedophiles were also on the loose, always with nails well-manicured, looking to fondle an innocent, unsuspecting penis. Mom shook her head, stretched open the collar of her dress and spat into her cleavage—*teh, teh, teh.*

Twisting and strangling her hankie, she continued. "These pedophiles would give little boys fistfuls of candy and lure them into dark corridors."

"Mom, how do you know all of this?"

"Your father would return home, trembling, and sometimes utter a word or two. Other husbands told their wives everything they saw, and these wives told me." She shook her head. "Trust me, I know."

Mom scrunched up her nose. "Your father said that when he saw clumps of semen float to the top of a pool, he'd turn around and come straight home."

I had now been told more than I cared to know.

"That's why when your brothers were young, your father would tell me to take them to the hammam with me on Women's Day, so they would be safer in female company."

Poor Pop. I wondered what he had seen and never revealed. I wondered if any men at the bathhouse had ever victimized or tried to victimize him. I couldn't ask Mom, and I knew I could never ask Pop. But just knowing this much helped explain his all-consuming distrust of the outside world and fears for his grandchildren. New-found compassion gurgled within me. I no longer scoffed. I understood, at least a bit.

CHAPTER 39

Gin Rummy

Mom kept a deck of cards in her handbag—in truth, two decks, deeply buried beneath keys, a can of pepper spray, Fendi wallet, comb, Chanel lipstick, pack of Wrigley's Doublemint chewing gum, and lace hankies. She said she needed to be prepared because she never knew when a couple of decks would come in handy.

Sitting cross-legged on her Persian Sarouk carpet, she was teaching five-year-old Miriam to play gin rummy. With matching intensity they each studied their hand, rearranged fanned-out cards, and carefully concealed sets from each other. While they shuffled and dealt, I listened to my mother invent outlandish stories with case-hardened confidence, just to keep her granddaughter doubled over, laughing. She repeated a tale she'd often told me as a child about the gorilla that attempted to kidnap her off of a train in India. In the version she told Miriam, it was a talking, love-struck gorilla trying to court her in broken Persian and English. I watched my daughter's thick blond ponytail, tied up in ribbons, bob and bounce with delight. Mom's theatrics kept Miriam laughing hysterically.

They were sitting, barefooted, on the same hand-knotted, vegetable-dyed Sarouk that I, as a child, had sat on. I remembered sprawling out on that carpet at age two, drooling saliva, stroking the thick wool, hypnotized by the mystifying patterns shimmering in Queens sunlight. Jacks and marbles, houses of cards, plastic Pick-Up Sticks, wooden alphabet blocks, and, later, high school textbooks were all pushed against the sturdy Persian pile as I stretched out and read. Like Mom and Pop, these earth-toned carpets were Iranian immigrants, uprooted and relocated, belonging to another place and time. They lay beneath me as I breathed in their confident geometrics and wistful florals.

Miriam, a hardy, happy kindergartener, had already completed two years of nursery school. So different from my early childhood. I had waited five restless years to finally enter school. Preschool wasn't common when I was a child; instead, children hung loose, shadowing their mothers. Mom and I would ride the subway to Delancey Street, shopping for Sabbath shoes, kosher meat, and dill pickles. We filled loads of time rummaging through Woolworth's. At home, days dragged as I learned to color within the lines, listened to nursery rhymes from scratchy records, and played with Jekyll and Hyde, my twin turtles.

When Mom sensed boredom she shot out of her steamy kitchen like a burly cannonball and squatted next to me on our Persian carpet with a drawing pad and crayon. "Vee now do art. Seet veet mee." She'd doodle stick-figured chickens with spread apart legs, releasing long trails of droppings, then cluck loudly, adding soundtrack to animation. I belly-laughed until I thought I would burst. This full extent of her drawing skills always left me clamoring for more.

As if she had read my mind, Mom reached for a pad and began drawing for Miriam the same stick-figured chickens she had once drawn for me, with spread legs and irregular droppings coming out of rear ends, and began clucking. Miriam rolled on the carpet kicking her legs uncontrollably, laughing with her feet.

I stood in my mother's living room admiring my blond-haired, silky-skinned daughter, with her large, hazel, almond-shaped eyes. Gazing at Miriam's smooth cheeks triggered another early memory of watching my mother through my curtain of overgrown bangs as she performed her celebrated role in our Kew Gardens émigré circle. Mom was the charismatic and talented hair-plucker who threw lavish, all-female *band andazan*[1] parties for soon-to-be brides. Using a special technique she had learned in Mashhad that involved biting one end of a twisted thread, pressing the other looped end against the skin and yanking, Mom tweezed bridal brows, mustaches, chins, cheeks, underarms, bellies, and sometimes ventured south of the border, transforming hairy virgins into soft and silky sirens for their fortunate grooms.

1. *band andazan* (Persian/Farsi)—all-female, prenuptial hair-removal party for the bride

Plates of *noghl*,[2] vats of *sharbat*,[3] saffron rice, stews, homemade cakes, pastries, and caramelized almonds always adorned her band andazan tables. Women slipped off their shoes and danced bare-footed on our Persian rugs, reliving bygone days in Mashhad.

One weekday, years later, weighed down by high school physics, calculus, and world history textbooks, I came home to a band andazan in progress. I found Mom, the designated percussionist, slapping her dayereh, pounding her palms, and wiggling her hips to the beat. One by one, she dragged each female into the center of the circle, insisting they dance to her slick tempo, smacking her tambourine so emphatically she'd forget to breathe. Spotting me as I slid my bookbag off my shoulder, she handed me a glass of sharbat and yelped, "Dance!" Unable to escape, I was hauled in nervously against my will.

Defending her own aggressive nature, she said, "Estaire, you need be tuff." I watched her palms leave sweat stains on our goat-skinned dayereh and bashfully shuffled my feet, rotated my wrists, followed her frothy lead, giving *tough* a try.

Between ladling stews and beating drums, Mom, an uncanny impressionist, made the women laugh as she nailed Queen Elizabeth, Nikita Khrushchev, and our local rabbi. At the end of each band andazan party, she would pull me aside, look up at the ceiling, spread open her arms and say, "Pleez God...Sum day I do dees for my daugh-tair... and her daugh-tair." I would nod in agreement just to see her eyes glisten.

Mom never did do it for me. I had grown up an American girl, shaving my own legs and underarms since adolescence. Watching Mom and Miriam play, I was grateful that my prayers for an un-hairy daughter had also been answered.

Now, here I was, admiring Miriam, knowing she would never see this bigger-than-life side of her grandmother, much less receive her depilatory services. In some ways, a sad thought. But I also knew Miriam was being spared having to witness Mom's fitful moods and be subjected to her twisted truths. Now that my mother had aged and mellowed a bit, Miriam wouldn't be exposed to either her deathly dark or her blindingly bright sides. The present was muting the past. And I was comforted knowing that what my daughter was experiencing today was a far better version of Mom.

2. *noghl* (Persian/Farsi)—Persian taffy
3. *sharbat* (Persian/Farsi)—sweet, chilled beverage flavored with fruits and rose water

An ice-cream truck chimed through an open window, jolting me back to the present. Sucking hard candies with soft fillings, Miriam and her grandmother were pursing their lips, arching their eyebrows, and cackling over their cards.

"Bibi, I won!" Miriam squealed, laying down three perfect sets.

"Yezz...verrie goood," Mom replied half-heartedly, and insisted on a rematch. They took a brief break as Mom cut us each a thick slice of walnut cake. I sat at the dining table with mine, and they settled back on the carpet with theirs. After taking big bites, they began their next round.

Miriam vigorously shuffled, dealt ten cards to Mom and herself, placing each card facedown. Suddenly, overcome with urgency, she popped to her feet.

"Bibi, I have to go to the bathroom."

"Go, sveetie. I vait for you. Go, goood girl. I loave you."

Thrilled that my mother and my daughter were having such fun, my eyes followed Miriam toward the bathroom and then returned to Mom, only to see her reach under her skirted thigh and pull out a second deck of cards. After selecting the cards she needed, she slipped the spare pack back under her buttocks.

Feeling doused by buckets of ice water, I sprung to my feet.

"Mom, you're cheating! What's wrong with you? Miriam's only five years old."

She deflated, then majestically reinflated. Talking through one side of her mouth, she eyed me hostilely. "Vie you hate me? You alvays tink I cheat. I nevair cheat!"

That quick, she was back, the Mom I had grown up with: marginally literate, driving to and from Idlewild Airport, purchasing Oscar de la Rentas under false pretenses, all after growing up in Iran, passing as Muslim while secretly living the life of a Jew. Duplicity, tons of examples, came rushing back.

I nevair cheat! Had she really just said that?

I used to believe that in order to stop lies they had to be exposed. But after years of witnessing my mother's dishonesty and distortions, I knew that, with her, it wasn't that simple, and I fell back on a conclusion I had reached years earlier. To her, it wasn't lying. These fabrications were artifacts, archaeological remains of her life in Mashhad—deeply engrained habits and impulses, tools that helped her survive.

Miriam cheerfully returned from the bathroom, sat down and

picked up her cards. Once again they laughed, shuffled cards, drew, and made sets.

When my mother won this rigged round, Miriam jumped into her grandmother's lap and kissed the crook of her neck, applauding.

"Bibi, you won, you won! That's great!" Miriam sang. She jumped up and danced a little jig.

I marveled at Miriam's innocence, her trust, her unquestioning belief that Bibi was telling her the truth. I vowed again that our family's legacy of fear, suspicion, and its ghostly call for duplicity would stop with me. 🔲

CHAPTER 40

Outnumbered

Pop distrusted all doctors. "They want you sick and make sure you are," he claimed. "Doctors manufacture problems just so they can be paid. It's a business—a moneymaking business. The reason I'm so healthy is because I stay far away from all of them."

For more than half a century, Pop's cynical outlook seemed to work. He remained strong and vigorous, never in need of a dentist, cardiologist, pulmonologist, or any other medical specialist, and completely dodged the world of medicine, faring quite well.

However, when he turned 87, he began experiencing an array of aches and pains. After weeks of gentle persuasion, Pop allowed me to take him to a physician. He agreed to have a thorough exam and permitted the attending nurse to draw vials of blood. When we returned the following week to learn the test results, Pop remained in the waiting room while I met with the doctor.

A large, ruddy hematologist wearing a white lab coat paced from desk to window to desk, studying a chart he was holding, as I sat in a chair watching and waiting.

"I'll cut to the chase," Dr. Stevens said finally. "Your dad has a very rare disease called Waldenstrom. There are only about fifteen hundred new cases a year. It's a cancer of the lymph cells that interferes with the production of healthy red and white blood cells. Right now, your father is treading water. There are treatments, but your father's illness is too advanced." His tone turned brittle. "There is no cure."

My face closed up. I crawled into a cold, empty space deep inside myself. *There is no cure.* A stinging sentence. *Warring blood cells. Rare disease.* My father had spent his life expecting foul play from the outside, and now he had been ambushed from within. Outnumbered by his own blood cells.

The doctor muttered under his breath, "Your father is eighty-seven. I give him three more years. Maximum, three."

I felt a sharp chest pain—an ice pick in my heart.

Dr. Stevens came around the desk, placed a heavy hand on my shoulder, and slowly walked me to the door. My pulse hammered in my ears as I made my way unsteadily back to my father in the waiting room.

My mother and brothers insisted on not telling Pop. They were certain that knowing he had an incurable disease would kill him even faster. Mom said there are certain unmentionables, and telling the dying that they're dying is one of them. I differed. I wanted words—his, mine, even if spoken sparingly. Pop had often retreated to some far-off disk of darkness in some distant galaxy. If he were told the facts, he could go there. He could slip beneath wool blankets, clutch his tattered bible, and curl up with God. And should be allowed to, I thought. It was his life, and his death. He could then do whatever he needed to do, once he knew.

I was overruled. Pop wasn't told. Instead, we joined him in his sphinx-like silence.

As his white blood cells battled his red, I battled me, reappraising all of my gripes. Who cares that he lived in fortressed silence, the firmest foundation he knew. So what! Accessibility is overrated, I told myself. He forced me to use my imagination, give it a constant workout. Who cares that he didn't know me and never would? Feeling erased was an advantage; it made me work harder at seeing myself. Who cares that he hated books and was in a constant Cold War with the outside world? Why did any of this matter?

Now, when he brayed, "Enough talk!" I no longer flinched. I didn't care. I just wanted to wrap my arms around his thin neck and agree with him: "Yes, enough talk!" I'd promise to give up speech. I'd become the daughter with an unresponsive tongue, if only he would live. Soon, I wouldn't be smelling his tea-stained breath or feel the graze of his short square fingers on my forehead. Never again would I catch him sniffing, spying, detecting, suspecting conspiracy, in ardent pursuit of predators—a climate to which I had grown so accustomed.

By the end of the third year after his diagnosis, Pop's face had turned ashen. On December 11, 1996, at age 90, snugly tucked in bed, curled in a fetal position, my father died.

Before his passing, Pop reminded Mom that he wanted to be buried in Jerusalem—in the Givat Shaul cemetery, where his parents had been laid to rest. And so he was.

Standing on a hilltop next to his grave, wearing a pilling brown cardigan, I heard the cawing of crows. I shivered, feeling hollow. I thought back to how my father had lived, shielding himself from people and places, eating tiny morsels, and sleeping as much as possible. He had wanted to be left alone, far from the pull and push of human affairs. Struggling to keep the *outside* world *out*—his lifelong battle. How wearing this must have been. The only *inside* that felt safe and warm to him was the inside of his sleigh bed. Under the covers, Pop breathed easy.

Through a stream of tears, I stared at the freshly shoveled soil atop his grave and prayed there would be no more outside pushing in, no more fight, no more fear. I prayed he was finally getting exactly what he wanted: uninterrupted sleep.

I sobbed as I thought of his frail bones wrapped in linen, lying underground. A place he knew only too well. 🔲

CHAPTER 41

Yateem

My mother asked that I stop by and help her write out some checks. Awaiting me on her dining table was a stack of Con Ed, Verizon, Cable TV, AARP, co-op, dentist, and doctor bills. We didn't get straight to business since, for her, that would have been crass. Instead, we sat over Nan-e Berenji and darkly brewed Swee-Touch-Nee tea in her French Provençal living room, while being serenaded by Persian music.

Mom was now in her 70s. For decades, I had listened to three stories she loved to tell about her childhood, always recited in exactly the same way. Each time, I'd seal my lips and suspicious-ly squint at her, hoping she'd break new ground, piece the past together differently, and draw different conclusions. *I need to be patient*, was my self-talk. *She'll get there. Eventually it'll happen. Patience.*

Sweeping crumbs off her lap, plumping the couch cushions, she returned to the story of her birth and the death of her mother. "I strong...my *mammon*[1] veak. I leeve, she die." Said like a Samurai warrior, with no trace of guilt or shame. I was once again told that she had killed her own mother, snuffed her out as she muscled her way through the birth canal.

Mom coughed phlegm, spat into an embroidered handkerchief, and turned to Farsi to express the depth of her disgust. "Mashhad is no more than the spit in this hankie." She fretted over wasted lives: those who had died unfairly, friends and close relatives needlessly

1. *mammon* (Persian/Farsi)—mother

lost to primitive conditions and lack of medical care. Her mother and father for starters.

Partway through the story, she led me into her bedroom, mounted a stationary bike parked next to her king-size bed, and started cycling.

"Estaire, Good for at-rite-tees."

In the corner of the bedroom, on a night table, stood a Persian enamel vase filled with long-stemmed peacock feathers. Hanging on the wall over her headboard were two framed photos: one of David, her turbaned father, and the other of Esther, her chadored mother. Late in life, my mother had somehow tracked down these photos of her deceased parents and had created a private shrine to them in her bedroom, with not one image anywhere in sight of Yocheved, the woman who had raised her.

I sprawled out on her red velvet bedspread, chin in hand, as she pedaled.

Once again I heard how her father had swiftly married Yocheved only to provide a last-minute mother for my mother, his newborn, after Mom's birth mother, Esther, had died; how Yocheved had quickly become pregnant with Solomon, Mom's half-brother; and how Solomon had been an infant and Mom only two when their father died, leaving two young children for Yocheved to raise single-handedly.

My mother had often told me that she loved Solomon, who now was an adult living in Italy, and that throughout their childhood they had been inseparable, not knowing at the time they came from the same father but different mothers.

Solomon had been a roly-poly, sunny-faced fellow who shadowed his sister wherever she went. If he had a stick of candy, he'd break it in two, always making sure Hana had the bigger half. Mom blotted her eyes and blew her nose, recollecting how kindhearted and sweet-tempered he had been. They shared their Nan-e Sangak, their roasted chick peas, plump raisins, sock puppets, and Yocheved— their beloved mammon-joon.

Mom began telling the story of a steamy Saturday afternoon when Yocheved was taking her usual Shabbat nap. Since Mashhad had not yet been introduced to electricity, there were no spinning fans to freshen the air. Hoping for a summer breeze, Yocheved had left the back door wide open.

While Yocheved was sound asleep, four-year-old Mom coaxed her two-year-old brother to step into their courtyard wading pool.

Always eager to be her playmate, Solomon happily followed her into the water, which only came up to his chubby knees. Once she had him where she wanted him, with both hands she gleefully pushed him under and sat on his head.

As Mom reached this storytelling juncture, her voice was laced with pride. Her toddler brother wrestled, squirmed, pushed, and pulled while totally submerged, frantically fighting to come out from under. As he fought for his life, swallowed mouthfuls of water, released noisy bubbles, cried from below, Mom comfortably sat on the crown of his head, maintaining her station. Knowing Solomon was drowning, she gave an extra shove, holding him down.

Hearing muffled sounds, Yocheved awoke and ran into the courtyard. Fully dressed in her Shabbat best, she jumped into the pool and peeled Hana off her son. Between gasps, coughs, and cries, Solomon told his mother what his sister had just done.

Mom especially enjoyed telling this part of the story. Yocheved scolded her two-year-old son for misbehaving, slapped his rear, and sent him off to his room whimpering. Hana, on the other hand, was caressed and allowed to continue playing outside in the garden.

Having heard this story many times, I was no longer shocked by it. However, now well into my 40s, my patience had run out.

"Mom, you were trying to drown your brother. You wanted him dead. Now that you're a grown-up, a mother of three, a grandmother of seven, you can think differently. Don't you think Yocheved was wrong? Wouldn't you discipline your own child for doing something this awful?"

Her eyes narrowed.

"Estaire. I vas *yateem*. Den, I not know she not *mammon-joon*. But *she* know. She know dat Solomon have real mommy. I no have real mommy. She know dat." Her forearms stiffened as she rapidly pedaled. "Becauz I *yateem*, she cor-rect. I must get all loave."

"But, Mom, wouldn't you want to teach your four-year-old that she isn't allowed to drown her brother? Don't you think you should have been scolded and sent to your room? Not left to play?"

Mom stopped cycling. Her eyes hardened as she drew her thinly tweezed brows together, suspecting treachery. Once again I had proven what she knew all along: She had given birth to her own adversary.

"Estaire, you hate me! You no loave me."

I sighed.

"Mom, I don't hate you. We're talking about parenting. How a mother should discipline a four-year-old daughter caught murdering her younger brother."

Batting her eyelids to make me vanish, she looked straight ahead and declared: "I *yateem.*"

The second childhood memory she liked to share was different, but, in truth, not so different.

By age 12, Mom knew that Yocheved wasn't her birth mother but instead her stepmother, her father's wife. Zan pedaer, as she now addressed Yocheved, was busy in the kitchen one day, bent over 40, 50 balls of dough—kneading them, flattening them into patties, then stretching each patty paper thin, making Goosh-e Fil pastries for Shabbat.

On this frigid Friday afternoon, Mashhad was buried under three feet of snow, bringing the city to a halt. Dirt roads had turned milky white. Winter winds were so strong, my mother said, that those who dared walk outside walked backwards against it. Shopkeepers, squinting under kerosene lamps, attended to bookkeeping, not expecting clientele. The outdoor stillness was occasionally pierced by the yelping of dogs roaming alleyways.

My mother entered the kitchen and demanded Zan pedaer immediately take her to a shoemaker to have custom-made, navy blue suede shoes designed for her 12-year-old feet. She had just seen photos of such shoes in a news broadsheet and wanted an identical pair. Zan pedaer pointed to her rows of time-sensitive dough balls and explained that she couldn't just jump up and run off through mountains of snow and leave all her baking behind. She also had too much other cooking to do before the onset of Shabbat. Couldn't the shoes wait?

No! Mom insisted. She began crying loudly, stamped her feet, and with tight fists pummeled Yocheved's arms and breasts. Zan pedaer caved. She rapidly covered her dough with dozens of dish cloths, hailed a buggy and driver, and, bundled under layers of thick wool blankets, traveled with my mother through streets filled with dense, unplowed snow. All so the shoemaker could trace Mom's tiny feet.

With overbearing pride and a lingering afterglow, she ended this telling of her story by removing her bottom denture and placing it in a mug of water. A half-toothless, entitled smile curved into place.

I found her wrongness compelling. Even in her 70s my mother stood behind her younger self, defending her actions by telling herself: *I was given what I wanted, whenever I wanted, because I was an orphan, cheated out of having a mother—double-crossed by life.*

Her marred and distorted justifications never changed. She had no desire to ferret truth, to shoulder blame, to say she was wrong. Nevertheless, I clung to a deep-rooted belief that she must know better. I refused to accept her for who she was. I told myself *She pretends to be proud of these stories, but in her heart of hearts she knows otherwise.* I refused to believe she was emotionally stuck at age four. I refused to have a child as a mother and demanded she be an adult. Even when I caught her sitting on a second deck of cards, cheating to beat five-year-old Miriam at gin rummy, and explained it away to myself as *She can't help it*, in my own heart of hearts, I clung to the belief that she knew better.

Trapped in circles of thought, I slowly arrived at: *She distorts truth, but so do I. To drown out pain I lie to myself, sidestepping the truth of who she is. I delude myself into believing I could have the mother I want—if only she'd try harder.* As if I could make her comply with *my* script, the one *I* wanted her to follow.

As a child, I had vowed to teach my mother to read and insisted she learn when she couldn't. Now I was doing the same: insisting she grow up when she couldn't.

Stretched out on her red velvet bedspread, I offered no rebuttal. As she continued pedaling her stationary bike, I left her bedroom and sat at the dining table. Sinking my teeth into unpaid bills, I asked myself, *What if she were a Treblinka death camp survivor? Would I feel the same way about her behavior? Isn't she doing the best she can with what little she has?*

I wasn't sure. ▨

CHAPTER 42

Broken Door

Four years after Pop died, Mom learned that she had an impaired aortic valve. One of her heart's doors was broken, at times not opening and at other times refusing to shut, an erratic flap with an unpredictable swing. She ran from doctor to doctor, only to be told the same by each: "Schedule surgery immediately. Time is of the essence." The question was whether to have a plastic or pig valve. As a former underground Iranian Jew, committed to Orthodox Judaism, Mom had spent her life strictly keeping kosher. No way was she now, at seventy-five, about to plant *treif*[1] in her heart and have ham on her breath. Frantically, Mom selected a Catholic hospital on Long Island and a surgeon who promised her plastic.

She spent the week prior to surgery petitioning Catholic, Protestant, Buddhist, Islamic, and Zoroastrian gods. Mom asked random strangers on the street, along with manicurists, cashiers, crossing guards, and Park Avenue doormen to go to their houses of worship and pray for her. "Pray I leeve affair op-er-rae-shione," she pleaded. She even stopped a dwarf stepping out of Duane Reade, thinking he might have special connections of his own.

She called Mashhadis in London, Milan, Tel Aviv, and Hamburg, asking them to insert her name in their community's morning, afternoon, and evening prayers. She even begged the Gristedes checkout clerk bagging her produce to pray for her. When I asked her why, she replied in Farsi: "The greater the numbers, the more likely God will listen." For Mom, God was a sleepy senile husband in need

---

1. *treif* (Yiddish)—unclean, not kosher

of vigorous shaking and a thick stick of dynamite to launch him into action.

By June 6, 2000, God's ears were ringing loudly as thousands prayed and chanted on Mom's behalf. Entering the hospital at 5:30 in the morning, Albert, Mom, and I were greeted by a short, round nun with gray hair wearing a silver crucifix over her black chador-like habit. She braced Mom's shoulders and said courteously, "Hana Amini, welcome, my dear. In the chapel this morning, I prayed to our Lord Jesus and asked that he watch over you." The nun crossed herself. "I prayed your new valve gives you a brand-new lease on life. I want you to know Jesus, Our Heavenly Father, and The Holy Ghost love you."

Mom said, "Tanks." All bases were covered.

Garbed in a flimsy hospital gown, lying flat on a gurney, Mom was rapidly wheeled into surgery. I sat next to Albert in a Lysol-scented waiting room feeling nothing. While downing seven cups of coffee, I was convinced I had come purely out of filial duty. I remembered when Pop's health was failing, Mom had actually said she yearned for widowhood, and after he died she had let out an emancipated sigh and claimed that her life was finally her own.

But living without Pop took a worse toll on her than living with him. During what she called her *freedom years*, her rages heightened as she accused, blamed, cursed, labeling everyone cruel and heartless, often defining herself by whom she hated. Her toxicity bubbled, pushing friends and family away. Being in her presence required rationing. I, too, distanced myself, visiting once weekly. We lived in separate hemispheres, five blocks apart.

A surgeon's gravelly voice snapped me back into real time. I looked up at a widow's peak—his hairline

"Successful," he announced, still in scrubs. "I gave your mother a pig valve. It will work much better for her. When she's out of recovery, I'll explain it to her."

My jaw fell open. My brain gridlocked. If surgery didn't kill her, hearing *pig* would. She had conceded to handing over her heart only if guaranteed plastic. I swiveled around and watched Albert's face turn sickly yellow.

"Al? What do we do? She'll think you, David, and I planned this all along behind her back. She'll think we lied to her, that we're co-conspirators and want her dead. Tissue valves last fifteen years. She'll live a life filled with fear of death for the next fifteen years.

She'll be unbearable. That's it. I'm moving to California—I'll join legions of runaway daughters. I'll head west, as far west as possible."

A line of sweat grew over Albert's upper lip. "We won't discuss valves," he responded. "We just won't bring it up. She'll be groggy when she regains consciousness. She'll still be sedated, parched. Pain management will be the primary concern. She'll need morphine. We'll wait for the doctor to explain it all to her tomorrow."

Al was right. Why rush into full disclosure? Let Mom bask in the fact that she had survived, feel grateful to be alive. Maybe then she'd be more accepting of the truth.

We stood by her bedside in the recovery room as her sticky eyes pried half-open. I lightly stroked her dry furrowed brow. With cheeks quivering, Mom's cracked lips parted, and in a hoarse whisper she very slowly mouthed, "Plastic?" Then her lids drooped and she fell into a deep morphine sleep. Trembling, we fled to the waiting room.

Hours later, an inflamed, gum-snapping nurse found us.

"What's mur-guh-zob? Your mamma's screamin' it in my face: 'Mur-guh-zob! Mur-guh-zob!' And she's insistin' on havin' a private room. I told her, 'Honey, this ain't no five-star hotel. You're in an I.C.U!'"

Feigning ignorance, we shook our heads, pretending not to know what *mirghazab*[2] meant, that it was gobbledygook—pure gibberish. The alternative was to give her the English translation: Tyrant!

The next day, when the surgeon explained to Mom that "pig fit you best," she became so distraught she had to be sedated. As expected, she accused me of lying, planning this all along, wanting her dead, never loving her, not now or ever. She didn't accuse Al or Dave. Only me. I was iced out of her damaged heart.

Each day, as she ate and gained strength, she discharged raw rage. She trashed the nurses and called each one "mean and meez-ra-bull" to her face. Determined to punish me, she avoided my eyes. Mom had decided I was the culprit, the dangerously disloyal, backstabbing daughter who had plotted to kill her via pig.

On the fifth day, without warning, a blood clot shot into her brain resulting in a stroke, leaving her in a hit-and-run coma. There were no last words, just a line of spittle dripping from the corner of her mouth. Standing there, I heard a woman's wail, a cri de coeur, coming from another room. My skin prickled. It was the tortured sound Mom would have released, if she could have. I stood by her

2. *mirghazab* (Persian/Farsi)—tyrant, executioner

bed, my heart ramming into my ribs. Her lovely cheekbones looked contorted, her jagged jaw hung open, tubes ran into her mouth and down her throat. Mom's eyes were shut. Her chest expanded and contracted as machines forced air in and out of her lungs. Her auburn-dyed hair, always teased and stiffly sprayed, lay flat and disheveled on her pillow. Root energy gone.

In a matter of days she was declared brain dead. My brothers and I withdrew life support. On June 24, 2000, with a skid and a thud, Mom died at age 75.

I leaned over my mother's lifeless body and squeezed her swollen, liver-spotted hands—hands that had never wanted to be touched. Swallowing tears, I thought about her life. Fatally flawed, she was heroic, living out her wretched misunderstandings. On poor terms with herself. A warrior, now taken hostage—her mind and body hijacked. Washed up on Catholic shores.

I thought of how she'd say she was hatched in Mashhad, a city that wrecked her life, a home of lies, persecution, and executions, not allowing her to be real, not permitting her to use her strong intelligence. Denying her the right to choose and chart her own life.

She had blamed her mother for the greatest female crime, what only a bad mother does: dying and leaving her infant behind. It's shameful, she'd tell me, to be motherless and fatherless. "I vhant my *mammon*. I nevair have my *mammon*," she'd wail even into her seventies—the hurt she had inherited and the hurt she sustained. And yet, seemingly proud that she was the cause of this shame—a murderess who had killed her own mammon-joon in the act of being born.

Staccato memories of her life jostled and tumbled. Mom, the child bride, goading Pop, roasting him on the spit as she mocked his penis. Her stilettos denting his forehead as he chased me up the stairs. Me at age five, trying to broker peace, trying to hold her in place as she hoofed out the door.

Mom storming Ithaca by Greyhound bus with warm Nan-e Taftuns on her lap. Coming to feed Albert and his Cornell pals freshly baked Persian cakes. Winning over my suitemates at Barnard with her treats and opinions. Throwing lavish dinner parties, shocking guests with her daring dress, uncensored tongue. Singing, dancing, slapping her tambourine, ululating "Kililili...." Supporting me through my divorce, and then demanding I live only for her. In later years, happiest when flopped on her back, skirt hiked, bouncing a grandchild on her knees, singing *"Kalagh, kalagh, labeh, labeh*[3]...."

I had lost myself in her theater. Bold, brash, and daring. A woman of spiky contradictions. Part snake oil, part visionary. Propelled by adrenaline, audacity, and missing parts, thrown into the world like a grenade. A rogue, a wild card, with titanic expectations, haunted by fears of abandonment. Her self-defining ethos: *You're not the boss of me.* Barreling on, contesting convention.

I wanted to place a gold medal around her neck and say, "Mom, you lost your battle on a triumphal note, leaving behind deep wounds and high bars."

Mom, a Persian Pilgrim, the lifeblood of our family, with multiple pasts, lumbers through me. Though gone, she's in my blood. Her great unfinished business left for me. How often have I harnessed her energy, her audacity, slapping the tambourine in my head, chanting, "You're Hana's daughter! Slug it out!"

I stifle a sob.

And then another memory, and a smile.

Mom, in her red and pink kitchen, pounding the pestle, mashing chick peas, belting out in a moment of manic glory: "I burn *chador* and come to *Am-ree-kah*! Estaire, it goood for you, no? I geeve you life!"

---

3. *Kalagh, kalagh, labeh, labeh* (Persian/Farsi)—Persian nursery rhyme that begins, "Crow, crow, on the roof, roof."

EPILOGUE

VISIBLE

Growing up in Queens, a Persian diaspora, I watched breasts lactate, wombs procreate, wives fry and cry. I witnessed Mom's bustle, her endless catcalls, her walkouts, her unrepentant tongue sour Pop even further on freedom. Mom, on a lifelong rampage, hell-bent on emancipation; Pop, trembling, pining for solitude and silence. Shackled to one another, they tugged in opposite directions, Pop dodging the outside world and Mom devouring it. Three Medeco locks and a just-in-case chain bolted our entrance as bullets fired within. In many ways they never left Mashhad, living their underground life here in the U.S. so close to the surface.

Inflating his lungs, Pop would bellow: "What will people think!"

Mom would ratchet up the heat: *"Jahannam!*[1]*"*

As a teen, I'd grimace and grunt, aching to get out from under, leave it all behind.

Mom had the misfortune of being born in a place and time that had no use for her masculine muscle. If she had been born a boy, her life would have been different. Instead, she used her might to get her family out of Iran—and lived the rest of her life smack at the intersection of medieval Mashhad and 20th-century philistine New York City, inventing her own rules.

Then there was Pop, eyes ablaze, tracking me with KGB precision. His curdling and meddling thoughts were unbearable, his world peopled by predators. And yet, a part of me sympathized, no matter how thorny and murderous I felt.

---

1. *Jahannam.* (Persian/Farsi)—The hell with it; you can go to hell.

Can we ever really know our parents? A nagging question. We can only try. Mom, pedaling a stationary bike, battling arthritis; me, listening, taking mental notes, hoping to decode.

"Rough justice," an elderly relative tartly observed at my mother's shiva. "Your folks were the leaven that raised your family. They're only the prequel to what will follow."

Flashing back and flashing forward, I wonder: Are my children next in line? Are they tiptoeing behind my back, hiding, plotting, planning an overthrow? Am I that first-generation American they'll satirize as too fired-up, too much, a bit too Iranian, as they reach in and take some for themselves? As they say, "Mom, tell us—but keep it brief."

Leaving my shadow behind, what will be their wash of nostalgia?

Mashhad, India, the Upper West Side—all that preceded me is mine. Raised by opposites is mine, twined into my fiber, leaving me with a soft spot for the irrational and unexplainable, a goading conscience, never quite at rest, that resists tidiness of thought and simple explanations. Mom thumps in my chest when I'm drawn to aching hearts, unbridled tongues, and law-breaking rebels. A keeper of her flame.

I think back to Tuti, Yocheved, Layla—all the women who came before me, reduced to silence, unable to read or write, unable to leave their stories behind. I think back to Pop, amplifying soundlessness and secrecy; not wanting to be known, and certainly not chronicled.

And I'm left feeling I must. To stand against illiteracy, against suppression, against piercing silence and fear of words, I must tell their story and mine—a story only I can tell.

As for feeling unmothered, I now know I was mistaken—because it was she who modeled defiance.

"Enough!" Pop would shout as he flicked off my bedroom light. "Enough books!"

Pop was right. There's nothing more dangerous than a girl with a book. 🔲

GLOSSARY

PART ONE: A FORCE OF NATURE

Chapter 1: CLOSET FULL OF OSCARS

1. *chador* (Persian/Farsi)—long, loose garment that covers a woman's head and body
2. *Kooft-e balah* (Persian/Farsi)—a curse, wishing someone pain, disaster, misery, and disease
3. Koran (Arabic)—*Quran*, central Islamic religious text
4. *namaz* (Persian/Farsi)—Islamic prayers sung five times a day
5. *HaShem* (Hebrew)—a name for God
6. *Ghormeh Sabzi* (Persian/Farsi)—Persian stew made with veal, dill, parsley, scallions, lima beans, turmeric, cinnamon, dried lemons, and mint
7. *tokhmeh sag* (Persian/Farsi)—from the egg of a dog
8. *Khoda hafiz.* (Persian/Farsi)—God protect you.
9. *Khejalat bekesh.* (Persian/Farsi)—Shame on you; be ashamed of yourself.
10. *Khanum* (Persian/Farsi)—Madame
11. *bar mitzvah* (Hebrew)—Jewish coming-of-age ceremony for boys
12. *bat mitzvah* (Hebrew)—Jewish coming-of-age ceremony for girls
13. *bris* (Hebrew)—Jewish circumcision ceremony
14. Torah (Hebrew)—Old Testament containing the Five Books of Moses
15. keep *kosher* (Hebrew)—follow Jewish dietary laws
16. *najib* (Persian/Farsi)—kind, caring, trustworthy

Chapter 3: SCALPED

1. *tuti* (Persian/Farsi)—parrot

Chapter 4: PUBLIC SECRET

1. *Shabbat* (Hebrew)—Sabbath, day of rest, Judaism's seventh day of the week
2. *mammon joon* (Persian/Farsi)—dear mother
3. *zan pedaer* (Persian/Farsi)—father's wife
4. *Allah Daad* (Persian/Farsi)—God's justice
5. *Eidgah* (Persian/Farsi)—Jewish ghetto in Mashhad
6. *reshveh* (Persian/Farsi)—monetary bribes
7. *Jadid al-Islam* (Persian/Farsi)—literally "new to Islam"; a term for Jews who had outwardly converted to Islam
8. *dayereh* (Persian/Farsi)—framed drum with jingles resembling a large tambourine
9. *challah* (Hebrew)—braided bread made with eggs and eaten on the Sabbath
10. *neh* (Persian/Farsi)—no
11. *aftabeh* (Persian/Farsi)—metal pitcher
12. *minyan* (Hebrew)—quorum of ten Jewish men age 13 or older required for communal worship in Orthodox Judaism
13. *torshi* (Persian/Farsi)—pickled eggplant and cauliflower
14. *mekhitzah* (Hebrew)—partition or divider separating men from women during a religious service
15. *khastegar* (Persian/Farsi)—matrimonial representative who speaks on behalf of the suitor

Chapter 5: RUNAWAY BRIDE
1. *pedaer sag* (Persian/Farsi)—fathered by a dog
2. *jendeh* (Persian/Farsi)—whore
3. *Bemir.* (Persian/Farsi)—May you die.
4. *yateem* (Persian/Farsi)—orphan

Chapter 6: SHEPHERD IN QUEENS
1. Purim (Hebrew)—festival commemorating the defeat of Haman's plot to kill the Jews
2. *sari* (Hindi)—length of cloth worn draped around the body as a skirt and shoulder or head covering
3. *graggers* (Yiddish)—noisemakers
4. *hamantashen* (Hebrew)—triangular Purim pastries
5. *ruach* (Hebrew)—spirit

Chapter 7: KOSHER AT CHRISTMAS
1. *Nan-e Berenji* (Persian/Farsi)—Persian rice cookies
2. *asoor* (Hebrew)—not allowed, forbidden
3. *Hanukkah* (Hebrew)—Festival of Lights marking rededication of the second Temple in Jerusalem
4. *menorah* (Hebrew)—eight-branched candelabrum with a central socket used during Hanukkah
5. *dreidel* (Hebrew)—four-sided spinning top played during Hanukkah
6. *Begu.* (Persian/Farsi)—Tell him.

Chapter 8: TUTI
1. *aroos joon* (Persian/Farsi)—dear bride
2. *harum zadeh* (Persian/Farsi)—bastard
3. *bibi* (Persian/Farsi)—grandmother
4. *shiva* (Hebrew)—seven-day period of mourning

Chapter 9: REARVIEW MIRROR
1. *sambooseh* (Persian/Farsi)—triangular pastry filled with chopped meat
2. *khaneh mandeh* (Persian/Farsi)—colloquial for old maid, spinster
3. *Nan-e Taftuns* (Persian/Farsi)—Persian scones
4. *doroshkeh* (Persian/Farsi)—horse and buggy
5. *Chelow Nokhod Aab* (Persian/Farsi)—Persian stew made with beef, meat balls, green vegetables, kohlrabi, lima beans, and mild spices

PART TWO: FROM MASHHAD TO MANHATTAN

Chapter 11: DAVID'S EARLOBE
1. *Babai Albairt* (Persian/Farsi)—Albert's father
2. *ghelyoon* (Persian/Farsi)—hookah, water pipe

Chapter 12: QUEEN ESTHER'S TOMB
1. *Esther HaMalkah* (Persian/Farsi)—Queen Esther
2. *Nan-e Sangak* (Persian/Farsi)—coal-oven-baked flatbread
3. *joon* (Persian/Farsi)—dear
4. *Vasta!* (Persian/Farsi)—Stop!

5. *Khak bar saram.* (Persian/Farsi)—I should die.
6. *Birkat HaGomel* (Hebrew)—Jewish prayer of gratitude recited after surviving a brush with death

Chapter 13: EXODUS
1. *divoone* (Persian/Farsi)—crazy
2. *málish* (Hindi)—rubber, masseur
3. *pungi* (Hindi)—flute-like instrument made from a gourd
4. *lungi* (Hindi)—sarong or wrap worn around the waist
5. *kilim* (Persian/Farsi)—pileless handwoven rug
6. *shechitah* (Hebrew)—the laws of kosher butchering
7. *aleph* (Hebrew)—the letter A
8. *bet* (Hebrew)—the letter B
9. *shochet* (Hebrew)—kosher butcher
10. *zudi, zudi* (Persian/Farsi)—quickly, quickly
11. *brakhah* (Hebrew)—blessing

Chapter 14: CROSSING
1. *Adar* (Hebrew)—sixth month of the Hebrew calendar
2. *Hamashun divoone.* (Persian/Farsi)—They are all crazy.

Chapter 15: WELCOME
1. *gabbai* (Hebrew)—synagogue attendant
2. *tallit* (Hebrew)—prayer shawl
3. *Shabbat Shalom.* (Hebrew)—Good Shabbos.
4. *bimah* (Hebrew)—raised platform in a synagogue from which the rabbi leads services

Chapter 16: THINKING GOATS
1. *khar* (Persian/Farsi)—donkey, ass, stupid fool
2. *siddur* (Hebrew)—Jewish prayer book
3. *Siman Tov u' Mazal Tov* (Hebrew)—Hebrew celebration song

PART THREE: OLD WORLD MEETS NEW

Chapter 17: SHOWERING WITH MOM
1. *mikvah* (Hebrew)—bathing facility used for ritual immersion
2. *aberu* (Persian/Farsi)—face, honor, reputation
3. *leef* (Persian/Farsi)—crocheted rectangular wash cloth or bath mitt
4. *hammam* (Persian/Farsi)—Persian bath house

Chapter 20: FRIDAY NIGHT CLEAVAGE
1. *Polo Shevid* (Persian/Farsi)—Persian rice with dill
2. *Gonteveh* (Persian/Farsi)—Persian hamburgers
3. *Khoresht Nokhod* (Persian/Farsi)—Persian stew made with tomatoes, tomato sauce, beef, chickpeas, and onions
4. *flanken* (Yiddish)—short ribs
5. *Tahdig* (Persian/Farsi)—Persian rice steamed in a pot with a bottom layer of crispy fried potatoes
6. *kafgir* (Persian/Farsi)—perforated metal skimmer used for cooking

Chapter 21: PROTÉGÉ
1. *Chi mige?* (Persian/Farsi)—What is he saying?

Chapter 22: KITCHEN CONFIDENTIAL
1. *Loze* (Persian/Farsi)—Persian marzipan
2. *Goosh-e Fil* (Persian/Farsi)—thin-dough pastry shaped like an elephant's ear, deep-fried, and sprinkled with powdered sugar

Chapter 24: ABOUT FACE
1. *chai* (Persian/Farsi)—Persian tea
2. *Aberu darim.* (Persian/Farsi)—We have honor and reputation to protect.
3. *Aberu mon raft.* (Persian/Farsi)—We have lost face.
4. *Aberu rizi.* (Persian/Farsi)—We are disgraced.
5. *porru* (Persian/Farsi)—cocky, sassy, arrogant
6. *bi haya* (Persian/Farsi)—shameless
7. *bi aberu* (Persian/Farsi)—without face
8. *bi dast u pa* (Persian/Farsi)—incompetent
9. *khejalat* (Persian/Farsi)—shame
10. *taarof* (Persian/Farsi)—complex form of Persian civility
11. *bad-bakht* Persian/Farsi)—ill-fated, unfortunate

Chapter 25: ORIGINS
1. *dhimmis* (Persian/Farsi)—inferior non-Muslim subjects of the Islamic empire
2. *tahara* (Persian/Farsi)—ritual purity
3. *najis* (Persian/Farsi)—impure, unclean
4. *Kooh-i-Noor* (Persian/Farsi)—Mountain of Light
5. *Darya-ye-Noor* (Persian/Farsi)—Sea of Light

PART FOUR: BREAKING AWAY

Chapter 26: BEHIND BARS
1. *beshert* (Hebrew)—preordained, life partner
2. *najabat* (Persian/Farsi)—kindness, gentleness, generosity, nobility

Chapter 27: BOOKLEGGER
1. Chumash (Hebrew)—Torah, Old Testament

Chapter 29: CHANGE SUBJECT!
1. *Va-veylah!* (Persian/Farsi)—Oh, my goodness! Oh, my gosh!

Chapter 30: BARNARD
1. *yarmulke* (Hebrew)—skullcap worn during prayer by all Jewish men and all day by Orthodox Jewish men

PART FIVE: LOST AND FOUND

Chapter 32: HOMECOMING
1. *Polo Safi* (Persian/Farsi)—Persian rice that has been soaked overnight in saltwater, then drained,boiled, and steamed so each grain is separate and firm

Chapter 34: JERUSALEM
1. **Ulpan** (Hebrew)—Hebrew language school
2. *shuk* (Hebrew)—outdoor market

Chapter 35: SCANDAL
1. *Sukkot* (Hebrew)—Festival of Tabernacles
2. *sukkah* (Hebrew)—temporary hut, booth

Chapter 36: SECOND CHANCE
1. *Mikhastam.* (Persian/Farsi)—I wanted to; I meant to; I did it on purpose.

Chapter 37: IRA
1. *Seder* (Hebrew)—ceremonial meal held on the first night or first two nights of Passover, commemorating the exodus of the Jews from Egypt

PART SIX: BIBI

Chapter 38: PERSIAN PARANOIA
1. *dallak* (Persian/Farsi)—hired washerwoman
2. *kiseh* (Persian/Farsi)—rough-surfaced, rectangular washing mitt
3. *sang e pa* (Persian/Farsi)—pumice stone

Chapter 39: GIN RUMMY
1. *band andazan* (Persian/Farsi)—all-female, prenuptial hair-removal party for the bride
2. *noghl* (Persian/Farsi)—Persian taffy
3. *sharbat* (Persian/Farsi)—sweet, chilled beverage flavored with fruits and rose water

Chapter 41: YATEEM
1. *mammon* (Persian/Farsi)—mother

Chapter 42: BROKEN DOOR
1. *treif* (Yiddish)—unclean, not kosher
2. *mirghazab* (Persian/Farsi)—tyrant, executioner
3. *Kalagh, kalagh, labeh, labeh* (Persian/Farsi)—Persian nursery rhyme that begins, "Crow, crow, on the roof, roof."

Epilogue: VISIBLE
1. *Jahannam.* (Persian/Farsi)—The hell with it; you can go to hell.

ACKNOWLEDGMENTS

All literature is a confession, more or less oblique. But it's the painfully private that's difficult to pen, making memoirs the hardest. Over the past five years, there were many kindnesses shown me, acquaintances ripening into friendships, as well as direct and indirect assists. I thank all who spurred me on, offering support and relentless reassurance.

Deep gratitude to Ronda Spinak, Co-founder and Artistic Director of Jewish Women's Theatre, who was the first to recognize dramatic potential in my stories and stage passionate performances of them in Los Angeles and elsewhere. Thank you also for more recently naming me JWT's 2019 Artist-in-Residence. What an honor!

Heartfelt appreciation to Adrienne Brodeur and Aspen Words for selecting me as one of the program's 2016 Emerging Writer Fellows based on an early draft of this memoir—a literary distinction that continues to give.

Thanks to those who took the time to read early versions of my manuscript and provide me with insightful feedback: Lin Rosenbluth, Carolyn Slaughter, Marcia Butler, Sheila Rahmanan, Peter Alson, Ada Alpert, Mary Cagney, Sharon Marson, Yvette Schwerdt, Adina Cimet Singer, Brenda Bernstein, Dana Jacobi, and many more. You know who you are. I can't thank you enough.

Endless gratitude to Catherine Adams, who has been staunchly at my side, reviewing multiple drafts, urging me on, insisting this story be told even when my resolve wobbled. You asked the hardest questions, forcing me to retrieve my thorniest memories. For that I'm eternally indebted.

Concealed would not have matured into a full-fledged memoir if not for Charles Salzberg, esteemed writing teacher and publisher of Greenpoint Press, who believed in my writing from the get-go and ushered this memoir into the world. Huge thanks, dear Charles, for your conviction, encouragement, and support.

Thank you to the extraordinary Gini Kopecky Wallace for her sagacious editing and for providing calm passage through the exacting publishing process. You cradled this baby as if she were your own. What a gem!

Thank you also to Bob Lascaro for diligently designing and producing *Concealed*, patiently pulling all the pieces together, and creatively transforming them into a beautiful, living, breathing book.

Deep gratitude to my remarkable publicist, Tanya Farrell, who instantly fell in love with *Concealed* and leaves no stone unturned in her efforts to make this story known to the world. Your energy and enthusiasm are unparalleled.

My most heartfelt thanks must go to Mom and Pop, both long gone, for courageously leaving Iran and enabling their three children to have lives filled with freedoms and opportunities they never knew.

To my brothers, Albert and David: How would I have survived without you? You were trailblazing giants who carried me on your shoulders, answered all my nagging questions, willingly served as surrogate parents, and kept me sane and centered by diligently issuing regular dispatches from Planet Rational. Special thanks, Albert, for sharing many of your early childhood memories so they wouldn't be lost.

Boundless love and thanks to my husband, Ira, who gently nudged me forward and gifted me a wondrous room of my own. My steadfast spouse and spine, without you I would have never inked a word.

Finally, a quick wink to Lillian Jacobs, up there in heaven, who whispered in my ear before her passing, "Esther, you must share your story with others. Do it for me, my dear."

ABOUT THE AUTHOR

Esther Amini is a writer, painter, and psychoanalytic psycho-therapist in private practice. Her short stories have appeared in *Elle, Lilith, Tablet, The Jewish Week, Bar-nard Magazine*, Washburn University's *In-scape*, and *Proximity*. She was named one of Aspen Words' two best emerging mem-oirists and awarded its Emerging Writer Fellowship in 2016 based on an early draft of this memoir. Her pieces have been per-formed by Jewish Women's Theatre in Los Angeles and in Manhattan, and JWT chose her as its Artist-in-Residence in 2019.

Photo: Aaron Levine

Esther Amini lives in New York City with her husband. *Concealed* is her debut memoir. Learn more at **EstherAmini.com**.

CPSIA information can be obtained
at www.ICGtesting.com
Printed in the USA
LVHW100320250322
714308LV00005B/900

9 780990 619420